THIRD EDITION

CONTROVERSIAL ISSUES IN SOCIAL POLICY

HOWARD JACOB KARGER

University of Houston

JAMES MIDGLEY

University of California at Berkeley

PETER A. KINDLE

University of Houston

C. BRENÉ BROWN

University of Houston

Editors

PEARSON

Boston   New York   San Francisco

Mexico City   Montreal   Toronto   London   Madrid   Munich   Paris

Hong Kong   Singapore   Tokyo   Cape Town   Sydney

Senior Series Editor: *Patricia Quinlin*
Series Editorial Assistant: *Nakeesha Warner*
Marketing Manager: *Laura Lee Manley*
Production Editor: *Won McIntosh*
Editorial Production Service: *Publishers' Design and Production Services, Inc.*
Composition Buyer: *Linda Cox*
Manufacturing Buyer: *Debbie Rossi*
Electronic Composition: *Publishers' Design and Production Services, Inc.*
Cover Administrator: *Elena Sidorova*

For related titles and support materials, visit our online catalog at
www.ablongman.com.

Between the time website information is gathered and then published, it is not
unusual for some sites to have closed. Also, the transcription of URLs can result in
typographical errors. The publisher would appreciate notification where these
errors occur so that they may be corrected in subsequent editions.

ISBN: 0-205-52846-5

Printed in the United States of America

10 9 8 7 6 5 4 3 2 1   11 10 09 08 07 06

CONTENTS

PREFACE

■ ■ ■ ■ ■

Back in 1993, when Bob Pruger invited us to compile this collection of debates on controversial issues in social policy, we had some misgivings but also a sense of excitement at the prospect of creating a forum for critically examining a number of key issues in the field. The idea of publishing different points of view on difficult social-policy issues seemed to offer us a unique opportunity to demonstrate that complex social-policy problems can best be understood when they are analyzed from radically different perspectives. We believe that debates are not only a great teaching device, but an important means of developing knowledge. A number of the social-policy scholars we invited to participate in the project have told us that their own understanding of the more subtle and difficult arguments in social policy has been deepened by participating in the debates. We hope that the book will also help our readers to appreciate some of the more intricate dimensions of thinking in the field of social policy today.

Although politically liberal, the editors believe in the *marketplace of ideas,* a concept first articulated by Supreme Court Justice Oliver Wendell Holmes in 1919. The marketplace of ideas concept holds that the best policy arises from the competition of divergent ideas in a free and transparent public discourse, an important element of liberal democracy. To that end, we have not "stacked the deck" in the debates and have tried to give both sides a fair hearing. In this third edition, we have intentionally expanded the politically conservative voices from organizations such as the American Enterprise Institute, Heritage Foundation, and Focus on the Family. It is our belief that eventually the most salient ideas will win out, regardless of where they sit on the political spectrum. Positions must stand the test of analytical scrutiny before they can be accepted. Critical debate facilitates the twin tasks of validation and refutation. It also heightens an understanding of the issues, permits contradictions to be resolved, and ultimately promotes correct rather than false knowledge.

Social policy is a dynamic field and innovations and revisions in policy thinking regularly occur. However, remarkably little has changed in social policy since the first edition of this book was published. The country remains split between hard-line conservatives and the more suffocating elements of politically correct thinking. Social policy is still shaped by rigid ideological commitments, even though these are often presented as thoughtful and original policy ideas that will improve social conditions. One example is the much-touted *compassionate conservatism* of the Bush administration, which seems to be reserved for the needy rich instead of the needy poor. Similarly, the government's new emphasis on marriage as a solution to the problems of poverty and family deprivation resurrects cultural themes in American social thought that are hardly new or innovative. There is an urgent need to examine these and other policy developments critically and to subject them to intense debate. Books of this kind are needed now more than ever.

Critical debate also has an important role to play in strengthening the social work profession. Unlike other disciplines, social work has not always encouraged critical debate and social-work educators have sometimes been criticized for propagating their own ideological points of view. Although controversial articles do appear in some social-work journals, they rarely result in rejoinders or ongoing debates. Much to the chagrin of many social-work authors, the ideas contained in controversial articles soon disappear from the journals. This has led many to believe that either social workers do not read their own journals, or they simply do not care enough about the issues. It is likely that neither of these suppositions are correct. Many social workers fail to respond simply because there is little culture of critical debate from which to draw. This problem is especially acute in the area of social policy, which is by nature open to multiple interpretations.

Another problem is the profession's propensity to adopt a single authoritative position on complex issues. For example, one is struck by the consistency of the position statements emanating from various professional associations. Often, particular views are espoused as if they were universally accepted. It is assumed, almost a priori, that everyone in the profession has the same opinion on key issues. This is clearly not the case, and the diversity of viewpoints among social workers on these issues needs to be recognized. While it is appropriate for the profession to take positions on political and social issues that affect their members, these positions are sometimes adopted with dogmatic authority, when in fact, there are widely differing opinions among social workers on important questions.

The tendency among social workers to propagate a single point of view has resulted in the avoidance of controversial discussions. For example, there are few articles in social-work journals that question whether the welfare state is in fact a failed social experiment, or whether social-welfare programs actually work. Although most social workers, including the editors of this book, are strongly committed to the values and principles underlying the welfare state, the absence of serious discourse on these issues within the profession isolates the membership from much-needed critical thinking about social-welfare policy. As a result, many social workers are ill informed about alternative viewpoints and ill prepared to respond to them.

This situation is unhealthy for the growth and vitality of social work as an academic subject. Social work must endorse and meet the challenges of rigorous intellectual discourse. The failure to do so will undoubtedly harm its growth as a respected field of academic endeavor and weaken its potential impact in federal and state policy debates. Not only is the vitality of the discipline compromised by a lack of critical debate, but its own strength and maturity is weakened as its dearly held tenets are isolated from critique. Whatever positions social workers adopt must be validated by the clarification that comes from rigorous debate. Indeed, the profession's beliefs and values may become calcified and ineffectual if it fails to exercise its intellectual abilities.

Exposing students to critical debate is also an effective teaching device. While rote learning has an obvious role in the educational process, the task of helping students gain an understanding of the most important issues in the field requires more than just the memorization of facts. In subjects such as social work and social policy, where judgment is as important as knowing facts, students need to think critically, to be able to grasp complex nuances, and to analyze issues and defend their positions. The lecture format is not always the most effective means to inculcate these kinds of intellectual skills. We hope that the debates in this book will assist instructors in promoting passionate discussions among students and in facilitating the critical thinking needed to enhance our field. Now more than ever, the profession needs innovative thinking that supports bold new ideas, not hashed-over "consensus" opinions that masquerade as truth.

We have included debates in this book that will encourage social-work students to think critically and to develop their analytical skills, in fact, many of these debates require careful and critical review. We also hope that instructors and general readers will also benefit from the debates. For this reason, many of the debates address very difficult issues. Indeed, some of the positions argued by our contributors are unpopular, but as was argued previously, it is important that social workers understand them. We believe strongly in the ability of our readers to determine for themselves which arguments are the most valid and relevant. For this reason, we do not avoid issues because of their contentiousness. It is hoped that instructors will use this book in the spirit in which it was written and expose students to the varied opinions found in the rich terrain of social policy. As stated earlier, one of the strengths of social policy is its openness to various interpretations, which makes it intellectually challenging and exciting. Indeed, we hope this book will communicate the exhilaration of analyzing the complexities of social-welfare policy.

OVERVIEW OF THE DEBATES

Controversial Issues in Social Policy is divided into three parts. The first part, Social Policy and the American Welfare State, focuses on general issues in social-welfare policy. Howard Jacob Karger and James Midgley examine whether the U.S. welfare system is compatible with the free-market system. Tatcho Mindiola and Howard Jacob Karger debate open borders with Mexico, a timely issue that is dividing the nation. Although moves to privatize

Social Security were stalled in the second Bush administration, the issue continues to remain salient. William Beach and Steven Rose debate whether Social Security should be privatized. Given the meteoric rise in health-care costs, another issue that will undoubtedly resurface is National Health Insurance (NHI). Manuel Zamora and Robert Moffit debate the pros and cons of NHI. The United States is pursuing drug interdiction and prosecution with a vengeance-like determination. The effectiveness of that policy is debated by Peter Kindle and Diana DiNitto. The idea of providing the poor with Individual Development Accounts (IDAs) was developed by social worker Michael Sherraden, and later adopted by the former Clinton administration and several states. Michael Sherraden and James Midgley debate whether IDAs can help the poor in the long run.

Part II looks at The Culture Wars: Discrimination, Stigma, and Social Policy. One hot-button issue in this war is same-sex marriage, debated by Lori Messinger and Focus on the Family's Glenn Stanton. Affirmative action is another hotly debated policy. Has it worked? If so, at what cost? American Enterprise Institute's José Idler and Jolyn Mikow of UTSA examine whether affirmative-action policies have gone too far. The Americans with Disabilities Act (ADA) was applauded as the most important piece of legislation ever passed for the disabled. But who has really benefited? Howard Jacob Karger and John Bricout debate whether the ADA is meeting its promise or is rife with abuse. Religion is one of the most powerful symbols in the culture wars. It has also been exploited on both sides of the political fence. David Hodge and Gary Anderson debate whether the social-work profession—emblematic of the larger society—discriminates against evangelical Christians. Should the social-work profession support a woman's right to abortion? While there is seemingly a consensus in social work around a woman's right to choose, there is also a constituency that questions that stand. Roland Meinert and the late John (Terry) Pardeck debate whether abortion rights should be an accepted social-work value.

Part III examines Social Work and Social-Service Delivery Issues. One divisive social-service issue is reflected in Gaynor Yancey and John Belcher's debate on whether the federal government's support of faith-based social services is consistent with social-work values. The privatization of social services has been hotly debated for 20 years. Ira Colby and David Stoesz examine whether privatization is ultimately viable and whether its promise has been realized. The Personal Responsibility and Work Opportunity Reconciliation Act (PRWORA) of 1996 was enacted a decade ago. Conservatives and some liberals claim it is a stellar success. Others doubt it. Kirk Johnson and Robert Rector debate Mimi Abramovitz on whether welfare reform has helped or hurt current and former recipients. Almost half of all child-abuse deaths are open cases or known to Child Protective Services (CPS). Kristine Nelson, Diane Yatchmenoff, and Katharine Cahn debate David Stoesz on whether CPS is still viable given its less-than-stellar record of protecting children. Last, Patricia Sandau-Beckler and Scott Burrus debate Michael Beckler on whether drug courts are working in child welfare.

The reader should not assume, despite the passionate tone or persuasive impact of these debates, that the authors personally endorse the issues they present. Controversy is the essence of intellectual discourse. Although it may produce sharp disagreements, the role of critical disputation in furthering knowledge is universally recognized. While scholars may strenuously promote particular positions, the capacity to do so requires mastery of both sides of an issue.

ACKNOWLEDGMENTS

This book could not have been written without the hard work and commitment of the contributors. We extend our heartfelt thanks to all who contributed to this book. Their professionalism made the book both manageable and possible. Apart from delivering their debates in a timely manner, many had the courage to publicly take an unpopular position. This demonstrates both their self-confidence and intellectual integrity.

Thanks to Pat Quinlin, Allyn & Bacon's senior acquisitions editor for believing in this project and for her support over the years. It has meant a lot.

Howard Jacob Karger

James Midgley

Peter A. Kindle

C. Brené Brown

PART I

SOCIAL POLICY AND THE AMERICAN WELFARE STATE

IS THE AMERICAN WELFARE STATE COMPATIBLE WITH THE MARKET ECONOMY?

Editor's Note:
Although the term *welfare state* can conjure up many meanings, it is widely used to connote a variety of government social programs designed to meet social needs and solve social problems. Most of these programs emerged at the time of the New Deal in the 1930s. Despite the popularity of these programs, critics argue that government involvement in social affairs is harmful to the economy, contrary to the U.S. values of hard work and individual responsibility, and detrimental to freedom of choice. Supporters of the welfare state have attempted to refute these arguments, but others believe that the welfare state needs an overhaul. They argue that the basic principles of the welfare state are not compatible with a modern market economy in which virtually everyone is expected to participate in the labor force. In effect, the New Deal's outmoded collection of social programs are no longer relevant in a modern free-market society.

James Midgley, Ph.D., is Harry and Riva Specht Professor of Public Social Services and Dean of the School of Social Welfare at the University of California at Berkeley. He has published widely on issues of social policy, social work, and international social welfare. His most recent books include: *Social Welfare in Global Context* (Sage, 1997), *Alternatives to Social Security* (with Michael Sherraden, Greenwood Press, 1997) and *The Handbook of Social Policy* (Sage, 2000).

Howard Jacob Karger, Ph.D., is Professor at the University of Houston. He is the author of *Shortchanged: Life and Debt in the Fringe Economy* (Berrett-Koehler, 2005) and, along with David Stoesz, of *American Social Welfare Policy: A Pluralist Approach* (5th ed.). He has published widely in the field of social-welfare policy including such areas as community economics, income maintenance policy, poverty policy, and social development.

YES

James Midgley

The question of whether government social policies and programs are compatible with a market economy has been widely debated by social-policy experts in the past. Although strong opinions have been expressed, the topic is a complicated one. Unfortunately, the issues have been oversimplified and conclusions seem to be based on sentiment rather than careful reasoning. This debate will show that it is only possible to reach a reasoned conclusion by addressing the complexities of the issue and by introducing caveats and qualifications. Taking these caveats and qualifications into account, it will be argued that welfare statism is compatible with the market economy, provided that the government is able to regulate the market, link it in a planned way to social welfare, and ensure that it functions to serve people's interests.

An attempt to decide whether the welfare state is compatible with the market economy requires that the terms *market economy* and *welfare state* be defined. Both terms are used in a very imprecise way not only in the academic literature but in the media and in ordinary discourse as well. However, both terms need to be understood if the relationship between the market economy and the welfare state is to be analyzed.

THE DYNAMICS OF THE MARKET ECONOMY

The term *market economy* refers to an economic system in which producers and consumers voluntarily engage in economic activities on the basis of prices determined by supply and demand (Pearce, 1992). Producers are motivated to respond to consumer demand because they wish to maximize profits, and consumers respond because they want to obtain goods and services at an optimal price. Prices are not determined by custom, personal considerations, or the government, but by supply and demand. Producers compete with each other to sell their goods and services and this not only ensures affordability but promotes efficiency. Price efficiency is also governed by the fact that consumers can choose between the goods and services offered by different producers and distributors. Supply and demand are, therefore, vital forces for determining the volume of goods and services produced, the way prices are determined, and the way the interests of producers and consumers are harmonized. Economists believe that the market economy has its own internal, self-regulatory dynamic. When supply and demand are out of balance, the market corrects itself and returns to a state of equilibrium in which the interests of both producers and consumers are satisfied. Supporters of the market economy argue that it works best when it is allowed to operate free of government control. When the market functions autonomously, competition, supply and demand, and the interests of producers and consumers ensure its smooth operation (Friedman, 1962; Friedman & Friedman, 1980).

The market economy may be compared to other economic systems where supply and demand do not play such a critical role. In traditional societies, goods and services may be produced and exchanged because of cultural obligations or because of personal relationships. Producers provide goods and services to consumers not because they are seeking to make a profit but because they are members of the same family or clan, or because particular economic exchanges are prescribed by the traditional culture. Similarly, in the former communist countries, economic exchanges were controlled and directed by the government. All citizens were expected to contribute collectively to production and it was claimed that they did so because of a shared commitment to the common good and not because of self-interest. Government economic planners and political leaders decided what should be produced and how much goods and services should cost. The role of the market in these countries was severely curtailed.

People have strong opinions on whether the market or the centrally planned economy is the best way of meeting the demand for goods and services. Supporters of the market economy argue that it is obviously more efficient. A centrally planned system, they argue, creates shortages, requires rationing, and will ultimately collapse, as occurred in the Soviet Union and other communist nations. On the other hand, critics argue that the market economy is based on greed, profits, and exploitation. They believe that claims about its effectiveness are exaggerated. It is not, they contend, a benign system of exchange based on the mutual satisfaction of the interests of producers and consumer, but on the exploitation of labor, the manipulation of consumers through advertising, and the promotion of crass consumerism (Kuttner, 1997). Price gouging, environmental degradation, and other deplorable practices are integral to the way the market economy functions. They argue that the market economy, particularly in the form of economic globalization, is morally debased (Gray, 1998; Hertz, 2001; Lutwak, 1999).

Despite opposing the market economy, many of its detractors have recognized its positive aspects. For example, Karl Marx and Friedrich Engels, who were perhaps the most famous critics of the market economy, recognized its dynamic character. They conceded that it had raised economic production to unimagined levels, and that it had obliterated oppressive feudal structures (Heilbroner, 1992). On the other hand, supporters of the market economy have recognized its limitations. The famous economist Joseph Schumpeter praised the market's creative power, but he also emphasized its destructive impact. He noted that entrepreneurs, in their relentless pursuit of profits, were constantly producing new products and technologies. Although this fostered innovation, it also resulted in obsolescence, waste, and the decimation of producers who were unable to compete.

There is, of course, a middle way between the supporters and opponents of the market economy. Many on the political left, who are critical of the market economy, believe that its dynamism can be harnessed for good. They want government to manage the economy not through centralized planning but through less intrusive economic-policy instruments such as interest-rate manipulation, monopoly limitation, labor and work regulations, the maintenance of fair prices, production incentives, and environmental protection. Many on the political right who are critical of government intervention also recognize that regulations and incentives have a role to play. For example, many are in favor of measures to limit monopolies and of efforts to stimulate economic growth and control inflation through manipulating interest rates.

THE ROLE OF THE WELFARE STATE

It is in the context of regulating and harnessing the dynamic power of the market economy that the role of the welfare state should be discussed. Many of those who believe in the positive potential of the market economy also believe that governments must link the market economy to social policies and programs in a planned and purposeful way. But before examining this argument in more depth, the definition of the welfare state should be considered.

The term *welfare state* is loosely used to connote an economically developed country where the government provides extensive social services to its citizens. The term was popularized in Britain in the years after the Second World War, when the recommendations of a committee appointed by the government to plan for postwar reconstruction were adopted (Glennerster, 1995). The committee was chaired by William Beveridge, and it urged the government to introduce comprehensive health, housing, education, social security, and welfare services. These recommendations were accepted and resulted in a massive expansion of government social services. The British National Health Service was created in 1948 to provide free medical care to all citizens; housing and educational programs were expanded; a comprehensive social security system was introduced in 1946 and social services for families, the disabled, and other vulnerable groups were strengthened (Hills, Ditch & Glennerster, 1994). Other European countries also expanded their social provisions after the war, and by the 1960s most European nations were described as welfare states by social-policy writers.

Before the Second World War, it was widely believed that people should be responsible for their own welfare. However, the Great Depression of the 1930s showed that even hardworking, responsible citizens could fall into poverty and deprivation. Many workers became unemployed and many business people lost their livelihoods. The horrors of the Depression convinced many political leaders, and many ordinary citizens as well, that government had a vital role to play in promoting the welfare of the people. As government social programs expanded, the prevailing individualist ideology, which opposed government intervention, was gradually replaced by a collectivist ideology, which stressed the importance of government provision.

It is important to note that the expansion of the social services in the European countries after the Second World War took place within the context of wider economic policies. In an effort to promote full employment and rapid economic growth, most European governments implemented policies based on the writings of the British economist John Maynard Keynes. Welfare statism was, therefore, closely linked to economic management. The social services were not intended to function in isolation from economic policy, but to complement and sustain economic development.

The term *welfare state* was also applied to other economically developed countries, such as Australia, Canada, New Zealand, and the United States. However, there has been disagreement about whether the United States is, in fact, a welfare state. Unlike the European countries, the United States has not introduced a comprehensive government-funded health service, and commercial health-care providers continue to dominate the system. Public housing and social-welfare services are also believed to be less extensive than in Europe. It is for this reason that some American scholars have described the United States as a residual or reluctant welfare state (Jannsen, 1993; Wilensky & Lebeaux, 1965).

On the other hand, social-policy writers such as Theda Skocpol (1995) point out that the United States has invested more extensively in education than many European countries and that its Social Security system is very well developed. The United States has also adopted a different approach to welfare than that favored by the Europeans. Instead of maintaining a large, centralized welfare bureaucracy, the U.S. government has promoted decentralization and it contracts out public services to nonprofit and commercial providers. It is not that the government has failed to promote the welfare of its people, but that it has done so in a different way.

In the United States, the term *welfare state* is historically associated with the first major expansion of government social programs, which took place during the Roosevelt administration of the 1930s (Berkowitz, 1991). However, in the 1950s, when Republican president Eisenhower served two terms, social programs were also expanded. Further expansion took place under the Great Society programs of President Johnson in the 1960s, and during the Nixon and Carter administrations (Berkowitz, 1991). Despite differences between U.S. and European approaches, the term *welfare state* was widely used to describe U.S. social policy during these periods.

On the other hand, the term began to be used in a derogatory way during the Reagan administration. Several social-policy scholars associated with the political right began to attack welfare statism. For example, Charles

Murray (1984) popularized the idea that government social programs caused more harm than good. By providing generous social services and benefits, the welfare state had undermined the work ethic, fostered the disintegration of traditional family obligations, engendered a culture of indolence, and promoted irresponsibility. Because of the welfare state, the United States had not made steady social progress but had, in fact, lost ground. Many other writers supported Murray's position and, by the mid-1990s, Republican leader Newt Gingrich (1995) had succeeded in demonizing the term. The goal of the Republican Party, he promised, was to replace the welfare state with the opportunity society.

Perhaps the most serious criticism of state welfare programs came from neoliberal or free-market economists. Some claimed that government social programs had reduced people's propensity to save, creating a shortage of capital for investment and impeding economic growth (Feldstein, 1974). Others argued that costs of social programs have required high levels of taxation. As more elderly and other needy people received social benefits, a heavy and unfair burden was being imposed on those who remained economically active (Bacon & Eltis, 1976; Freeman, 1981). Social programs were also accused of harming work incentives and undermining self-reliance. Because people were no longer required to meet their own social needs, they were becoming dependent and irresponsible (Mead, 1992; Murray, 1984; Payne, 1998).

During the 1970s, as taxation levels increased and as the United States and many other industrial countries experienced recession and other economic difficulties, these arguments gained support and resulted in the election of governments that had little sympathy for the welfare state. The most important of these were Mrs. Thatcher's Conservative government in Britain, President Reagan's Republican administration, and the military regime of General Pinochet in Chile (Glennerster & Midgley, 1991). In addition, since the 1980s, the market economy has been elevated to a new level of importance. The maximization of profits, tax reductions, deregulation, and the retrenchment of social programs has been promoted (Kuttner, 1997). In this situation, the question of whether the welfare state and the market economy are compatible assumes a new and urgent significance.

THE MARKET ECONOMY AND THE WELFARE STATE

The most widely accepted position today is that the welfare state and the market economy are not compatible. Ironically, this opinion is shared by many of those on the political right with those on the political left. Free-marketeers, libertarians, and traditionalists agree with Marxists and radical populists that capitalism and welfare statism are contradictory ideals.

Marxists have traditionally claimed that the welfare state is subservient to the market and that it is used by capitalists to promote the interests of the wealthy and powerful. For this reason, they argue, it is unable to create a just and equal society in which people's social needs are met (Ginsberg, 1979; Gough, 1979). Radical populists agree that the global market economy is harming people's welfare.

Libertarians, traditionalists and neoliberal proponents of the free market have a strong dislike of government, believing that people should be free of its constraints and regulations. The libertarian position is summed up in the aphorism that the best government is the government that governs least. Of course, the arguments supporting this idea are more complex than this simple maxim implies (Nozick, 1974).

Traditionalists agree! They believe that the American people have historically met their own social needs and that traditional institutions such as the family, church, and local community have been effective in providing support to those who were unable to help themselves. Traditionalists want the government to curtail its welfare programs and to encourage the churches and charities to play a greater role in meeting social needs (Olasky, 1992, 1996).

Neoliberal economists focus largely on the way welfare programs allegedly harm the economy. As was noted earlier, they contend that social programs require high levels of public spending and impose exacting taxes on working people. Because of high taxes, the incentives of business firms and hardworking people are undermined. This problem is exacerbated when people realize that their taxes are being used to support a large underclass of people who are dependent on welfare. Unless government welfare programs are scaled back, free-marketeers believe, the economy will steadily decline, resulting in slumping production, high unemployment, falling standards of living, and a higher incidence of poverty.

One variation of the free-market position concerns the privatization of social programs. Many neoliberal economists have urged government to transfer social-welfare programs to commercial providers. However, many believe that governments funds should be used for this purpose. The extensive contracting out of services to commercial providers, which characterizes American social policy today, suggests that market proponents do not oppose government spending if commercial providers are the beneficiaries of this spending. The campaign to privatize Social Security in the United States is supposedly about ensuring the program's long-term viability but, in reality, it is about transferring huge resources to commercial insurance firms (Baker & Weisbrot, 1999; Kingson & Williamson, 1998).

The free-market position enjoys widespread popularity and support at the highest political levels today, and those who believe that the market economy and the welfare state are compatible are in a small minority.

Nevertheless, they continue to argue that the market economy can be harnessed to promote full employment, higher standards of living, and the well-being of the population as a whole. A managed market economy that is harmonized with a social-service system can, they believe, function effectively to enhance people's welfare.

Those who believe that the market economy can be harnessed for social purposes draw on the historical experience of the European countries and the United States to show that attempts to regulate and manage the market economy and to link it with social policies and programs were successful. They place particular emphasis on social investments that enhance people's abilities to participate effectively in the productive economy. They show that New Deal programs in the United States provided jobs and a livelihood for hundreds of thousands of unemployed people and that the educational and job-training programs of the time enhanced the skills of many people. Many communities in the United States today continue to reap the benefits of New Deal public-works programs.

Those who believe in the compatibility of the market economy and the welfare state also point out that European Social Democratic parties were able during the last 50 years to raise standards of living to unprecedented levels. Unlike Marxists, who favored revolution and dictatorial government, European Social Democrats were able to achieve economic and social transformation without bloodshed, secret police terror, or concentration camps. Similarly, unlike the free-marketeers who favored unrestricted profit maximization, Social Democratic governments in Europe achieved economic development without the widespread poverty, inequalities, and social deprivation that characterize unregulated capitalist economic development.

However, those who claim that the market economy and the welfare state are compatible are not so naive as to believe that the Social Democratic formula of the postwar years continues to be viable today. They recognize that fundamental economic, demographic, cultural, and social changes have taken place since the mid-20th century. Nevertheless, the basic principles that governed the Social Democratic approach can, they argue, be reconceptualized and modernized to meet the challenges of our time. A variety of innovations that propose a reconceptualization of this kind have already been formulated, and some are being adopted by Social Democratic and other progressive governments in Europe and elsewhere. Anthony Gidden's Third Way approach (1998, 2001), Amartya Sen's (1999) concept of human capabilities, James Midgley's (1995, 1999) developmentalist or social investment theory, the new egalitarianism of Samuel Bowles and Herbert Gintis (1998), and similar proposals offer strategic opportunities to once again harness the market economy for social purposes. Whether these approaches will be adopted in the United States remains to be seen.

NO

Howard Jacob Karger

At least as reflected in the Social Security Act of 1935; the U.S. welfare state was designed to complement rather than replace the free-market economy. This debate will argue that the American economy has changed dramatically since the 1930s, making anachronistic the premises on which the welfare state was built.

THE AMERICAN WELFARE STATE
IN HISTORICAL PERSPECTIVE

To understand why the welfare state is incompatible with the modern U.S. economy, it is necessary to examine the ways in which the welfare state has changed in relation to the national economy. When Franklin Roosevelt assumed the presidency in 1933 he faced a country divided between right- and left-wing political factions, an industrial sector on the verge of collapse and violent labor strikes, a class society at its breaking point, and a banking system that was virtually bankrupt (Cohen, 1958). FDR's response to the Depression involved a massive social experiment with the objectives of relief, recovery, and reform. Roosevelt was not a socialist nor was the philosophy of the New Deal welfare state Marxist. Far from radical, FDR's New Deal programs (the foundation of the American welfare state) were designed to salvage capitalism.

FDR's policies helped create the foundation for the modern welfare state in important ways. First, federal policy was used to ameliorate some of the more egregious inequities in the labor market. This occurred through minimum-wage laws and the establishment of the right of workers to strike and collectively bargain. The New Deal welfare state established important precedents in others areas. First, it established the *right* of eligible citizens to receive public assistance. The New Deal took public assistance from the realm of "we will provide what we have" to an entitlement in which resources *must* be provided to those in need. Second, it removed the provision of public assistance from the states and planted it firmly in the federal government. Certain public-assistance rules and eligibility (but not the determination of cash benefits) were standardized and applied more evenly. FDR's New Deal programs contained an implicit policy directive that established the responsibility of the federal and state governments to provide for the needs of citizens deemed worthy of receiving aid (Karger & Stoesz, 2006). Third, the New Deal welfare state firmly established the precedent of using social programs to quell social unrest (Piven & Cloward, 1993). This policy would be applied as late as the Los Angeles riots of 1992. Fourth, it established the precedent of using welfare-state programs to subsidize a seg-ment of the unemployed population or those who could not compete in the labor force. Welfare-state programs such as unemployment insurance subsi-dized displaced workers until the economy could reabsorb them. On the other hand, this safe haven provided little more than subsistence. Neverthe-less, FDR's programs created a social compact that lasted for more than 60 years.

Despite sustained attacks by conservatives, the U.S. welfare state grew from the 1950s to the 1970s. Apart from some economic blips, the U.S. econ-omy was generally on an upward trajectory. American innovation had intro-duced a wide range of products and services and the productivity of U.S. workers was unsurpassed globally. The U.S. economy was in the driver's seat, so we could afford to idle a small percentage of our workforce, espe-cially since our growth and productivity more than compensated for the costs.

The strategy of using welfare programs as a palliative for social unrest grew during the 1960s. Driven by massive urban riots in African American communities during the middle and late 1960s, former president Lyndon Johnson's War on Poverty and Great Society included a host of programs designed to ameliorate social unrest. Not only did these welfare programs buy off social discontent, but by the end of the Great Society the number of people living below the poverty line was cut almost in half, from about 25 percent in the early 1960s to around 12 percent by 1969 (Karger & Stoesz, 2006). Much of this cut paralleled the enrollment growth in Aid to Families with Dependent Children.

Although former president Richard Nixon rapidly dismantled the Great Society, the welfare state grew more under his administration than it had under preceding presidents. Between 1965 and 1975, America's national fiscal priorities were reversed: In 1965 defense expenditures accounted for 42 percent of the federal budget while social-welfare expenditures accounted for only 25 percent. By 1975, defense expenditures accounted for only 25 percent of the federal budget while social-welfare outlays accounted for 43 percent. Even in Ronald Reagan's conservative budget of 1986, marked by large increases in defense spending, only 29 percent was defense related, com-pared to 41 percent for social welfare (DiNitto & Dye, 1987). The American welfare state was clearly in a growth mode from 1935 to the middle 1970s.

THE GLOBAL ECONOMY AND THE WELFARE STATE

By the middle 1970s, America's secure economic position in the world had become more uncertain. Throughout the 1970s, inflation coupled with reces-sion (stagflation) began to erode the economic advances to which Ameri-cans had become accustomed. By the late 1970s inflation had reached double digits and the unemployment rate was rising precipitously. The productivity advances of European and Asian nations were nipping at the heels of American industry, and the productivity edge was being eroded in the face of foreign competition (Reich, 1983). The term *global economy* was finding its way into the American vernacular as more legislators and policy analysts began realizing the economic playing field had changed (Barnet, 1994). Independent national economies were no longer the rule; instead, an economically interdependent world was the norm. This new international competition made Americans less smug about their economic dominance of the world, and, by the middle 1980s, all but the most daft were aware that Americans had to change their understanding of the economy.

Concomitant with changing economic sensibilities was a transformation in our understanding of welfare. Not surprisingly, welfare-to-work programs were promoted vigorously during former president Jimmy Carter's administration. Welfare reform was also an important issue for the Reagan administration. This followed on the heels of a growing consensus among conservatives and many liberals that America would be left behind if it did not adapt to the global economy. But how should America make the adjustment? For one, economists looked at how human resources were deployed in Asian nations, most of which did not subsidize a large percentage of their population, especially those who could conceivably work.

Idling a percentage of the workforce through welfare and public-assistance programs was viewed as a luxury that was no longer affordable. Subsidization could only be entertained when the United States was the undisputed economic leader of the world, and when the huge productivity gap between it and the rest of the world compensated for that indulgence. Instead, a more rational method for deploying human resources became paramount in the new world economic order.

Redeploying human resources in the global economy meant cutting— or at least stabilizing—taxes (Karger, 1992). When economists looked at Asian competitors, it was obvious that tax burdens—on both industry and individuals—were considerably lower than in the United States. By redeploying human resources through compelling the able-bodied to work, government was able to stabilize or lower welfare spending, which in turn helped reduce tax rates. Given this, it is no surprise that while the 1990s was a period of robust economic growth, Congress passed no new welfare-program initiatives that required significant funding. The few welfare-related programs that did pass, such as AmeriCorps, were funded at a paltry amount compared to other social programs (Karger & Stoesz, 2006).

Another adaptation to the global economy was the reliance on economic insecurity to boost productivity. This was grounded in the belief that job security lowers motivation and damages productivity. Ergo, workers threatened by the specter of dismissal are more productive. As a result, concepts such as lifetime employment became an anachronism. Middle managers and workers were let go as profits dipped, operations moved over-seas, production was outsourced, or cheaper employees could be hired. Even academics were threatened as tenure became a hot button in state legisla-tures, resulting in several bills to weaken or eliminate it. In the welfare sector, economic insecurity was evident in the Personal Responsibility and Work Opportunity Reconciliation Act of 1996 (PRWORA), which put a 5-year fed-eral lifetime cap on the receipt of public assistance (Karger & Stoesz, 2006). Welfare recipients were now subject to the same economic insecurity faced by most of the American workforce. The new economic order offered no guarantees.

THE EVOLUTION OF AMERICAN WELFARE POLICY

Over the past 20 years, welfare policy has undergone a radical transforma-tion in response to changing economic conditions. For instance, New Deal public-assistance programs shifted from maintaining people outside of the labor force to programs and policies designed to force the poor into the labor market (Karger & Stoesz, 2006). Labor force participation was fast becoming the only vehicle the majority of the poor could rely on for subsistence. In effect, the welfare state was transformed into the work state (Kaus, 1992). Traditional social-welfare programs providing benefits to those unable to participate in the labor force were replaced by labor and tax policies designed to subsidize low-wage employment and compel the poor to work. This trend is illustrated by three recent and important welfare-related developments: the growth in the Earned Income Tax Credits (EITC), the passage of the Per-sonal Responsibility and Work Opportunity Reconciliation Act (PRWORA), and the Child Tax Credits program.

The Earned Income Tax Credit (EITC) was enacted in 1975 after the fail-ure of the negative income tax advanced by the Nixon administration. A refundable tax credit, the EITC instructs the IRS to send a check to low-wage workers, especially those with children, who have earned income below a certain level. In 2003, a worker with two children could receive a maximum refund of $4,204. Since the creation of the EITC, other work-related tax cred-its have also been introduced: a child-care tax credit allows low-wage work-ers to deduct the costs of day care, and several states have introduced tax credits for low-income workers, some of which are refundable (Karger & Stoesz, 2006). It is no coincidence that the only stable public-assistance pro-gram is EITC, which is tied to labor-force participation.

On August 22, 1996, President Bill Clinton signed the PRWORA, a com-plex 900-page document that was the most important welfare legislation since the Social Security Act of 1935. The complexity of the act masked three important features. First, the responsibility for providing public assistance devolved from the federal government to the less-than-generous states. Second, the act disentitled the poor from receiving public assistance. In contrast to the former AFDC program, which operated under the principle of entitlement (anyone eligible for assistance received it), under the PRWORA the poor are not entitled to receive public assistance, and in the event that funds run out, states can turn them away. Third, the PRWORA introduced a 5-year lifetime cap on the receipt of public assistance even though states had an option to reduce that cap and most opted for 2 years or less (Karger & Stoesz, 2006).

Although called welfare reform, the PRWORA was in fact labor policy. The intent of the bill was to remove the safety net of the New Deal welfare state, thereby forcing the poor into the labor market. By devolving public assistance to the states, removing the protection of entitlement, and legislating a lifetime cap, the welfare state became the work state and hence was no longer served as the protected economic haven that New Deal architects had envisioned. The rules of welfare receipt were subordinated to the rules of the new marketplace. In the same way that no one was entitled to hold a job, no one was entitled to receive public assistance.

The conversion of public assistance into labor and tax policy is shored up by the expansion of EITC benefits (the largest public-assistance program in the nation and the only one purposely enlarged in the last 20 years) (Karger & Stoesz, 2006). By concomitantly expanding EITC benefits and eliminating AFDC, the public policy focus shifted from the non-working poor to the working poor. The PRWORA forced poor people into the labor market and the EITC subsidized their low wages. This scheme was part of the new deployment of human resources that would mark the nation's accommodation to the global economy. It would also become a mainstay in the U.S. strategy of creating a domestic Third World labor force in the hope of becoming more globally competitive. However, labor and tax policy are not welfare policy and the work state is not equivalent to the welfare state.

The transformation of the welfare state into the work state represents the deconstruction of the public assistance portion of the New Deal and the final victory of the market over humanitarian concerns. In no small measure, this victory is an important step in the total marketization of American society, and without the safe harbor of public assistance, almost all Americans are now more vulnerable to the vicissitudes of the marketplace.

CONCLUSION

Several years ago, General Motors ran an ad promoting their new line of cars by saying, "this isn't your dad's Oldsmobile." Well, this is not your dad's economy. The global marketplace has transformed the American economy in important ways that make it incompatible with the welfare state. Like the old Pac-Man video game, the new economy devours everything in its path. Not only has it converted the welfare state into the work state and replaced welfare policy with labor and tax policy, but the programs it cannot deconstruct are turned into for-profit ventures by privatization and subcontracting social services.

State, local, and federal governments pay more than half a trillion dollars in salaries to public workers to deliver goods and services (Donahue, 1989). If only half of these services are good candidates for privatization, corporations stand to realize huge revenues. As early as 1994, thirteen top human-service corporations (Columbia/HCA, CIGNA Corp., United Health Care, FHP International, PacifiCare Health, Humana, U.S. Healthcare, Tenet Healthcare, Wellpoint Health, Beverly Enterprises, Wackenhut, Community Psychiatric Centers, and Kinder Care) had revenues in excess of $72 billion and employed more than 471,000 people (Standard and Poors, 1995). What American corporations cannot beat they join.

While this debate has focused on the public-assistance part of the welfare state, the Social Security system, arguably the last bastion of the American welfare state, is also affected by the global marketplace. The intent of the Social Security Act of 1935 was to protect workers from destitution in old age. This was accomplished by compelling workers to invest a portion of their earnings in the Social Security system. The money collected is then invested in U.S. Treasury bills. Although a worker's contribution to Social Security does not provide a rate of return commensurate with private investment, it is safe and guarantees retired workers a stable fixed income.

For an increasingly voracious economic system, the protected Social Security trust funds are analogous to a chicken coop threatened by a hungry fox. With about a $1.5 trillion surplus, the Social Security trust funds are an irresistible temptation for corporations, investment houses, and stock portfolio managers. The result is several reform plans that allow workers covered under Social Security to invest at least a portion of their trust funds in the private market. Under these plans, if the economy does well the Social Security trust funds will be fiscally healthier than before. However, if the economy does poorly, recipients will suffer. Although the Bush Social Security plan was clearly rejected by the public, the idea of privatizing Social Security is by no means dead. Privatization will replace security as workers are asked to tie their economic future to the vicissitudes of the marketplace.

While this debate has focused on the American welfare state, its implications are international. Most industrial countries are forced to compete in the global economy and most have made concessions by cutting welfare benefits and other social programs. Welfare-state programs in virtually all industrial countries have either been stagnant or pared back (Midgley & Glennester, 1991). The global economy has made the growth of the welfare state in the United States and abroad a thing of the past.

The humanitarian drive behind the original welfare state has changed. The social unrest that led to the development of the New Deal welfare state in the 1930s (and its growth in the 1960s) has been replaced by relative social quiet and widespread apathy, which has resulted in the erosion of benefits and social provisions. The outrage of Americans toward poverty and social injustice has been replaced by an acceptance of the status quo. Not only has the U.S. economy adapted to the global economy, but the sensibility of citizens has been transformed. The welfare state thrives in periods of compassion, concern, and outrage. Conversely, it withers when apathy and self-interest rule the day. The irony is that the welfare state is needed now more than ever given the havoc wreaked by the global economy.

Is the U.S. welfare state compatible with the free market? The resounding answer is *no!* At least, as the U.S. economy is presently structured.

REFERENCES

Bacon, R., & Eltis, W. (1976). *Britain's economic problems: Too few producers.* London: Macmillan.

Baker, D., & Weisbrot, M. (1999). *Social security: The phony crisis.* Chicago: University of Chicago Press.

Barnet, R. (1994, December 19). Lords of the global economy. *The Nation,* 754–757.

Berkowitz, E. (1991). *America's welfare state from Roosevelt to Reagan.* Baltimore: The John Hopkins University Press.

Bowles, S., & Gintis, H. (1998). *Recasting egalitarianism.* New York: Verso.

Cohen, N. (1958).*Social work in the American tradition.* New York: Holt, Rinehart and Winston.

DiNitto, D., & Dye, T. (1987). *Social welfare: Politics and public policy.* Englewood Cliffs, NJ: Prentice-Hall.

Donahue, J. (1989). *The privatization decision.* New York: Basic Books.

Feldstein, M. (1974). Social security, induced retirement and aggregate capital accumulation. *Journal of Political Economy, 83*(4), 447–475.

Freeman, R. A. (1981). *The wayward welfare state.* Stanford, CA: Hoover Institution Press.

Friedman, M. (1962). *Capitalism and freedom.* Chicago: University of Chicago Press.

Friedman, M. (with Friedman, R.). (1980). *Free to choose.* London: Secker and Warburg.

Giddens, A. (1998). *The third way: The renewal of social democracy.* Cambridge: Polity Press.

Giddens, A. (2001). *The global third way debate.* Cambridge: Polity Press.

Gingrich, N. (1995). *To renew America.* New York: Harper.

Ginsberg, N. (1979). *Class, capital and social policy.* London: Macmillan.

Glennerster, H. (1995). *British social policy since 1945.* Oxford, England: Blackwell.

Glennerster, H., & Midgley, J. (Eds.). (1991). *The radical right and the welfare state: An international assessment.* Lanham, MD: Rowman & Littlefield.

Gough, I. (1979). *The political economy of the welfare state.* London: Macmillan.

Gray, J. (1998). *False dawn: The delusions of global capitalism.* London: Granta Books.

Heilbroner, R. K. (1992). *The worldly philosophers: The lives, times and ideas of great economic thinkers.* New York: Simon & Schuster.

Hertz, N. (2001). *The silent takeover: Global capitalism and the death of democracy.* London: Heinemann.

Hills, J., Ditch, J., & Glennerster, H. (Eds.). (1994). *Beveridge and social security.* Oxford, England: Clarendon Press.

Jannsen, B. (1993). *The reluctant welfare state: A history of American social welfare policies.* Pacific Grove, CA: Brooks/Cole.

Karger, H. (1992). Welfare, the global economy and the state: The American experience. *Social Development Issues, 14*(1), 83–95.

Karger, H., & Stoesz, D. (2006). *American social welfare policy: A pluralist approach* (5th ed.). Boston: Allyn & Bacon.

Kaus, M. (1992). *The end of equality.* New York: Basic Books.

Kingson, E. R., & Williamson, J. B. (1998). Understanding the debate over the privatization of social security. *Journal of Sociology & Social Welfare, 25*(3), 47–62.

Kuttner, R. (1997). *Everything for sale: The virtues and limits of markets.* New York: Alfred A. Knopf.

Lutwak, E. (1999). *Turbo capitalism: Winners and losers in the global economy.* New York: HarperCollins.

Mead, L. M. (1992). *The new politics of poverty: The nonworking poor in America.* New York: Basic Books.

Midgley, J. (1995). *Social development: The developmental perspective in social welfare.* Thousand Oaks, CA: Sage.

Midgley, J. (1999). Growth, Redistribution and welfare: Towards social investment. *Social Service Review, 77*(1), 3–21.

Midgley, J., & Glennester, H. (Eds.). (1991). *The radical right and the welfare state.* London: Wheatsheaf Books.

Murray, C. (1984). *Losing ground: American social policy, 1950–1980.* New York: Basic Books.

Nozick, R. (1974). *Anarchy, state and utopia.* New York: Basic Books.

Offe, C., & Keane, J. (1984). *Contradictions of the welfare state.* Boston: MIT Press.

Olasky, M. (1992). *The tragedy of American compassion.* Washington, DC: Regnery.

Olasky, M. (1996). *Renewing American compassion.* Washington, DC: Regnery.

Payne, J. L. (1998). *Overcoming welfare: Expecting more from the poor and from ourselves.* New York: Basic Books.

Pearce, D. W. (1992). *The MIT dictionary of economics.* Cambridge, MA: MIT Press.

Piven, F. F., & Cloward, R. (1982). *The new class war.* New York: Pantheon.

Piven, F. F., & Cloward, R. (1993). *Regulating the poor.* New York: Vintage Books.

Reich, R. (1983). *The next American frontier.* New York: Times Books.

Sen, A. (1999). *Development as freedom.* New York: Knopf.

Skocpol, T. (1995). *Social policy in the United States: Future possibilities in the United States.* Princeton, NJ: Princeton University Press.

Social Security Administration. (2000, April). *A summary of the 2000 annual reports.* Retrieved June 11, 2001, from www.ssa.gov/OACT/TRSUM/trsummary.html.

Standard and Poors. (1995). *Standard and Poors directory.* New York.

Wilensky, H., & Lebeaux, C. (1965). *Industrial society and social welfare.* New York: Free Press.

SHOULD WE OPEN THE SOUTHERN U.S. BORDER TO IMMIGRATION?

Editor's Note:

In the period following the first World War, immigrants comprised 12 percent of the residents of United States. Reactive legislation restricting immigration from Asia and southern and eastern Europe was passed in the early 1920s. The discriminatory intent of these restrictions—privileging white immigrants from western Europe over all other migrant candidates—was repealed in the mid-1960s, yet the racial and ethnic biases underlying immigration law remain. Perhaps it is merely a lack of national reflection, but legalized discrimination has always been a part of immigration restrictions.

In recent decades the inflow of migrants from Mexico and other Latin American countries has escalated so that the proportion of foreign-born residents of America rivals that of 1920. Public concerns about immigration have escalated as well, with restrictive proposals dominating the national news and legislative debate. In the 1920s America privileged western Europeans; who will we choose to privilege in the early 21st century?

Opponents of open borders frame the debate in terms of security and economic costs. Proponents contend that few individual decisions rival migration for the sacrifice it demands. Some migrants arrive in the United States with ample family ties, financial resources, and human capital (e.g., education and work experience). Others arrive with little more than hope and courage. It is possible, though not conclusive, that immigrants place some economic burdens on America; but these costs may be minor in comparison to the social benefits gained by the vitality hidden within immigrant dreams and ambitions.

Tatcho Mindiola, Ph.D., is the director of the Center of Mexican American Studies and Associate Professor of Sociology at the University of Houston. His primary research and teaching interests are in race relations, with particular emphasis on Mexican Americans and other Latinos. He is the author of

Black-Brown Relations and Stereotypes along with Yolanda Flores Neiman and Nestor Rodriguez (University of Texas Press, 2003).

Howard Jacob Karger, Ph.D., is Professor at the University of Houston. He is the author of *Shortchanged: Life and Debt in the Fringe Economy* (Berrett-Koehler, 2005) and, along with David Stoesz, of *American Social Welfare Policy: A Pluralist Approach* (5th ed.) (Allyn & Bacon, 2006). He has published widely in the field of social-welfare policy, including community economics, income maintenance policy, poverty policy, and social development.

YES

Tatcho Mindiola

The border should be opened, and it inevitably will be. This opinion is based on two interrelated variables: (1) the economic power of U.S. capital and its need for inexpensive Mexican labor, and (2) the long-term trend of integration between the economies of Mexico and the United States. The economic power of U.S. capital and its need for cheap Mexican labor will ultimately redefine the border as less of a rigid boundary and more of a symbolic marker of sovereignty. A formal process is already underway.

The opening of the border may occur in two phases. The North American Free Trade Agreement (NAFTA) signed by the United States, Canada, and Mexico, which took effect in 1994, represents the first phase and removes all tariffs and administrative barriers to the free movement of capital, products, technology, and ideas across each country's border. This has led to more commercial interaction between the two countries than ever before. The second phase may remove all barriers to the free movement of labor, but this has been put on hold amidst security concerns resulting from 9/11. Nevertheless, this may be only a temporary delay in the long-term vision of turning the North American continent into a single economic unit where there are no restrictions on the movement of labor across the Mexico–U.S. border. Under this scenario, Mexico's economy will become an even more complete part of the U.S. economy. It will also result in more social and cultural integration between the two countries. The overall trend is for both countries to become more, not less, integrated and the force driving the process is economics.

ECONOMIC INTEGRATION

The absorption of Mexico's economy by the United States has been underway for more than 150 years. The United States has always had the more dominant economy, and Mexico has not been able to withstand the pull of U.S. economic might. Today, the U.S. economy is the most powerful in the world, and the disparity between it and that of Mexico can be seen by comparing their respective Gross Domestic Products (GDP). The United States' GDP is $12 trillion, while Mexico's is $700 billion, or 6 percent of the U.S. GDP (Villarreal, 2005).

Mexico's economy reflects the relationship between capital and labor (both are an essential part of the equation), with capital being the more powerful force. Capital expands by utilizing inexpensive labor. The less industry has to pay for labor the greater the capacity to earn profits and expand. The inherent "logic of capital" is, therefore, to seek the cheapest labor. Mexico is a reservoir of cheap labor and the United States is the reservoir of excess capital. The process of capital and labor "finding each other" occurs primarily in the U.S. marketplace, where there is a great demand for cheap labor.

The economic integration with Mexico began in 1823 when Anglos colonized Texas with Mexico's permission. Anglo colonization eventually led to the U.S.–Mexico war of 1848, where a defeated Mexico was forced to sell half of its land (now the Southwestern states of Texas, New Mexico, Arizona, Colorado, California, and parts of Utah and Idaho) to the United States for $18 million.

This did not satisfy some of the owners of capital, who wanted to take all of Mexico, by force if needed, and make it a protectorate of the United States. Others argued that force would not be necessary, and that the best way to conqueror Mexico was by taking control of its economy. It was this strategy that prevailed.

The takeover of Mexico's economy began in 1888 with the presidential election of Porfirio Díaz, who, as dictator, ruled the country for 30 years. Díaz wanted to modernize Mexico through industrialization and opened up the country to foreign investments. Not surprisingly, U.S. capitalists became, and continue to be, the major source of foreign investment. The initial investments were in railroads, but they quickly spread to oil, mining, agriculture, and then to telephones, telegraphs, and urban transportation. Investment was so heavy that by 1910 about half of Mexico's economy was owned by foreign investors, the major ones being from the United States (Gonzales & Fernandez, 2003).

Major U.S. investments in Mexico have continued to grow. In 1980, U.S. investments totaled $5.9 billion; by 2004 that rose to $66.5 billion. (U.S. Census Bureau, 1991, Table 1395; 2006, Table 1283). In addition to these investments, U.S. investors in Mexico now own or control the production or manufacture of copper, aluminum, petroleum products, industrial chemicals, electrical and nonelectrical machinery, transportation equipment, automotive, rubber, food and beverages, commerce, tobacco, computers, office equipment, pharmaceuticals, and television programming, and dominate tourist hotels and related services (Cockcroft, 1998). There is no major economic sector in Mexico not wholly or partly owned by a U.S. corporation or its subsidiary. A symbol of the U.S. economic influence in Mexico is Vicente Fox, the current president and former CEO of Coca-Cola in Mexico.

Mexican labor has responded to these investments by finding and gravitating to U.S. capital both within Mexico and the United States. U.S. investments in Mexico in the late 19th and early 20th centuries spurred the movement of labor by displacing it from ancestral lands. These lands were confiscated to claim the acreage needed to lay rail and build the infrastructure needed for its operations and maintenance, and triggered one of the first mass migrations of Mexicans. Many went to work for the railroads, laying the track that runs from the northern part of Mexico into its interior. Others went to work on the haciendas whose owners were convinced by U.S. capital to begin producing cash crops for export. Still others migrated to Mexico City, or to the north to work in the mines being developed by U.S. capital. The northern movement rapidly increased the size of the border cities, which eventually became today's staging areas for crossing into the United States. The border cities also received a mass influx of people when U.S. capital started developing the agricultural regions in northern Mexico in the 1940s, and in the 1960s when U.S. corporations established the assembly plants known as maquiladoras along the Mexican side of the border.

In the early 1900s Mexican workers responded to the demands of the U.S. labor market by crossing the border, a trend that continues today. Most Mexican labor has been undocumented, but there have also been numerous contracts signed between the U.S. and the Mexican governments to legally allow Mexican labor to enter the United States. The migration of Mexican labor into the United States has not been without conflict, but it has nevertheless continued and increased.

Mexican labor moved across the border relatively freely until the Great Depression of the 1930s, when these workers were blamed for the economic malaise, rounded up, and sent back to Mexico. During WWII, Mexican labor again migrated to the United States in large numbers due to the labor shortage created by the war. This movement continued throughout the Korean War, but the postwar years saw an economic recession, and Mexican workers were again blamed, rounded up, and sent back to Mexico.

During the early 1960s undocumented labor once more crossed into the United States in large numbers. These numbers increased during the late 1980s, and continued through the turn of the century. The recent number of Mexicans crossing has been called the largest movement of Mexican labor into the United States. Not coincidentally, it was spurred on by one of the most expansive growths of the U.S. economy in history. Although many economic sectors in the United States have integrated Mexican workers, the sectors most dependent on this labor are manufacturing, agriculture, construction, hospitality, and the service industry (Kochhar, 2005; Passel, 2005).

SOCIAL AND CULTURAL INTEGRATION

The concepts of capital and labor should not obscure the fact that it is human beings who are crossing into the United States from Mexico. They bring not only their labor but their culture and, in many instances, their families. Whether they stay depends on several factors; settling in the United States is only one possible outcome. Some return to Mexico and will cross again in the future. Others establish transnational communities and live in both countries, moving back and forth as circumstances dictate. And others decide to stay in the United States and raise their families. The settlement of immigrants and their descendants is especially evident in the states that border Mexico, where both Mexican and Anglo cultures have mingled for almost two centuries.

Approximately 15.3 million people of Mexican origin reside in the Southwest, comprising 74 percent of the 20.6 million Mexicans who live in the United States (U.S. Census Bureau 2000, Table 2). The Southwest has the strongest Mexican influence since they lived there before the Anglo colonizers arrived. The Mexican presence in the Midwest began in the 1900s, and in the last 30 years Mexicans have migrated to New England and the Southern states.

Mexicans who settle in the United States are eventually assimilated into U.S. culture, and they and their offspring typically follow a pattern of integration not unlike that followed by the European immigrants at the beginning of the 20th century. However, while European immigrants have stopped coming to the United States in large numbers, Mexicans have not only continued migrating, but their numbers have grown. Mexican culture is, therefore, always being replenished and kept alive by immigration.

The immigrant generation is integrated through participation in the labor market. The majority learn to speak English in varying degrees of fluency the longer they remain in the United States, but for the most part their acculturation is partial. The second and later generations become more assimilated and integrated into American culture. The vast majority of immigrants born or raised in the United States view it as their country and are patriotic. Many are bilingual, especially the second generation. Since bilingual and bicultural people can move easily between two cultures, they have become a symbol of what it means to be a Mexican American.

Second, third, and later generations typically increase their level of education and experience upward mobility. Over time, a significant middle class develops, which leads to more integration into the United States. There is more participation in the civic life of the host country as Mexican Americans begin to vote and achieve representation in government. In turn, Mexican culture becomes more diffuse and integrated into the United States.

Spanish is the second most-spoken language in the United States and it is the language most studied in high schools and colleges. Mexican cuisine is the number-one ethnic food in the United States, and is so popular that it is becoming a mainstream food, even in many non-Mexican eating establishments. But the most significant indicator of integration is intermarriage rates. The number of Mexican Americans who marry non-Mexicans increases over time. In 1970, for example, 23 percent of all Mexican Americans married a non-Mexican. By 1990, that rate jumped by 11 percent to 34 percent. In cities such as Houston, the intermarriage rate is higher, averaging 46 percent between 1960 and 1990 (Rosenfeld 2002; Valdez, 1993). The increase in intermarriage rates suggests that these groups are interacting on a regular basis in a variety of settings—workplace, school, churches, leisure venues, and entertainment establishments—and indicates a great deal of acceptance on the part of each group. It also implies that the discriminatory and prejudicial barriers of the past are breaking down.

THE BORDER

Some fear that an open border will make it easier for terrorists to enter the United States. This concern is leading to a variety of proposals designed to stop undocumented immigration, including one that seeks to build a fence on the U.S. side of the border. Obviously, no one wants a border that allows terrorists to cross into the United States or Mexico freely. But terrorism is only one of several security issues of concern to both countries. To date, there has been no published data indicating that terrorists have tried to enter the United States through the Mexican border; nevertheless, the possibility exists that it may occur in the future. What we need is not symbols, rhetoric, or exclusion, but cooperation, negotiation, and concrete efforts to bilaterally make the border as safe and secure as possible.

Security involves more than just being concerned about terrorists. It also includes recognizing that both countries need the safety valve that immigration provides. By any measure, Mexico is a poor country that shares a 2,000-mile-long border with the richest country in the history of the world. If the border were somehow miraculously sealed and undocumented immigration stopped, there is the real danger that the Mexican economy would collapse because of its inability to absorb those prevented from migrating. An economic collapse raises the possibility of chaos, which could stimulate an even greater migration into the United States. It also raises the specter of a group hostile to the United States coming to power in Mexico. Given the U.S. interest in protecting its southern border, it would in all probability intervene militarily to prevent this from happening. In turn, this could spark a greater crisis, not only in Mexico but also in the United States, especially among Mexicans and Mexican Americans. Thus, a completely sealed border could pose more dangers than many people imagine.

CONCLUSION

The opening of the Mexico–U.S. border is inevitable given the countries' economic integration and the U.S. domination of the Mexican economy. A border that impedes the free movement of labor when all other aspects of economic integration are underway represents a contradiction that will eventually give way to the power of capital. As indicated by signing the NAFTA agreement, economic interests in both countries recognize this contradiction and are committed to keeping a relatively open border.

In all probability, an open border will be phased in over a long period of time. The president of Mexico has speculated that full integration of the Mexican and U.S. economy may take up to 40 years, and that the first steps toward the free movement of labor can begin within the next 10 years by increasing the number of legal immigrants. The hope, of course, is that completely integrated economies between Mexico, the United States, and Canada will lead to an increase in Mexico's standard of living, thereby reducing the number of people who migrate to the United States. Only time will tell if this will occur, but the prospect for an open Mexico–U.S. border is inevitable and cannot be denied. It is only a matter of when this will happen.

NO

Howard Jacob Karger

Open immigration between the United States and Mexico is obviously a highly charged political and social issue. If people call for closing U.S. borders to anything but legal immigration, they are immediately assumed to be racist, bigoted, Nazis or Ku Klux Klan members. However, in the world of practical politics the fault line around this issue is less clear.

In his 2006 State of the Union address, George W. Bush stated, "We hear claims that immigrants are somehow bad for the economy, even though this economy could not function without them. All these are forms of economic retreat, and they lead in the same direction, toward a stagnant and second-rate economy" (White House, 2006). Bush's 2005 State of the Union speech characterized America's immigration system as "outdated, unsuited to the needs of our economy and to the values of our country." He argued that "we should not be content with laws that punish hardworking people and deny businesses willing workers and invite chaos at our border. It is time for an immigration policy that permits temporary guest workers to fill jobs Americans will not take. . ." (White House, 2005). In the 2004 presidential race both George Bush and John Kerry agreed on the need to curb illegal immigration.

THE POLITICAL RIFT AROUND ILLEGAL IMMIGRATION

The vague stance—and erratic enforcement record—of the Bush administration on illegal immigration has been a sore spot for conservatives who demand a tightly closed border with Mexico. Their argument is based on a twin premise. First, illegal immigrants drain the public treasury through high demands for social-welfare benefits, school and hospital/medical services, and increased correctional costs. These conservative groups argue that Americans are tired of sharing their public resources with illegal immigrants. Second, conservatives point to the security threat posed by porous southern borders and to the possibility that terrorists will exploit this weakness to infiltrate the nation. For these conservatives, illegal immigration is tantamount to an illegal invasion of the United States.

Americans for Legal Immigration PAC (ALIPAC) is a conservative political action committee formed to address the supposed disparity between the public's desire for more control of illegal immigration and the inaction of lawmakers. ALIPAC (2006) claims that polls show that more than 75 percent of Americans want more done to control illegal immigration. They also charge that elected officials willing to address this problem constitute only a minority of the Congress and Senate.

The American conservative movement is caught in a double bind. On the one hand, grassroots conservatives and a handful of lawmakers are demanding more barriers along the United States–Mexico border and more job-site raids to uncover undocumented workers. On the other hand, business groups, such as the U.S. Chamber of Commerce, a strong conservative ally, want a temporary-worker program, saying they desperately need immigrant labor to fill the jobs Americans will not take. But in the absence of such a program, they seem content to accept a porous border that allows anywhere from 250,000 to 3 million undocumented workers a year to enter the United States. This is in addition to the 11 million undocumented workers already here (Americans for Legal Immigration PAC [ALIPAC], 2006).

The issue of open borders sharply divides both conservative and liberal camps. Jim Gilchrist's Minuteman Project has mobilized thousands of volunteers to patrol the Arizona, California, and Texas borders to report sightings of illegal immigrants to the Border Patrol. Although the Minutemen claim to be "lawn chair" observers, critics have ascribed more pernicious motives to the group. Nevertheless, Gilchrist, a retired California accountant and former Marine, is highly critical of the Bush administration's "soft approach" to illegal immigration. This outrage was aggravated by the Enhanced Border Security and Visa Entry Reform Act of 2002, which omitted provisions for cracking down on undocumented workers from Mexico. The goal of Gilchrist's Minutemen is straightforward—seal the border from California through Texas (the longest border in the world between a developed and developing nation) to anything other than legal immigration.

Daniel Griswold, the director of the Cato Institute's Center for Trade Policy Studies, a conservative think tank, has a different take on the issue. According to Griswold (2003):

> America's immigration laws are colliding with economic reality, and reality is winning. Migration from Mexico is driven by a fundamental mismatch between a rising demand for low-skilled labor in the U.S. and a shrinking domestic supply of workers willing to fill those jobs. The Labor Department estimates that the total number of jobs in our economy that require only short-term training will increase from 53.2 million in 2000 to 60.9 million by 2010, a net increase of 7.7 million.
>
> Meanwhile, the supply of American workers willing to do such work continues to fall because of an aging workforce and rising education levels. By 2010, the median age of American workers will reach 40.6 years, while the share of adult native-born men without a high school diploma continues to plunge: from more than half in 1960 to less than 10% today. Older, educated Americans understandably have better things to do with their work time than to wash windows, wait tables and hang drywall. (p. 4)

In a plea for more liberal immigration laws, Griswold (2003) asserts that:

> Current immigration law has made lawbreakers out of millions of hard-working, otherwise law-abiding people—immigrant workers and native employers alike—whose only "crime" is a desire to work together in our market economy for mutual advantage. Death in a boxcar is perverse punishment for seeking a better life. (p. 5)

The knotty problem of illegal immigration has also divided the liberal movement. While most liberals are relatively soft on illegal immigration, Senator Hillary Clinton has taken a far stronger position than even the Bush administration. In one interview, she proudly proclaimed "I am, you know, adamantly against illegal immigrants" (Hurt, 2004). To stop illegal immigration, Clinton has called for an advanced radar system on the border and biometric and other kinds of identification systems.

THE CASE FOR CURBING ILLEGAL IMMIGRATION

There are compelling reasons to believe that an open border with Mexico is deleterious to the well-being of low-wage American workers. A 2004 study by Harvard economist George Borjas (2004) found that when immigration increases the supply of workers in a skill category, the earnings of native workers in that same category falls. This negative effect will occur regardless of whether the immigrant workers are legal or illegal, temporary or permanent. Conversely, reducing the labor supply by strict immigration enforcement increases the earnings of native workers. Borjas found that between 1980 and 2000 immigration reduced the average annual earnings of native men by an estimated $1,700 or roughly 4 percent. The wages among native workers without a high school education—roughly the poorest 10 percent of the workforce—were reduced by 7.4 percent. Borjas also found that the negative effect on native black and Hispanic workers is significantly larger than on whites since a much larger share of them are in direct competition with immigrants.

As a result of this wage pressure, native workers may be "voting with their feet." Borjas maintains that for every 10 immigrants that move into a state, eight natives either move out or choose not to move into the state. This theory is supported by Congressional reports concluding that in California, immigration accounted for just under 60 percent of population growth from April 2000 to July 2004. The reports also found that newly arrived immigrants filled all net new U.S. jobs created since 2000 (Lochhead, 2005).

Some liberal and procorporate pundits claim that illegal immigrants are doing jobs that Americans will not do. At best, this statement is hyperbole. For instance, 79 percent of all service workers are native, and 68 percent of all workers are in jobs requiring only a high school education. Illegal immigrants make up only 17 percent of workers in building cleaning and maintenance occupations, 14 percent of private household workers, 13 percent of accommodation industry workers, 13 percent of workers in food manufacturing, 12 percent of the workers in construction and extraction occupations, 11 percent of workers in food preparation and serving occupations, and 8 percent of workers in production occupations (Hostettler & Smith, 2005). The remaining workers in these job categories—the lion's share—are native.

Seventeen million adult U.S. citizens lack a high school degree, 1.3 million are unemployed, and 6.8 million discouraged workers have stopped looking for work. The percentage of 16- to 19-year-olds with jobs is now at its lowest point since 1948. American workers in building, cleaning, and maintenance have an 11 percent unemployment rate, as do 13 percent of those in construction and 9 percent of food preparation workers (Hostettler & Smith, 2005). The data clearly repudiates the canard that illegal immigrants take jobs that Americans refuse to touch. On the contrary, the evidence suggests that illegal immigrants are in direct competition with native workers for many of the same types of jobs. The data also suggests that native American workers are losing the battle.

Illegal immigration devastates not only low-income workers but also legitimate small businesses. Small businesses that hire undocumented workers often work on a cash basis, thereby avoiding taxes on profits and on their employees' pay. This puts legitimate small-business owners—those who pay taxes and provide benefits—at an extreme economic disadvantage. In turn, businesses that hire primarily undocumented workers have driven legitimate companies out of gardening, and are doing the same to other service industries such as house painting, roofing, and car repair. Illegal immigration has created a robust underground economy and a hole in society's tax pocket through which a lot of loose cash falls out.

As long as undocumented workers are allowed to stream across porous borders, there is no reason for farm, hotel, and restaurant owners to pay anything above the minimum wage. Sadly, America's service economy is increasingly being built on the backs of a constant stream of poorly educated undocumented immigrants willing to work for a pittance. In fact, the American service industry has become a race to the bottom in terms of wages.

Illegal immigration has created a new tier of second-class exploited labor. It is a system of oppression whereby undocumented workers are afraid to demand even the most rudimentary employment rights, including payment for overtime. In fact, undocumented workers have no workplace rights whatsoever. The two primary beneficiaries of this system are rapacious domestic companies and the Mexican ruling elite who benefit from the steady flow of remittances these workers send home—remittances that now constitute the country's second-largest source of foreign income.

Illegal immigration has also put a severe burden on the nation's health and social-welfare systems. In large measure, funding for America's social welfare and educational system is predicated on available tax resources rather than need. Since tax dollars are finite, the increased service needs of undocumented workers do not automatically translate into more services. According to a study by the Federation for American Immigration Reform (FAIR, 2004), illegal immigration cost California's education system an estimated $7.7 billion, and its health-care system another $1.4 billion. Given the sad state of California's budget, illegal immigration accounts for a sizeable chunk of red ink. The drain on public services caused by illegal immigration has led to fewer and more parsimonious tax-based health and social-welfare services for America's indigenous poor.

The regulation of legal and illegal immigration must be calibrated to a tax base capable of supporting the increased need for services and the documented labor shortage within the society. These prerequisites are not being currently met. Opening the United States–Mexico border in an economic context where wages have been stagnant since the late 1990s and where the minimum wage has been frozen since 1997 will further depress the wages of indigenous low-income workers. Moreover, it is not that Americans will not work; it is that they will not work for slave wages under intolerable working conditions. The right to a fair, safe, and clean workplace has been a hard-fought gain for U.S. workers. Wisely, most U.S. workers are reluctant to give up that right.

Undocumented workers make the lives of the middle class more comfortable. We get to have cheap hamburgers, gardening, and maid service. We can get our cars fixed more inexpensively and our houses roofed and painted. Illegal immigration makes it possible for us to live better on less. But can we afford to pay the hidden costs in the long run?

REFERENCES

Americans for Legal Immigration PAC. (2006). *Help stop illegal immigration!* Retrieved from http://alipac.us/modules.php?name=Content&pa=showpage&pid=16.

Borjas, G. (2004, May). *Increasing the supply of labor through immigration: Measuring the impact on native-born workers.* Washington, DC: Center for Immigration Studies.

Cockcroft, J. D. (1998). *Mexico's hope: An encounter with politics and history.* New York: Monthly Review Press.

Federation for American Immigration Reform. (2004). The costs of illegal immigration to Californians: Executive Summary. Retrieved from www.fairus.org/site/PageServer?pagename=iic_immigrationissuecentersffec.

Gonzales, G. G., & Fernandez, R. (2003). *A century of Chicano history: Empire, nations, and migration.* New York: Routledge.

Griswold, D. (2003, February 19). *Capitol Hill panel discussion on Mexican immigration.* Washington, DC: Center for Trade Policy Studies, CATO Institute.

Hostettler, J., & Smith, L. (2005, December 2). *We must put citizens and legal immigrants first. U.S. Border Control.* Retrieved from www.usbc.org/profiles/2005/fall/first.htm.

Hurt, C. (2004, December 13). Hillary goes conservative on immigration. *The Washington Times,* p. 16.

Kochhar, R. (2005). *Survey of Mexican migrants: The economic transition to America.* Washington, DC: Pew Hispanic Center.

Lochhead, C. (2005, May 5). Immigration hurts American workers, lawmaker says. *San Francisco Chronicle,* p. A4.

Passel, J. S. (2005). *Unauthorized migrants: Numbers and characteristics, background briefing prepared for task force on immigration and America's future.* Washington, DC: Pew Hispanic Center.

Rosenfeld, M. J. (2002). Measures of assimilation in the marriage market: Mexican Americans 1970–1990. *Journal of Marriage and Family 64,* 152–162.

U.S. Census Bureau. (1991). *Statistical abstract of the United States: 1991.* 111th ed. Washington, DC: Government Printing Office.

U.S. Census Bureau. (2000). *The Hispanic population: Census 2000 brief.* Washington, DC: Government Printing Office.

U.S. Census Bureau. (2006). *Statistical abstract of the United States: 2006.* 126th ed. Washington, DC: Government Printing Office.

Valdez, A. (1993). *Intermarriage among Mexican Americans in Harris County, 1960–1990.* Unpublished paper, Graduate College of Social Work, University of Houston.

Villarreal, A. M. (2005). *U.S.–Mexico economic relations: Trends, Issues, and implications.* (CRS Report, RL32934.) Washington, DC: Government Printing Office.

White House. (2005, February 6). *State of the Union Address.* Office of the Press Secretary, United States Capitol, Washington, DC. Retrieved from www.whitehouse.gov/news/releases/2005/02/20050202-11.html.

White House. (2006, January 31). *President Bush delivers State of the Union Address.* Office of the Press Secretary, United States Capitol, Washington, DC. Retrieved from www.whitehouse.gov/news/releases/2006/01/20060131-10.html.

SHOULD SOCIAL SECURITY BE PRIVATIZED?

Editor's Note:

Social Security is a social insurance system that provides income supplements for retirees, the disabled, surviving spouses without an employment history, and surviving children. It has been unequaled as a means for spreading the risks of old age, disability, and premature death across all levels of U.S. society.

Social Security is funded out of "premiums," which are paid through employee wage deductions matched by an equal amount from the employer. The advantages of this system have been strong public support, relatively low wage deductions, and confidence that retirees would get more in benefits than they paid in. When Social Security benefits were added to corporate pensions and personal savings—the intent of the 1935 legislation—retirement no longer meant poverty for the vast majority of Americans.

All of this is changing. Corporate pensions are almost an anachronism, and many Fortune 500 firms are substituting employee savings plans for traditional pension programs. Moreover, those entering the workforce since the early 1990s may get less in retirement benefits than they paid in premiums. In effect, they are paying for retired workers who didn't pay their fair share during their working careers, and paying more in anticipation of the retirement of the baby-boomer generation. What can we do about it?

Proponents of privatization want to sever retirement benefits from the insurance components. They claim that the higher rates of return earned in stock-and-bond markets will help younger workers accumulate more for retirement than Social Security provides. Opponents are against dismantling the most successful social insurance program in the nation's history, decrying the erosion of the social compact and the potentially greater financial risk to the younger generation.

William W. Beach, M.A., is the director of the Center for Data Analysis at The Heritage Foundation and a Visiting Fellow at the University of Buckingham in Great Britain.

Steven Rose, Ph.D., is Professor of Social Work at George Mason University. His research areas include child, youth, and family services; social services in school and community systems; and group processes, interventions, and outcomes. His books include *Task Groups in the Social Services* (Sage, 1995), *Group Work with Children and Adolescents* (Sage, 1998), and *Social Work with Children and Adolescents* (Allyn & Bacon, 2003).

YES

William W. Beach

President George W. Bush devoted most of his public policy energy in 2005 to making the case for Social Security reform. Indeed, much of the policy community in Washington—think tanks, prominent news outlets, interest groups, lobbyists—devoted enormous resources to the debate over Social Security's future. In the end, Congress refused to act and put off for another day the passage of reforms that would assure the future of the nation's premier public-pension system.

Despite the lack of legislative action, the great Social Security debate of 2005 proved enormously useful. It is probably fair to say that voters are more informed today about the future of Social Security than at any time in the recent past. More Americans than ever appear to appreciate the need for updating Social Security and doing so before the giant wave of baby-boom retirements enter the system over the next 15 years.

Social Security's Old-Age and Survivors Insurance (OASI) program—certainly the United States' most important old-age income program—is quickly becoming one of the country's most expensive public policy liabilities. After 71 years of providing nearly certain income maintenance during retirement or after the premature death of a spouse, the oncoming retirement of the baby-boom generation threatens to undermine the system. If Congress and the president fail to act soon, Social Security will be unable to meet its obligations by the time the boomers' children start to retire (H. R. Rep. No. 109-18, 2005, p. 8).

Social Security's financial challenges are hardly news. Indeed, nearly a decade of debate and discussion by advocates and critics of the system have made these challenges clear to anyone interested in the subject. If any aspect of the current disputes over Social Security's future is settled, it is that dark financial clouds hang over the retirement system's next 50 years. So why have Congress and the president failed to act?

Most questions about politicians' behavior can be answered by studying voters' behavior. The truth is that the politics behind the debate over

Social Security's financial future have been shaped by a false opposition: that the current system is secure and that reform would be too risky. The widespread public acceptance of this opposition has, in turn, spawned complacency among political leaders. They have failed to act in the system's best financial interests.

SOCIAL SECURITY'S RATES OF RETURN

Many analysts begin their case for reforming Social Security with the simple and utterly true observation that demographic fundamentals of the program have changed, well, fundamentally. They point out that Social Security transfers income from current workers to current retirees, which means that the system needs at the very least four workers for each retiree to produce the promised retirement benefits at today's tax rates. However, there will be fewer workers in the future than Social Security requires. That means that Social Security must increase its tax rate or cut its future benefit to retirees or change; and change means, to some analysts, the introduction of a savings element, such as a Personal Retirement Account, inside Social Security.

The reform debate of 2005 focused principally on the demographic imbalances inherent in Social Security. As important as this feature is, it is not the only reason why Social Security needs to be changed as soon as possible. Lurking behind all the talk about unsustainable worker-to-retiree ratios is the inescapable fact that Social Security taxes fall heaviest on low- and moderate-income workers who will one day depend more on Social Security for retirement income than their higher-income counterparts. This would be all right were it not for Social Security's excessively low rate of return.

If Americans were allowed to direct their payroll taxes into safe investment accounts similar to 401(k) plans, or even supersafe U.S. Treasury bonds, they would accumulate far more money in savings for their retirement years than they are ever likely to receive from Social Security. For example:

- *Social Security pays a very low rate of return for two-income households with children.* Social Security's inflation-adjusted rate of return is only 1.42 percent for an average household of two 30-year-old earners with children in which each parent made just under $26,000 in 2006, assuming both adults were born in 1976. Such couples will pay a total of about $391,787 in Social Security taxes over their lifetimes (including employer payments) and can expect to receive benefits of about $571,781 (before applicable taxes) after retiring at age 67, the retirement age when they become eligible for full Social Security Old-Age benefits. Had they placed that same amount of lifetime employee and employer tax contributions into conservative tax-deferred IRA-type investments—such as a mutual fund split equally between U.S. government Treasury bonds and equities—they could expect a real return rate of about 4.7 percent per year prior to the payment of taxes after retirement. In this latter case, the total amount of income accumulated by retirement would equal approximately $1,094,150 (before applicable taxes).

■ *The rate of return for some ethnic minorities is negative.* Middle-income, single African American men born after 1959 face a negative real rate of return from Social Security. For every dollar he has paid into Social Security, a single, 37-year-old black man who earned about $50,000 per year would have a −2.25 percent rate of return (see The Heritage Foundation Social Security Calculator at www.heritae.org.research/features/socialsecurity/SSCalcWelcome.asp). This negative rate of return translates into lifetime case *losses* of $102,800 on the taxes paid by the employer and the employee.

Black women typically live longer than their male counterparts, yet even they have a rate of return lower than that of the general population. A 21-year-old African American single mother who in 2006 made just $25,000 can look forward to a real rate of return on her Social Security taxes of only 0.69 percent. Under conservative assumptions, if she had saved those same tax dollars in a private investment account composed of government bonds, she would have received a real return of around 3 percent per year. With a mixed portfolio of bonds and equities, she could expect a return on her investments of at least 4.8 percent. Social Security promises (though it may not be able to pay) a monthly benefit of $2,776 for this individual. However, if her payroll taxes had been invested in a portfolio composed of Treasury bonds and equities, she would have a monthly retirement annuity (before taxes) of $5,402, or $2,626 more than Social Security.

WHY RATES OF RETURN MATTER

Defenders of Social Security argue that rates of return are irrelevant to the OASI portions of the program. Social Security, they suggest, was intended to provide a basic but decent retirement income to beneficiaries and stopgap incomes for surviving spouses. Future Social Security beneficiaries, they argue, should be saving now for additional retirement income to supplement OASI benefits. Thus, they maintain that comparing rates of return on private pension investments with those from a public retirement program intended to pay out at least 35 percent of the wages an average worker earned is akin to comparing apples with oranges (H. R. Rep. No. 104-228, 1997, Table R1, p. 36).

This line of reasoning contains a fundamental flaw. If Social Security taxes were low enough to enable workers to save these additional dollars for their retirement, apologists for the system might conceivably be correct in characterizing Social Security as a pension program of last resort. But Social

Security taxes are not low, and they are crowding out the ability of most low- and middle-income Americans to save for retirement. Thus, the rate of return on these taxes is vital, especially for those Americans for whom Social Security is their main retirement savings.

As payroll taxes have risen, many more Americans have fewer dollars left over for supplemental retirement investment. Over the past 25 years, Congress and the president have increased Old-Age and Survivors benefits so often and so much that today the high payroll taxes needed to pay those current benefits crowd out private retirement investments (Feldstein, 1996). In 1972, the average worker with his or her employer paid 8.1 percent in Old-Age and Survivors payroll taxes on the first $9,000 of wages and salary equivalent to about $42,050 in 2005. In 2005, that worker paid 10.6 percent on the first $90,000 of earned income (or the first $19,260 in 1972). In other words, the tax rate increased by 1.3 times between 1972 and 2005 and the taxable income limit increased 2.1 times after adjusting for inflation over that same time period. Moreover, between 2020 and 2046, the Old-Age and Survivors tax rate will have to rise to 14.4 percent from today's 10.6 if the growth of benefits is not slowed.

Because of rising payroll taxes for retirement, increasing numbers of poor and middle-income workers do not have the after-tax funds needed to create private supplemental pension investments, and many firms have been discouraged from providing employee pensions due to rising taxes and costly regulations. In fact, Social Security taxes now consume as much of the average family's budget as do outlays for food, and nearly three times more than annual health-care expenses (Bureau of Labor Statistics, 2005).

Because of the long-term financial problems of the Social Security trust fund, calculations of the rate of return for Social Security are likely to prove optimistic. The fact is that Social Security will not be able to pay out old-age benefits to the baby-boom generation without additional tax increases on workers or benefit cuts. These tax increases or benefit cuts will further reduce Social Security rates of return for those workers currently in their 20s, members of the so-called Generation X, and their children. As these return rates fall, the relevance of rates of return on private pensions rises. That is, members of Generation X are not simply going to ignore the decaying prospects for adequate income during their retirement years. Rather, they will insist on more opportunities to create pensions to supplement Social Security's Old-Age benefits. Thus, comparing rates of return for private and public pensions will become even more important to each new generation.

In addition, the rate of return is important because the crowding-out effect of high Social Security taxes on private savings for low- and middle-income workers affect the wealth that such individuals can leave to the next generation. Few aspects of Social Security are as unintended or as damaging to low- and moderate-income workers as the squeeze that high payroll taxes have put on the formation of intergenerational wealth transfers. The inability of poor workers to accumulate enough savings to leave a nest egg to their children can mean that those children will be as dependent as their parents could be on their monthly Social Security check. It means that poor communities will not have as much "homegrown" capital with which to create new jobs and sources of income. Without these new jobs and income, members of the next generation will be less able to save for their retirement as well. Thus, by taxing away one generation's opportunity to help the next generation start earning at a high level, the Social Security system acts as a drag on future generations.

SOCIAL SECURITY MAY IMPEDE WEALTH TRANSFERS

It is one thing for those most dependent on Social Security's retirement program to be bound to a system that yields rates of return below those for passbook savings accounts. It is quite another thing if this system also impedes the growth of supplemental retirement savings. For middle- and upper-income workers, Social Security's low rates of return are less of a problem. These workers usually have access to pension plans and other company-sponsored retirement savings programs. They also make sufficiently high wages and salaries to be able to purchase Individual Retirement Accounts (IRAs) and participate in 401(k) and 403(b) tax-advantaged savings programs. Thus, the ability of these workers to save for retirement and pass on wealth to their children is seldom impeded by Social Security's high taxes or low rates of return.

For low- and moderate-income workers, however, employers often do not provide pension plans. These individuals' incomes are so low that they seldom have any reason to purchase tax-advantage savings vehicles like IRAs or U.S. savings bonds. Indeed, millions of workers who pay taxes to Social Security pay little if any income tax. Thus, for them, the tax system is FICA, or the 10.6 percent of wages that go to pay for retirement and survivors insurance.

Economists in the Center for Data Analysis (CDA) have published research that shows how Social Security affects wealth creation in low- and moderate-income households. Center analysts used data from the Current Population Surveys of the U.S. Bureau of the Census and the Survey of Income Program Participation to trace the wealth-creation patterns of households at various income levels and demographic types. The construction of this database provided the CDA with a baseline of how covered workers, or those workers who pay FICA taxes, currently accumulate assets.

Center analysts then contrasted this set of baseline outcomes with those that would have occurred had these same workers had access to a Social Security system consisting of Personal Retirement Accounts (PRAs) and the traditional pay-as-you-go program. In other words, workers had the ability (in this experimental world) to invest a portion of their 10.6 percent payroll tax that currently pays for the OASI program in a Personal Retirement Account (PRA), or an IRA that they controlled and could access only at retirement. The buildup in that account would pay for part of the worker's retirement. The remaining amount up to the full amount the worker would have received anyway from Social Security would be paid by Social Security from the remaining payroll taxes (Beach, Goyburu, Rector, John, Johnson, & Bingel, 2004). This work shows that even this modest substitution of the PRA for a portion of the current Social Security substantially enhances low- and moderate-income families' ability to create greater retirement income or a nest egg for their children.

CONCLUSION

When the Social Security system began, its aim was to help ordinary Americans and those in disadvantaged positions to have adequate financial security in their retirement years. However, as this analysis and a gathering body of research shows, the current system may actually decrease the lifetime well-being of many socioeconomic groups—even under the most favorable assumptions. Among the groups who will lose out under the current system are single mothers, low-income men, average-income married couples with children, and even affluent professionals. Indeed, many ordinary Americans already understand that the Social Security system is a bad deal.

This analysis of the Social Security system almost certainly underestimates its total economic costs. For instance, it makes no attempt to include the benefits from faster economic growth, higher wages, and increased employment generated by a retirement program in which individuals are allowed to invest their Social Security tax dollars and build the wealth necessary to sustain them in their old age.

The debate on Social Security reform at times may feature technical terms (such as the "replacement ratio" and the trust fund's "long-range actuarial balance") that mean little or nothing to most American families. However, there is little doubt that the outcome of the debate will have profound importance for them.

But this debate is also a concern to the 30-something married couple who earned a combined income of $52,000 in 2005 and who struggled to put away enough for retirement while paying over one-eighth of their income into a Social Security system that is likely to yield a real return of less than 1.7 percent on their contributions. Moreover, the outcome of the debate will influence the life of people, perhaps not yet born, who quite possibly could become employed by a business that is created by the retirement investment of young, high-income couples.

For almost every type of worker and family, retirement under Social Security means receiving fewer dollars in old age and passing on less wealth to the next generation than they could if they placed their current Social Security tax dollars in private retirement investments instead.

NO

Steven Rose

Economic insecurity is growing in this country. It has been estimated that a majority (58 percent) of the U.S. population will be poor at some point between the ages of 20 and 75 (Rank, 2004). While the poverty rate has decreased for the elderly, many hover near the poverty line.

Social Security, of course, has a significant role to play in keeping the elderly out of poverty. Social Security was designed to provide bedrock coverage for many people (not just the elderly). It represents a legitimate function of the federal government even though, for the past half century, and particularly since the 1980s, it has been reexamined and privatization has been considered.

The ongoing debate about the privatization of Social Security is significant because so much is at stake, not least of which is the economic well-being of so many people. It appears that if Social Security were to be privatized, either entirely or in part, it would accelerate privatization in other social service areas as well. The consequences of privatization would likely be closely observed by other governments, including those of countries whose economies are less affluent or stable. I will attempt to show how the arguments made in favor of privatization do not necessarily require privatization to occur, and how the public system is less risky, more efficient, and better for both society and individuals than a privatized system.

HISTORY AND POLITICS

Fears about the changing age demographic, or the graying of America, and indeed considerable parts of the world, has exacerbated society's challenges in caring for its elderly population. However, care of the elderly is not a brand-new social problem. Social Security has a long history. Originally intended to countervail socialism, the first insurance program for old age was introduced by Bismarck in Germany in 1889 (Karger, 1996). It is perhaps ironic that in the United States it is being fought by those who call it socialistic. Born out of the nation's experience with the crash of the stock market in 1929 and the ensuing Great Depression, and sandwiched between World Wars I and II, it was a social necessity. Although some government safeguards are in place that would make the reoccurrence of a stock market crash less likely to reoccur, an economic disaster is still possible, and despite the gains in economic science and econometrics, economic depressions are still not readily amenable to prediction. Social Security enhances the financial security of the elderly by alleviating retirement incomes of the risk associated with free-market economic forces.

In more recent decades, political changes in the United States reflect a shift to the right, corresponding to the ascendance of a conservative ideology encompassing advocacy for a free-market economic system following the defeat of communism in the Cold War. The scoffing by the political right of public social-welfare programs lessened the acceptance or support for anything that can be made to appear like communism, including Social Security, and has undercut public support for social assistance. The right has been eager to dismantle Social Security, which it sees as a vestige of an earlier liberal era; however, the right has yet to propose a privatization option that provides the elderly financial security on a par with that provided by Social Security.

BUSINESS AND THE ECONOMY

The federal government has made attempts to get out of or minimize exposure to the social-welfare business. Efforts include attempting to restrict the funding available for social welfare. Devolution of federal responsibility has transferred the financial outlays and programmatic administration to state governments, as well as to other sectors of society, including the religious, the family, and the business sectors. The ascendance of family values in the conservative agenda suggests that families ought to take care of the elderly and the government should be relieved of overseeing that responsibility. Given that extended families are no longer very common in the United States and given that many families no longer directly house the elderly nor routinely provide for their basic living needs, elder care is increasingly subject to monetization. Considerable sums of money are expended for care provided by paid caregivers. The increased monetization of American society forms the backdrop of the Social Security debate (Martin, 2002).

The ascendance of business in society and its influence on the social services has contributed to making the consideration of the privatization of Social Security possible by its advocates. Business is on a quest for new domestic markets, such that social services and benefits, a huge item in the large federal budget, are new targets for business entrepreneurs. Increasingly, business and social values have been converging. Moreover, it has been bidirectional such that while social services have been influenced by business, the latter has seen social services as a prospective market. Business interests are not only interested in capturing the revenue associated with the provision of social services, business interests are also interested in tapping into the massive availability of capital represented by the Social Security trust fund. The advantages of these changes to the business sector are evident, but the advantages to the elderly are more circumspect. Higher rates of return require the assumption of greater risk, but the elderly are particularly averse to risk due to lower levels of financial resiliency and their incapacity to return to employment.

PRIVATIZATION IS LIMITED ASSISTANCE

Privatization changes Social Security from a defined-benefit plan, in which recipients receive guaranteed distributions based on cost-of-living adjustments, to a defined-contribution plan, in which recipients receive only their individual investment plus interest earned. It is neither desirable nor necessary to change our current Social Security system to a defined-contribution program. As it currently exists, the Social Security system is a useful complement to the increasingly prevalent employer-based defined-contribution pension plans and individual savings plans. Changing Social Security to a defined-contribution plan shifts all the risk for retirement income to the individual. Will our society accept an increase in elder poverty? If not, privatization could easily result in future costs that ultimately would need to be absorbed by society.

A move to privatization could usher in an unwelcome change in the social contract. It would involve a disruption in the current pattern of multi-generation family caretaking and in the employer–employee relationship. Ironically, privatization may represent a threat to the ideal of the traditional nuclear family advocated in the profamily stance by the right and require higher levels of intergenerational caregiving. It could affect employers' sense of responsibility for caring for their employees. Ultimately, privatization represents a change in the expectations and roles of governmental responsibility to the elderly, the widowed, dependent children, and persons with disabilities.

In other countries where privatization has been tried, such as Chile and Sweden, the national government has had to pay private companies through tax breaks to assume the administrative burdens associated with privatization. If these costs were to be borne by individuals, it would hinder the accumulation of retirement savings. A changeover to a privatized system would also entail huge transitional costs estimated by some to be as large as $2 trillion over the first 10 years (Karger & Stoesz, 2006). Privatization would be a very expensive choice for government and the taxpayer.

Changes involving privatization could also transfer the additional administrative burdens to employers. Employers do not usually relish having more paperwork to complete, particularly in complex and time-consuming matters such as individualized retirement options. It could easily become a great burden on small businesses and quite costly to them. They will not willingly assume the administrative burden without some relief or compensation from the government.

EQUITY, ACCESS, AND EFFICIENCY

Potentially, enormous financial benefits would accrue to corporations in managing the accounts in a privatized Social Security system. Currently, 44 million people collect Social Security benefits (Burtless, 2002). This prospect has led several companies to spend millions of dollars to convince the American public that the Social Security system is broken in a big way and that it must be reformed or privatized. Evidence suggests that the current Social Security system is readily accessible and user-friendly. Moreover, it is a very cost-efficient program.

No one argues that Social Security is a perfectly fair and equitable system. It does attempt to provide some redistribution of wealth from those segments of the population with shorter life expectancies (e.g., the poor and African American males) to those with longer life expectancies (Davis, 2005). Issues of gender (Herd & Kingson, 2005) and intergenerational equity (Williamson, McNamara, & Howling, 2003) continue to remain vexing problems. A privatized system would appear to solve these problems, but would create new ones.

Those people who already have a great deal of income or wealth and already are knowledgeable about investment matters, or are in the position to hire a capable financial investment advisor to oversee their accounts would clearly benefit from privatization. But what of those who do not have such means and knowledge? How will they be protected from the vicissitudes of market fluctuations, embezzlement, fraud, theft, unscrupulous accounting practices, and hidden and illicit activities by white-collar executives? Ultimately, the privatization controversy represents two different systems of values and of views of society. Keeping Social Security in the public domain affirms it as a program for all.

Potentially, privatization might spur the development of different programs for different classes of individuals in different geographical regions, potentially reducing the social cohesiveness of the country and misrepresenting the potential benefits as occurred in Great Britain (Walker, 2001). Indeed, market forces might push it in that direction so that it would not in actuality provide equal access and service. This would change a program that is a public good into one that would enrich the few and impoverish, or at least underserve, the many. It may bring forth many choices of providers whose differences in program features, values, costs, and benefits would be a challenge for the public to fathom. More choices often impede rather than facilitate decision making, as evidenced by the recent experience with Medicare prescription plans.

Privatization would increase the complexity of the program, thereby making it more difficult to access for many people. Wittingly or unwittingly, a privatized version of Social Security would likely place new organizational obstacles in the way for potential recipients. Individuals would have to learn about new financial management operations and organizations. Working knowledge requirements of English or Spanish language, American culture, and of contemporary computer applications, as well as either access to or ownership of computers with Internet access, would likely place privatized Social Security well beyond the range of those persons who are likely to need it. A privatized Social Security system would result in a further widening of the gap between the have and have-not sectors.

Under a privatized Social Security system, providers would likely be selected as the result of a political process. In such a model it is likely that the costs of administration for a profit-making provider would be borne by participants in the Social Security system. The net result would be a reduction in benefits for recipients in a privatized system due to the costs of managing the system accounts. Even apparently small percentages, such as the recently proposed 1 percent, can have large consequences for actual net benefits. Of course, over time escalation in administrative costs seems likely.

Social Security is designed to provide economic stability. Any suggestion that the gains would be greater under a system that allows for investments in stocks has yet to be proven. What is known is that privatization would result in the loss of employment of many Social Security employees and require public oversight. Hard-to-reach people who actually are more likely to need Social Security would be those least desirable in a privatized system. Ultimately, the federal government would likely be placed in the position of assuming responsibility for helping persons for whom the administration of benefits would be the most costly.

OBLIGATIONS AND RESPONSIBILITIES

Privatization of Social Security is suspect in regard to its motivation, which largely appears to be that of increasing the wealth of corporations. It is difficult to see much true regard for the public good. Certainly it is not to improve benefits or services for Social Security beneficiaries.

It appears that privatization of Social Security represents an unrealistic attempt by the Federal government to transfer its obligations to help its citizenry. This would be in line with a narrow view and minimalist definition of the scope of responsibilities of the federal government. The consequences of such a view of government would create a society with much larger holes in its safety net.

Furthermore, it appears highly likely that privatization would result in a less stable service-delivery system. This would portend considerable difficulties in receiving benefits regularly by many recipients who depend on Social Security for all or even a significant portion of their limited incomes. They cannot afford any disruption, because even the loss or significant delay of one payment may have drastic repercussions in their lives. Many Social Security recipients are unlikely to be well equipped to weather the storm induced by such changes, communicate with providers, and satisfactorily resolve issues.

CONCLUSION

The real nature of Social Security's current problems are difficult for the public to determine given the proclivity and propensity for the selective use of information by businesses who would reap huge profits through management fees. The extent to which Social Security is broken has been exaggerated by the proponents of privatization (Herd & Kingson, 2005). Basically, the system works and just requires some tinkering or fine-tuning (Diamond & Orszag, 2005). Privatization of Social Security is a drastic choice, which would not solve predicted future financial problems and may, in fact, create many new challenges. Drastic changes are unnecessary. The forecasted economic problems of Social Security can be readily addressed while minimizing the probability of creating new problems associated with individual accounts.

Retirement security requires financial guarantees the scope of which only the federal government is able to assume. Forecasting long-term political and economic events is notoriously inaccurate. Privatization would inevitably involve the use of speculative investments in stocks or other high-risk strategies, which are inappropriate for a social assistance intended to be a safety net. Essentially, privatization would be a grandiose social experiment whose likely outcome would be increased wealth for financial corporations and wealthy individuals, and increased social insecurity for the nation's elders and many others who depend on it. Social Security is a remarkably successful program, indeed a model program. Experimenting with alternatives is unwarranted at this time.

REFERENCES

Beach, W. W., Goyburu, A. B., Rector, R. A., John, D. C., Johnson, K. A., & Bingel, T. (2004). *Peace of mind in retirement: Making future generations better off by fixing Social Security.* (Center for Data Analysis Report no. CDA04-06). Washington, DC: The Heritage Foundation.
Bureau of Labor Statistics. (2005). *Report no. 986: Consumer expenditures in 2003.* Retrieved May 22, 2006, from www.bls.gov/cex/csxann03.pdf.

Burtless, G. (2002). Social security privatization and financial market risk: Lessons from U.S. financial history. In T. Ihori & T. Tachibanaki (Eds.), *Social security reform in advanced countries: Evaluating pension finance* (pp. 52–80). London: Routlege.

Davis, E. (2005). Social security and the African American male (a cash transfer system). *Journal of Sociology & Social Welfare, 32,* 71–84.

Diamond, P. A., & Orszag, P. R. (2005). Saving social security: The Diamond-Orszag plan. *The Economists' Voice, 2,* 1–8.

Feldstein, M. (1996). The missing piece in policy analysis: Social Security reform. *NBER Working Paper Series, No. 5413,* 1–14.

H. R. Rep. No. 109–18. (2005).

H. R. Rep. No. 104–228. (1997).

Herd, P., & Kingson, E. R. (2005). Reframing social security: Cures worse than the disease. In R. B. Hudson (Ed.), *The new politics of old age policy* (pp. 183–204). Baltimore: The Johns Hopkins University Press.

Karger, H. J. (1996). The challenge of financing social security in the United States. In J. Midgley, & M. B. Tracy (Eds.), *Challenges to social security: An international exploration* (pp. 19–34). Westport, CT: Auburn House.

Karger, H. J., & Stoesz, D. (2006). *American social welfare policy: A pluralist approach* (5th ed.). Boston: Allyn & Bacon.

Martin, R. (2002). *Financialization of daily life.* Philadelphia: Temple University Press.

Rank, M. R. (2004). *One nation underprivileged: Why American poverty affects us all.* New York: Oxford University Press.

Walker, C. (2001). The forms of privatization of social security in Britain. In J. Dixon, & M. Hyde (Eds.), *The marketization of social security* (pp. 123–142). Westport, CT: Quorum.

Williamson, J. B., McNamara, T. K., & Howling, S. A. (2003). Generational equity, generational interdependence, and the framing of the debate over Social Security reform. *Journal of Sociology & Social Welfare, 30,* 3–14.

DOES AMERICA NEED NATIONAL HEALTH INSURANCE?

Editor's Note:
The U.S. health-care system is driven by ideological and fiscal concerns. Primary among them is whether access to health care should be a right or privilege. Conservatives generally believe that health is not a right but a privilege that must be earned through past or present labor force participation. Grounded in a European context, liberals argue that health care is a right and should be bestowed on each individual at birth.

In recent years, the American health-care system has been severely criticized. Many people are unable to afford health insurance, the numbers of families without any insurance coverage has reached alarming proportions, and growing numbers of ordinary citizens are dissatisfied with the cost of medical treatment. Numerous proposals for reforming or replacing the health-care system have been formulated. One proposal calls for a federal single-payer health insurance program similar to Canada's. This proposal has been rejected by those who believe that the health-care system functions more effectively when it is open to competitive market forces. Critics of a national health-care policy want little or no federal involvement in health care.

Manuel F. Zamora, Ph.D., is a lieutenant with the Houston, Texas, Police Department assigned to the Crime Analysis Division. He is also a graduate of the FBI National Academy and the 2006 president of Phi Alpha Social Work Honor Society. Dr. Zamora's research interests include conflict resolution, anger/aggression, workplace violence, and crisis intervention. He authored a 2005 task force committee report for the U.S. Department of Justice and Houston activist organizations, including the NAACP, on Use of Force and a Coalition Memorandum for Justice.

Robert E. Moffit, Ph.D., is Director of the Center for Health Policy Studies at the Heritage Foundation, and a 25-year veteran of Washington policymaking. A former senior official at the U.S. Department of Health and Human

Services and the Office of Personnel Management, both under former president Ronald Reagan, Dr. Moffit specializes in Medicare reform, health insurance, and other health-policy issues.

YES

Manuel F. Zamora

American health care costs $1.9 trillion and employs 10 percent of the U.S. workforce (Department of Health and Human Services, 2006, National Coalition on Health Care, 2006; National Association of Social Workers [NASW], 2002). However, the inherent problems in the health-care system are quickly reaching a crisis point. In turn, the debate around a national health insurance (NHI) program will inevitably gain momentum.

Despite its world-class medical personnel and sophisticated medical technology, primary health care in the United States is becoming less accessible as the costs spiral out of control and the coverage contracts. This is leading to a substandard level of health care compared to other, similar nations. According to Jill Quadrango (2004), the United States is the only Western industrialized nation that fails to provide universal coverage and the only nation where health care for the majority of the population is financed by for-profit, minimally regulated private insurance companies (p. 25).

THE COSTS OF THE PRESENT HEALTH-CARE SYSTEM

For the unemployed, underemployed, and temporarily employed, health-care coverage is becoming more inaccessible. According to the U.S. Census Bureau (DeNavas-Walt Proctor, & Lee, 2005), the number of U.S. citizens lacking health insurance has increased to 45.8 million, 9 million of whom are children. These Americans lack access to Medicare and Medicaid, much less private insurance. They also cannot access benefits involving consumer-directed health care, such as flexible spending accounts (FSAs, pre-tax deductions for health care); Archer Medical Savings Accounts (MCAs, trusts for medical care that roll over from year to year and may be invested); Health Reimbursement Arrangements (HRAs, deductions to employee compensation set aside for medical use); and Health Savings Accounts (HSAs, part of a tax-exempt, high-deductible health plan) (Hermer, 2005). For the 30 million Americans who are underinsured, the safety net of available charitable health care includes for-profit and nonprofit hospitals.

In 2004, about 174 million U.S. workers and their families (approximately 60 percent of the population) received health insurance through their employment. However, as premiums rise, prescription coverage is curtailed, and referrals to specialists or surgical procedures are denied, citizens question whether companies making large profits are reducing costs (if they are being reduced at all) at the expense of access, education, and the delivery of comprehensive quality care (NASW, 2002, p. 170).

Jill Quadrango (2004) cites stakeholder mobilization as a predominant reason why the United States lacks a national health insurance plan. Powerful stakeholder groups, such as the American Medical Association, the American Hospital Association, the Insurance Economic society, and employer groups are able to defeat every effort to enact national health insurance across an entire century because they have superior resources and an organizational structure that closely mirrors the federated arrangements of the American state (p. 25).

Health-care costs are clearly spiraling out of control. In 2004 the nation's total national health expenditures rose by 7.9 percent—over three times the rate of inflation. Total spending was $1.9 trillion dollars ($6,280 per person, compared to $2,164 for a resident of Britain), and comprised 16 percent of the gross domestic product (GDP). In 2005, annual employer health insurance premiums rose by 9.2 percent, with a family of four paying close to $11,000 and a single person paying $4,000 (National Coalition on Health Care [NCHC], 2006). This $11,000 eclipsed the total wages for a minimum-wage earner ($19,724). From 2000 to 2005, employer-based insurance premiums rose by 73 percent, while cumulative inflation rose 14 percent, and cumulative wage growth rose 15 percent. Health insurance costs are the fastest-growing business cost and, at the current rate, will exceed profits by 2008.

Administrative costs for health-care programs consumed approximately one-sixth of the $1.9 trillion spent on U.S. health care in 2005. This amounts to an estimated $300 billion per year. Redirecting the hundreds of billions of dollars squandered each year on the health-care bureaucracy would be enough to cover all the uninsured, pay for full drug coverage for seniors, and upgrade coverage for the 10s of millions who are underinsured (Woolhandler & Himmelstein, 2005). The only industries hurt would be the big HMOs and drug companies (Sirota, 2006b). By the way, in contrast, government expenditures on public health-care programs such as Medicare amount to about 4 cents for every dollar.

A single-payer national insurance system would contribute to stability in long-term financing for health care. It would cut costs by streamlining health-care paperwork and by making universal, comprehensive coverage affordable. For example, Massachusetts' three largest private insurers spend over $1.3 billion annually on billing, marketing, high executive salaries, and administrative costs. This amounts to 10 times as much overhead per enrollee as Canada's national health insurance program. Hospitals and doctors spend billions more fighting with insurers over payments for each aspirin tablet, X-ray and doctor's visit. Cutting bureaucracy to Canada's levels would save at least 11 percent of current health expenditures, enough to cover all the uninsured in Massachusetts and improve coverage for other patients (Physicians for a National Health Program, 1999).

The State of California contracted with Lewin Group, a private independent consulting firm, to analyze 10 alternative proposals to increase health-care coverage to its citizens. The firm concluded that pay-or-play models, which require employers to finance coverage, would increase state health-care costs by $2 billion, while a single-payer plan would reduce overall costs by $7 billion and provide comprehensive coverage for residents of California. The single-payer plan would trim $18 billion in unnecessary administrative costs and excessive prices for prescription drugs and medical supplies. This is more than enough to fund universal coverage (Grumbach & Lee, 2003).

WHY WE DON'T HAVE NHI

HMOs nearly doubled their profits from 2002 to 2003, adding $10 billion to their bottom line. That year, top executives at the 11 largest health insurers made a combined $85 million in salaries (Sirota, 2006b). In 2004 alone, the four biggest health insurance companies reported $100 billion in revenues ($273 million per day, every day, 365 days of the year). That level of revenues allowed the health industry to spend more than $300 million on lobbying in 2003, and another $300 million on campaign contributions since 2000. On the other hand, CEOs mindful of rising costs are raising copays, trimming benefits, or cutting health insurance altogether. Some companies, like Wal-Mart, are encouraging their lower-wage workers to sign up for Medicaid (Emanuel & Fuchs, 2005, p. 20).

Physicians do not receive a tax benefit or relief from medical malpractice when providing charitable care to an uninsured or Medicaid patient. Low physician-reimbursement rates, rising overhead costs, and increasing malpractice premiums are fueling entrepreneurial activity by physicians. Many primary-care physicians are choosing to limit their practice to insured patients willing to pay additional retainers for specialty work, such as in cardiac care, neurosurgery, and orthopedics (Gunnar, 2006). The net effect is a lucrative field for insured-patient health care. Such specialty hospitals are not emergency medical facilities and therefore do not have to admit the medically indigent.

THE HEALTH STATUS OF AMERICANS COMPARED TO INDUSTRIALIZED COUNTRIES WITH AN NHI PROGRAM

In 2004 the Institute of Medicine attributed 18,000 unnecessary U.S. deaths to the lack of health insurance. In comparing U.S. and British national health-care approaches, a 2006 study published by the *Journal of the American Medical Association* reached an unambiguous conclusion after controlling for age, race, obesity, income, education, and other variables: At every point in the social hierarchy, there is more illness in the United States than in England, and the differences are really dramatic, said study coauthor Dr. Michael Marmot, an epidemiologist at University College London, in England. The upper crust in both countries proved healthier than middle-class and low-income people in the same country, but richer Americans' health status resembled the health of the low-income British (Banks, Marmouth, Oldfield, & Smith, 2006). British health-care expenditures are roughly half that of the United States.

In 2003 the Canadian Institute for Health Information found that the nation spent, on average, $3,839 for each resident's health care. The amount reflects the Canadian government's contribution of over 71 percent to health-care costs, compared to 44 percent in the United States, and 85 percent in Denmark, Norway, and Sweden (Canadian Institute for Health Information, 2005). Canada's cost of national coverage totaled $121 billion, or slightly less than 10 percent (9.7 percent) of its GDP. The Canadian plan provides government health insurance for most critical services, leaving the option open for citizens who want additional coverage or additional services.

In comparison, the de facto health-care rationing in the United States results in unnecessarily expensive tax-supported public emergency-room services, disproportionately inferior service to the lower socioeconomic strata of society, serious quality issues in rural-based health care compared to urban areas, and low levels of patient compliance with medication protocols. Moreover, health-care providers, particularly physicians, have little motivation to care for the Medicaid population because of the exceptionally low reimbursement rates (Gunnar, 2006). Medicaid often reimburses physicians at a rate lower than the cost of service provided. Each of these adverse consequences of financial rationing could be prevented through rational regulation. A more intelligent approach to health-care regulation can improve health outcomes.

THE CURRENT APPROACH TO HEALTH CARE IS FRAGMENTED, COMPLEX, AND COSTLY

Countries with single-payer systems lack the convoluted health-law landscape found in the United States. For example, The False Claims Act was created to address fraud and abuse, kickback measures, and trust violations. A 1999 Mayo Clinic study found that hospitals must comply with 132,720 pages of Medicare rules alone (Hermer, 2005, p. 39). Laws and regulations are constantly changing, and providers are required to remain current on them. Penalties for noncompliance can be severe. Ironically, there are no similar government regulations in countries with universal health-care coverage. According to Hermer (2005), many expenses associated with navigating our web of overlapping and duplicative legislation at the state and federal levels would no longer apply, leading to reduced health-care costs (p. 40).

The policy logic of having a Medicare-for-all NHI system is compelling. Medicare remains extremely popular with seniors, who rate it higher than working adults rate private health plans. Health-care-industry experts concede that the simplest way to guarantee coverage for all Americans is to make every resident automatically eligible for coverage under a single public plan, thereby avoiding the chaos of eligibility linked to specific employers or degrading and cumbersome "means testing" of family income. Single-payer systems have appealing economic virtues, operating with lower overhead costs than private insurance and exercising greater control of health-care inflation.

AMERICANS WANT CHANGE

In a 2003 ABC News/*Washington Post* poll of 1,000 adults, Americans by a 2 to 1 margin (62 percent to 32 percent) preferred a universal health insurance program over the current private employer-based system (Sirota, 2006b). The same percentage reported they would support a universal health-care system even if it meant waiting for some non-emergency treatments (Hermer, 2005). A Gallup poll in 1993 found that 80 percent of Americans believed that government should be responsible for medical care for people who can't afford it, while a Harris poll found that 91 percent of Americans agreed that "everybody should have the right to get the best possible care—as good as the treatment a millionaire gets" (www.en.wikipedia.org, 2006). Even many doctors support an NHI plan. In 2003, the *Journal of the American Medical Association* published a proposal for government-sponsored universal health care that was endorsed by more than 8,000 physicians (including two former surgeon generals) (Sirota, 2006b).

Many business leaders also support government intervention. For example, Ford, GM, and Chrysler all endorsed Canada's single-payer system. Some small-business owners also support such a plan, even if funded with a small tax increase. In short, the health insurance industry is not only gouging patients, it is also gouging employers who provide health-care benefits to their workers (Sirota, 2006b).

Since 1991, the Physicians for a National Health Program (PNHP, 1991) have championed a proposal to cover all Americans under a single, comprehensive public insurance program without copayments or deductibles, and with free choice of providers. In addition, Mantone (2006) reported that some state officials are working on plans to address needs of the 46 million people without health insurance. About 25 states are considering expanding coverage through employer mandates, 7 states are considering bills with different forms of universal coverage, and 6 states are examining bills that establish commissions for a universal health-care plan.

THE ARGUMENTS AGAINST NHI

Conservatives have made myriad arguments against NHI, including the following:

> *National health insurance is too expensive.* An examination and audit of administrative expenses alone is sufficient to address this concern. An intelligent approach to health care will enable the most effective and efficient application of funding.
>
> *An NHI plan will lead to socialized medicine.* This fear has been created by the AMA and the insurance industry in a well-organized, well-published, grassroots anti-welfare strategy. In other words, they claim that NHI is part of a communist plot to destroy freedom, where patients surrender their liberty in return for low-grade, assembly-line medicine.
>
> *NHI will lead to health-care rationing.* As noted earlier, health-care rationing already exists for the uninsured, and for those covered under private health-care plans that disallow many medical procedures and services. Similar to the Canadian and British models, universal coverage would be available to all residents, while a private alternative would coexist with the regulated health-care system.
>
> *An NHI plan will eliminate incentives for innovation.* NHI would not unduly limit America's open and competitive health-care market. Researchers would continue to have opportunities for medical and technological breakthroughs, while businesspeople could invest in new technologies and pharmaceuticals. Research grants and funding will not necessarily be cut. Moreover, pharmaceutical and medical breakthroughs are quite common in European nations with NHI systems.
>
> *A national insurance program will hurt the economy.* The contrary may be true. Longley (n.d.) argues that NHI would reduce the cost of U.S.-made products. Employers naturally pass on soaring costs of employee health premiums to consumers, resulting in U.S. consumers paying more. This also increases the price of U.S. goods internationally and results in the reduced ability of U.S. goods to compete in global trade (Longley, n.d.).

CONCLUSION

The United States spends trillions on a health-care system characterized by little real connection between health outcomes and expenditures. Health-care expenditures have a negative impact on the market economy since they comprise a significant portion of the GDP yet do little to boost America's productivity, economic strength, or influence in the global economy. Rising health-care costs, including meteoric rises in prescription drug and hospitalization costs, and the shrinking coverage of private insurance plans, strongly suggest that a national health insurance crisis is imminent. This crisis is particularly acute since the baby boomers are aging and thereby requiring more health-care services. However, this imminent crisis can be averted or at least reduced by an intelligently structured NHI program. Without NHI, the best the uninsured and underinsured can hope for is that Congress will guarantee access to emergency medical care, charitable care will be provided from nonprofit hospitals who seek tax incentives, assistance will come from physicians with financial incentives to provide care in underserved areas, and the safety nets provided by federal, state, and local funding entities will hold. A sound NHI plan would improve the health status of Americans while enabling the nation to become a stronger and more competitive player in the global economy.

NO

Robert E. Moffit

"National health insurance," also known as "single-payer," refers to a system of national health-care coverage administered or supervised by the national government, which pays for most or all health-related expenditures. Compared to other proposals to expand health coverage in the United States, single-payer care is deceptively appealing for its apparent simplicity.

While single-payer systems may differ in structure (e.g., Britain's National Health Service is unlike the Canadian or American Medicare systems), their economic dynamics are the same. Coverage is universal. Citizens pay the government taxes, and the government gives them health care. Care is free, or nearly so, at the point of service, and health-care providers become, in effect, public utilities.

Sounds great? It's not. The simple appearance of single-payer care masks the real mechanisms by which it operates: government coercion and rationing of health care.

WHAT THE RECORD SHOWS

Ignore the lofty promises about national health insurance and look at this kind of system's actual performance. The experiences of Great Britain,

Canada, and other countries teach a great deal about how the economic dynamics of single-payer care work in practice. Importing single-payer into the United States will have inevitable consequences.

Politics, Not Medicine, Will Control Health Care

If health care becomes an entitlement, it becomes, for all practical purposes, a "free good." Free goods have certain characteristics. Consumers, although they pay taxes, don't have to pay when they receive a free good and so treat the good as if it were costless—which explains the high utilization of medical services in single-payer systems. If health care is a free good, then demand for it will be almost unlimited. Because no real market is left to match supply and demand, health care is no longer subject to the market's price discipline, which keeps down costs.

When costs are not controlled by the market, they are controlled by politics. Politicians cannot, of course, control *demand*. What people want—or need—is simply beyond politicians' control. They can, however, control *supply* in a variety of ways. Canada, for example, limits health-care spending with an annual budget cap. A variation on the Canadian approach is to limit payments to doctors and hospitals with a complex system of price controls. In response, the supply of medical services within the single-payer system shrinks, shifting costs outside the system and onto patients and their families. Periodically, Congress and state legislatures do this when they alter the pricing schedules in Medicare and Medicaid.

Political control of health-care decisions under single-payer is inevitable. When unlimited demand collides with limited supply, rationing is the result, and someone has to do the rationing. Government officials—not doctors or patients—have to make big and often painful (to patients, that is) decisions about where, how, when, and to whom care is provided. For example, economist Paul Krugman (2005), a supporter of a government-run system, is quite frank about this: "For decades we've been lectured on the evils of big government and the glories of the private sector. Yet health reform is a job for the public sector, which already pays most of the bills directly or indirectly and sooner or later will have to make key decisions about medical treatment."

Government Will Ration Access to Care

Universal government health insurance does not automatically translate into universal access to care. Beyond the political machinery of global budgets and price controls, single-payer systems require patients to queue and wait for medical treatment. This is inevitable when supply is restricted in the face of rising demand.

Rationing causes the quality of care to fall. Doctors are rushed, and patients' conditions fester as they wait for treatment and follow-up. In

Britain, waiting-list numbers reached 1.2 million in England alone by 1999 (Aaron, Schwartz, & Cox, 2006), and British politicians are now obsessed with fixing the National Health Service (NHS).[1] NHS's most serious problem is its substandard treatment of major diseases, such as heart disease and cancer. British cancer patients have much lower survival rates than U.S. cancer patients. The treatment of cardiovascular disease is also poor within the NHS, with only 5 percent of British medical specialists having access to specialized stroke units (Adam Smith Institute, 2005).

Not surprisingly, a recent survey of British doctors found that a stunning 41 percent of senior hospital physicians are enrolled in private health insurance (Templeton, 2006). For example, Dr. Sarah Burnett, a London radiologist diagnosed with breast cancer and 15-year NHS doctor, had harsh words for her former employer: "NHS treatment is not a pleasant experience in any way—from the standard of the food, to ward cleanliness . . . I was lucky enough to have exceptionally prompt treatment because I chose to pay for insurance. Under the NHS I would not have been screened until 50 for breast cancer and would not have been able to catch my cancer at such an early stage. The type of surgery I had is only rarely available on the NHS, depending on the expertise of your local surgeon" (Templeton, 2006). The British Medical Association, *The Sunday Times* reported, does not consider the large number of British doctors enrolled in private health insurance to reflect a lack of confidence in the NHS: "They want speedy treatment so they can get back to looking after their NHS patients as soon as possible" (Templeton, 2006).

Waiting lists are also routine in Canada. According to a recent analysis by the Fraser Institute, a Canadian think tank, the median wait time for a referral from a general practitioner to a specialist is 17.7 weeks.[2] The longest median waiting time was for orthopedic surgery, at 40 weeks, and the shortest for medical oncology, at 5.5 weeks. While waiting times for more serious medical conditions were shorter, a Canadian Medical Association survey revealed that less than two-thirds of Canadian physicians rated access to urgently needed acute care as excellent, very good, or good (Goodman, Musgrave, & Herrick, 2004).

---

[1]With heavier spending and tax increases, the Blair government has reduced that number. Britain's labor party made an election pledge in 1997 to treat 100,000 more patients, but despite these initial efforts, the number waiting actually increased by an additional 100,000 patients within 2 years of Labor's 1997 election victory. The objective has been to raise British health-care spending from 6.8 percent of the GDP (in 1997) to 9.4 percent by 2007–08. See Reform strategies for the English NHS, by Simon Stevens, 2004, *Health Affairs, 23*(3) (May/June), p. 38.

[2]The study focused on 12 medical specialties in 10 Canadian provinces. See *Waiting your turn: Hospital waiting lists in Canada*, by N. Esmail and M. Walker, 2005, The Fraser Institute, October. Retrieved from www.fraserinstitute.ca/share/readmore.asp?sNAV=pb&id=801.

The Quality of Hospital Care Will Decline

Hospitalization is usually the largest single area of spending in health care, and the quality of hospital care is crucial in the treatment of major illness. A major international survey published by *Health Affairs* in 2004 focused on the views of hospital administrators in five countries—Australia, Canada, New Zealand, the United Kingdom, and the United States—on issues of quality of care (Blendon, Schoen, DesRoches, Osborre, Zapert, & Raleigh, 2004). On the provision of intensive-care units, 51 percent of Americans said their facilities were excellent, compared to 23 percent of the British, 30 percent of the Canadians, 35 percent of the New Zealanders, and 42 percent of the Australians. On the quality of operating rooms, 47 percent of Americans said that they were excellent, compared to 9 percent of the British, 25 percent of the new Zealanders, 21 percent of the Canadians, and 29 percent of the Australians. On diagnostic imaging equipment and medical technology, 51 percent of Americans ranked the facilities as excellent, compared to 13 percent of the British, 11 percent of the New Zealanders, 17 percent of the Canadians, and 20 percent of the Australians. The lesson: If you are really sick, you want to be in an American hospital.

In countries with single-payer care, patients are far less likely to get crucial preventative care in a timely fashion. For example, in scheduling a biopsy for a 50-year-old woman with an "undefined mass" in the breast, 74 percent of Americans said that the procedure would be performed in "less than one week," but only 6 percent of the British, 20 percent of the New Zealanders, 30 percent of the Canadians, and 49 percent of the Australians said so. According to the same survey, waiting for hospitalization, emergency services, elective surgery, and post-discharge care is far more common in government-run health-care systems than in the United States. If you want quick, responsive care, check into an American hospital—as so many foreign dignitaries do.

Personal Freedom Will Be Limited

Single-payer proponents promise "free care for all," but it doesn't quite work out that way. While systems differ, under single-payer, the government usually decides what health benefits and services you get, when and how you get them, what you pay for them, and how you pay for them.

Until a recent court decision, Canadian citizens have had no right to spend their own money on medical services that are covered by Canada's Medicare system. Canadians may pay out of pocket for extra services, such as cosmetic surgery, or buy supplemental private insurance for services that are not provided by the government. But Canada is the "only Western country" where it is *illegal* to buy a health insurance policy that covers health benefits provided by the government (Pipes, 2004). Canadians can't even go to private clinics and pay privately for covered but restricted medical services, such as magnetic resonance imaging (MRI) tests. Moreover, Canadian physicians can't provide private care and remain in the government program, like British doctors can.

These restrictions on Canadians' personal freedom are being challenged. In 2005, the Canadian Supreme Court ruled that the ban on private health insurance in Quebec resulted in the unnecessary suffering and death of Canadian patients and thus violated Canada's Chart of Rights and Freedoms (Cherney, 2006).

Oddly enough, American seniors in Medicare are the only class of American citizens who are statutorily restricted in spending their own money on medical services. In 1997, the United States Congress, under pressure from the Clinton Administration, introduced Canadian-style restrictions into the American Medicare program, the huge government health program for seniors and the disabled. Under Section 4507 of the Balanced Budget Act of 1997, a Medicare patient can contract privately with a Medicare doctor only if the doctor signs an affidavit, submits it to the Secretary of the U.S. Department of Health and Human Services within 10 days, and agrees to drop out of Medicare, foregoing all Medicare reimbursement from all other patients, for two full years. Thus, Medicare patients are unable to spend their own money on their health care. The liberal National Capital Chapter of the American Civil Liberties Union and the United Seniors Association, a conservative group, challenged this provision as an unconstitutional violation of personal liberty and privacy. Unfortunately, the challenge was unsuccessful.[3]

Inequalities Will Persist and May Expand

A key argument for single-payer is that all citizens would be treated the same, regardless of their wealth or income. Single-payer proponents often point to Britain and Canada, for example, as having health-care systems that are more "fair" than in the United States.

The reality is different. In Britain, the Labor Government conceded that there were "inequalities" in the British National Health Service and promised to correct them. One of the areas British officials targeted was the gap in medical outcomes between middle- and lower-class Britons. According to the *British Medical Journal,* infant mortality rates, and average life expectancy for men and women were lower for working-class citizens than for British citizens in managerial and professional groups (Dyer, 2005). Inequalities in outcomes—especially mortality rates between social classes and between geographic areas—have actually widened in recent years (Aaron et al., 2006).

[3]For a discussion of the current Medicare restrictions on private contracting, see Congress should end the confusion over Medicare private contracting, by R. E. Moffit, 2000, Heritage Foundation *Backgrounder,* No. 1347, February 28. Retrieved from www.heritage.org/library/backgrounder/bg1347es.html.

Seniors in Britain also have great difficulties getting quality care. Instead, they receive what British authorities recently described as "devastatingly poor care" (Lilley, 2006). Sir John Grimely Evans, professor of clinical gerontology at Oxford University, says that age discrimination is widespread in the National Health Service (Laville & Hall, 1999). Dr. Adrian Treolar, a senior lecturer in geriatrics at Greenwich Hospital, observes that, "There are severe pressures on beds and in order to relieve this there may be a tendency to limit care inappropriately where you feel doubtful about the outcome. Are the elderly being served properly? No. They are not getting what they deserve and I think they are being sold short. I think that is becoming clearer and clearer. If old people start to resist early discharge they are seen as an encumbrance" (Laville & Hall, 1999).

Inequality of care is also a problem in Canada. According to a survey published in the *Annals of Internal Medicine*, 80 percent of doctors and 53 percent of hospital administrators had been involved personally in cases involving preferential treatment; 79 percent said that the "community standing" of the patient ("big shots") would embarrass the hospital if they were dissatisfied with the care; and 71.2 percent said that a patient with a "community standing" could be helpful to the hospital.[4]

In Britain or Canada, patients with financial resources can go outside of their single-payer health-care systems. Often, the prominent and the powerful, such as former Quebec premiere Robert Bourrassa, who was diagnosed with melanoma, travel to the United States for consultation and surgery (Frogue, 2000).

Taxes Will Soar

Right now, taxes—federal, state, and local—consume more than 29 percent of Americans' income (Hintz, 2000). A single-payer system would replace voluntary premium payments for private health insurance with hefty new taxes. In Germany, mandatory "contributions" to the German "sickness fund" total 13.5 percent of payroll, and in France, the health-care tax is 13.6 percent of payroll.[5] In the United States, health-care spending already accounts for 16.5 percent of the Gross Domestic Product (GDP). Just equaling this level of spending would require a massive payroll tax on top of existing taxes.

[4]A survey of provider experience and perception of preferential access to cardiovascular care in Ontario, Canada, by D. A. Alter, 1998, *Annals of Internal Medicine, 129*(7) (October), pp. 567–572. Cited in A high price for patients: An update on government health care in Britain and Canada, by J. Frogue, 2000, Heritage Foundation *Backgrounder,* No. 1398, September 26. Retrieved from www.heritage.org/library/backgrounder/bg1398.html.

[5]Goodman et al., *Lives at risk,* p. 144. See Perspectives on European health care systems: Some lessons for America, by R. E. Moffit, P. Maniere, D. G. Green, P. Belien, J. Hjertquist, and F. Breyer, 2001, *Heritage Foundation Lecture,* No. 711, July 9. Retrieved from www.heritage.org/Research/healthCare/HL711.cfm.

Advocates of a single-payer system argue that America could maintain its current level of health-care spending but that lower administrative costs and greater economic efficiency would lead to net savings. Those savings, however, are likely to be illusory or transitional. One reason is that single-payer systems often have hidden administrative costs, such as the transactional costs of complying with government regulations that are shifted to doctors, hospitals, and other medical professionals and never appear in the government's budget. Another reason is that new taxes for health care would have to compete with every other demand in the congressional budget, including preexisting entitlements, education, energy programs, government pensions, social programs, and national defense. A U.S. version of the single-payer system would be unable to maintain the current level of spending on health care without raising taxes further still.

Some evidence of this is visible in the current Medicaid and Medicare programs, which lurch periodically from one fiscal crisis to the next. They are hardly models of fiscal responsibility. Medicaid, the joint federal and state program for the poor and the indigent, is a major financial problem in almost every state of the Union. Meanwhile, Congress' benefit expansions in Medicare have led to a long-term unfunded liability of almost $30 trillion (including an $8.7 trillion liability attributable to the new Medicare drug entitlement alone), a massive debt that no member of Congress has yet explained how to finance. Paying this debt directly with a Medicare payroll tax increase would result in today's 2.9 percent Medicare payroll tax jumping to 13.4 percent, with devastating consequences for the U.S. economy (Foertsch & Antos, 2005). Any new taxes to pay for a single-payer system would have to be imposed on top of this.

Patients Will Have Less Access to Newer, More Effective Drugs, Therapies, and Technologies

In Britain, the National Institute for Health and Clinical Excellence (NICE) determines whether new treatments are cost effective and thus available within the NHS. As well, NICE offers guidance to NHS doctors about when treatments should be used and avoided. This guidance is a form of government rationing that can and does save money. It appears that in making its approval decisions, NICE uses a cutoff price of $53,000 per quality-adjusted life year (QALY) for publicly funded medical treatments (Reinhardt, Hussey, & Anderson, 2004). By comparison, current U.S. health-care practices imply a much higher value per each additional quality-adjusted life year.

Since 1999, NICE has reviewed 93 drug and medical treatments and procedures and recommended full use of treatments in 28 cases, restricting use in 57 cases, and no use in 8 cases (Whalen, 2005). As an example of how the system works, NICE determined that Herceptin, a drug used in the treatment of early stage breast cancer, was too expensive but allowed local health services to provide it. Thus, patient access to Herceptin is a function of cost and geography. Anne Marie Rogers, a cancer patient, borrowed $8,700 to pay for the drug herself and filed suit in the British courts for relief from NHS. Because she could not remortgage her house to pay for the drug due to her grim diagnosis, Rogers was forced to discontinue use of the drug (Lyall, 2006).

American patients' access to medical technology on a *per capita* basis is routinely far greater than that of Australian, British, or Canadian patients, according to a major *Health Affairs* survey. For example, there are 8.1 magnetic resonance imaging (MRI) units per million people in the United States, but only 4.7 in Australia, 3.9 in Britain, and 2.5 in Canada. Americans have far greater access to CT scanners, coronary angioplasty, renal dialysis, and many other technologies (Anderson, Reinhardt, Hussey, & Petrosyan, 2003). Many say that Americans spend too much on medical technology—a questionable assertion given the effectiveness of newer treatments and medications—but it may be the case that single-payer systems spend too little.

SOME PERSPECTIVE

The United States spends roughly $1.9 trillion on health care—one out of every 6 dollars of GDP—more than any other country in the world, on a per-capita basis. One reason Americans spend more on health care is simply because Americans can afford to spend more.[6] Health care is a desirable good produced by highly complex and labor-intensive sector of the American economy. American physicians and medical professionals are quickly responsive, and also better paid than those of other countries.

Roughly 85 percent of Americans have health insurance coverage and access to a wide range of medical treatments and procedures. Most of those with insurance are generally satisfied with their coverage. Those Americans without health insurance are legally entitled to hospital care, whether they can pay for it or not.[7]

Not all is perfect with the U.S. health-care system—far from it. It is not even a "system" in the normal sense of the word. There are too many medical errors, malpractice laws are out of date, and patients too often lack crucial quality and safety information and the ability to act on that information to be good consumers. These problems, however, are not confined to the United States, and they do not constitute the biggest complaint with health care in America. The biggest complaint—too many Americans go without

[6]See U.S. health-care spending in an international context, by U. E. Reinhardt, P. S. Hussey, & G. F. Anderson, 2004, *Health Affairs, 23*(3), (May/June), p. 12. Retrieved from http://content .healthaffairs.org/cgi/content/full23/3/10t.

[7]Legal requirements to provide care to Americans regardless of their ability to pay have been reinforced by both litigation and government regulation.

insurance coverage—is a valid one. But the number of Americans without insurance can be dramatically reduced without resorting to a single-payer system and its inevitable consequences.

A Superior Alternative

The best solution to cover the large minority of Americans without health insurance is to give every American direct tax relief for the purchase of health insurance or to provide a health-care subsidy for poor families. The current tax treatment of health insurance benefits upper-income families, while providing little or nothing for poor, working families. Ideally, a universal tax credit system would replace the entire existing tax regime for health benefits (including employer-based coverage), which amounts to more than $210 billion annually.[8] Another option, though less comprehensive, would be to provide a targeted, refundable individual health-care tax credit to those who do not or cannot get health insurance through their employers. A generous and progressive health-care tax credit would enable families to buy the health plans they want, and receive direct assistance from the government in doing it, just as individuals and families receive generous health-care tax relief today when their employers purchase their health coverage.

CONCLUSION

A single-payer health system could work in the United States, but it would resemble single-payer systems elsewhere because the economic dynamics would be the same. Americans would have to be willing to accept much higher levels of taxation, a loss of personal freedom, and government control over personal health-care decisions. Moreover, they would have to lower their expectations about the kind and quality of health care they receive. They can expect long lines, long waits for treatment, less access to advanced medical technology, wider gaps in their quality of care, and fewer opportunities to take advantage of newer and more effective pharmaceuticals.

These things are inevitable under a single-payer system because, despite the rhetoric of its proponents, single-payer care is not based on universal equality in the delivery of health services, fairness, or anything like friendly persuasion. Rather, what makes single-payer systems work is their reliance on cold-eyed government discipline. The coercive power of government to restrain, guide, and direct doctors and patients and to control costs by limiting medical services is key to single-payer health care. Individual

---

[8]For the most recent version of the Heritage proposal for universal coverage, see Reforming the tax treatment of health care to achieve universal coverage, by S. M. Butler, 2001, in *Covering America: Real remedies for the uninsured*, Vol. I, Economic and Social Research Institute, June 2001, pp. 21–42. Retrieved from www.esresearch.org/rwj11PDF/full_document.pdf.

choice, in contrast, plays a tiny role. Only if Americans can accept government control over health-care decisions concerning themselves, their parents, and their children could single-payer work in the United States. But that is a lot to ask of independent-minded Americans when easier and less-intrusive methods of expanding health insurance coverage are available.

REFERENCES

Aaron, H. J., Schwartz, W. B., & Cox, M. (2006). *Can we say no?: The challenge of rationing health care.* Washington, DC: The Brookings Institution Press, p. 20.

Adam Smith Institute. (2005). Public, private . . . and people. Briefing Paper. Retrieved from www.adamsmith.org.uk.

Anderson, G. F., Reinhardt, U. E., Hussey, P. S., & Petrosyan, V. (2003). It's the prices, stupid: Why the United States is so different from other countries. *Health Affairs, 22*(3) (May/June), 99.

Author unknown. (2004). Minnesota ranks as healthiest state. (Brief article.) *Cappe's, 126*(24), 1.

Banks, J., Marmot, M., Oldfield, Z., & Smith, J. P. (2006). Disease and disadvantage in the United States and England. *Journal of the American Medical Association, 295,* 2037–2045.

Blendon, R., Schoen, C., DesRoches, C. M., Osborne, R., Zapert, K., & Raleigh, E. (2004). Confronting competing demands to improve quality: A five country hospital survey. *Health Affairs, 23*(3) (May/June), 119–135.

Canadian Institute for Health Information. (2005). *Exploring the 70/30 split: How Canada's health care system in financed.* Hawa, Ontario: Author.

Cherney, E. (2006). Canada relents on health-care. *The Wall Street Journal,* (March 7), p. A-7.

DeNavas-Walt, C. (2004). *U.S. Census Bureau: Income, poverty, and health insurance in the United States: 2004,* 16. Retrieved from www.census.gov/prod/2005pubs/p60229.pdf.

DeNavas-Walt, C., Proctor, B. D., & Lee, C. H. (2005). *Income, poverty, and health insurance coverage in the United States: 2004.* Washington, DC: U.S. Census Bureau.

Department of Health and Human Services. (2006). *Health, U.S., 2005,* Retrieved May 22, 2006, from www.cdc.gov/nchs/datahus05.pdf#executivesummary.

Dyer, O. (2005). Disparities in health widen between rich and poor in England. *British Medical Journal, 331* (August).

Emanuel, E., & Fuchs, V. R. (2005). Solved! *Washington Monthly, 37*(6), 20–24.

Foertsch, T., & Antos, J. R. (2005). Paying for Medicare: An economic look at the program's unfunded liabilities. Heritage Foundation *WebMemo* #880, October 11.

Frogue, J. (2000). A high price for patients: An update on government health care in Britain and Canada. Heritage Foundation *Backgrounder,* No. 1398, September 26. Retrieved from www.heritage.org/library/backgrounder/bg1398.html.

Goodman, J. C., Musgrave, G. L., & Herrick, M. L. (2004). *Lives at risk: Single payer national health insurance around the world.* Lanham, MD: Rowman and Littlefield, p. 70.

Grumbach, K., & Lee, P. R. (2003, April 27). *The long road to a national health plan. San Francisco Chronicle,* Retrieved from http://sfgate.com.

Gunnar, W. P. (2006). The fundamental law that shapes the U.S. health-care system: Is universal health care realistic within the established paradigm? *Annals of Health Law, 15,* 151–181.

Hermer, L. D. (2005). Private health insurance in the United States: A proposal for a more functional system. *Houston Journal of Health Law and Policy, 6,* 1–114.

Hintz, C. (2000). The Tax Burden of the Median American Family. March 1. Retrieved from www.taxfoundation.org/research/show/137.html.

Ingoglia, J. N. (2005). Supporting collaboration between mental health and public health. *Journal of Public Health Management and Practice, 11*(6), 577–580.

Krugman, P. (2005, December 26). Medicine: Who decides? *The New York Times.*

Laville, S., & Hall, C. (1999, December 6). Elderly Patients left starving to death in NHS. *The Telegraph.* Retrieved from www.telegraph.co.uk/html/Content.jhtml?html=/archive/1999/12/06/neld06.html.

Lilley, R. (2006, March 28). A bad time to be very young or old. *The Telegraph.*

Lyall, S. (2006, February 16). British clinic is allowed to deny medicine. *The New York Times.*

Longley, R. (no date). *Should U.S. adopt a nationalized health care system?* Retrieved from http://usgovinfo.about.com.

Mantone, J. (2006, May 1). Stating the case for coverage; Frustrated with federal efforts to solve the uninsured problem, many states are taking it on themselves to find solutions, *Focus,* p. 6.

National Association of Social Workers. (2002). *Social work speaks: National Association of Social Workers, Policy Statements,* 6th ed. Washington, DC: NASW Press.

National Coalition on Health Care. (2006). Health Insurance Cost. Retrieved May 24, 2006, from www.nchc.org/facts/cost.shtml.

Physicians for a National Health Program. (1991). *Liberal benefits, conservative spending.* Retrieved from www.pnhp.org.

Pipes, S. C. (2004). *Miracle cure: How to solve America's health care crisis and why Canada isn't the answer.* The Fraser Institute and The Pacific Research Institute, Vancouver, p. 139.

Quadrango, J. (2004). Why the United States has no national health insurance: Stakeholder mobilization against the welfare state, 1945–1996. *Journal of Health and Social Behavior, 45,* 25–44.

Reinhardt, U. E., Hussey, P. S., & Anderson, G. F. (2004). U.S. health care spending in an international context. *Health Affairs 23*(3) (May/June), 16.

Sirota, D. (2006a). *Hostile takeover: How big money and corruption conquered our government—and how we can take it back.* New York: Crown.

Sirota, D. (2006b). How corporate America perpetuates the health care crisis. Retrieved May 22, 2006, from www.alternet.org/story/36341.

Templeton, S. K. (2006, March 26). Doctors opt to have private operations. *The Sunday Times.* Retrieved from www.timesonline.co.uk/article/0,2087-2104091,00.html.

Whalen, J. (2005, November 22). Britain stirs outcry by weighing benefits of drugs versus price. *The Wall Street Journal,* p. A-1.

Woolhandler, S., Campbell, T., & Himmelstein, D. U. (2003). Costs of health care administration in the U.S. and Canada. *The New England Journal of Medicine, 349,* 768–775.

Woolhandler, S., & Himmelstein, D. U. (2005). Uninsured in America: Life and death in the land of opportunity. *Journal of the American Medical Association, 293,* 2538–2539.

■ ■ ■ ■ ■ ▬▬▬▬▬▬▬▬▬▬▬▬▬▬▬▬▬▬▬▬▬▬▬▬▬▬▬▬▬▬

IS THE WAR ON DRUGS EFFECTIVE?

Editor's Note:
The War on Drugs has become a "moral panic," the sort of melodrama that an insecure middle class creates in order to retain its social standing. A moral panic is manifested by policies and professionals that seek to reestablish social control over a phantom threat. In the case of the War on Drugs, conservative politicians and law enforcement officers have convinced the public that the nation suffers from a new generation of violent minority youth that must be held in check. The evidence presented for the law-and-order agenda consists largely of the arrest rates for violent and repeat offenders; yet most "violent" offenses were the result of overzealous police overcharging miscreants, and most "repeat" offenders were rearrested for drug-related offenses. Not coincidentally, many black leaders, including Jesse Jackson, argue that minorities are the target of the War on Drugs. In that sense, the "war" has become a war on minorities as much as a war on drugs.

Peter A. Kindle, M.A., M.Div., is a doctoral candidate at the University of Houston. He is an Adjunct Instructor in psychology at the University of Houston–Clear Lake. Peter's work has appeared in *Families in Society,* the *Journal of GLBT Family Studies,* the *Journal of Family Social Work, Social Work and Christianity,* and the *Journal of Human Behavior in the Social Environment.*

Diana M. DiNitto is Cullen Trust Centennial Professor in Alcohol Studies and Education and University Distinguished Teaching Professor at the University of Texas at Austin School of Social Work. She teaches courses on alcohol and other drug problems and is coauthor of *Chemical Dependency: A Systems Approach,* 3rd ed. (Allyn & Bacon, 2005).

YES

Peter A. Kindle

In 2001, an adult sample of Americans confirmed attitudes entrenched since the late 1980s that the country is losing the War on Drugs (Pew Research Center for the People and the Press, 2001). Pessimism dominates, with four times as many respondents believing that the country is losing ground (54 percent) compared to those who believe there has been progress (13 percent). Clearly any argument that affirms the effectiveness of the War on Drugs is a minority position.

Since the Harrison Narcotics Act (1914), the federal policy toward the use and distribution of illicit drugs has been one of prohibition (Boyum & Reuter, 2005). Prohibition has a single goal—prevalence reduction; that is, the elimination of illicit drug production, distribution, and use (MacCoun & Reuter, 2001). Because the production, distribution, and use of illicit drugs have not been eliminated, especially during a period in which federal resources committed to this purpose have increased from $4 billion to $18 billion (1985–2001), pessimism may be warranted (Boyum & Reuter, 2005); however, to measure the effectiveness of prevalence-reduction strategies against a metric that requires full elimination of illicit drugs is artificial at best. When contextualized within the economic realities of global markets, the addictive properties of the illicit substances, and the larger domestic experience with legal drugs, federal prevalence-reduction strategies have clearly been effective.

RESTRAINT OF PREVALENCE

Illicit drugs are not the only addictive substances. The most recent figures from the National Survey on Drug Use and Health (NSDUH) show that 121 million Americans over age 11 are current drinkers of alcohol and 70.3 million currently use tobacco products but only 19.1 million currently use an illicit drug (Department of Health and Human Services [DHHS], 2005). Even this surface comparison suggests that prevalence-reduction strategies are having some effect.

When the prevalence of drug and alcohol use is considered in the context of the addictive potential of the separate substances, the effectiveness of prevalence-reduction strategies is further enhanced. Ridenour, Maldonado-Molina, Compton, Spitznagel, and Cottler (2005) summarize the evidence that cocaine and opiates are significantly more addictive than alcohol and marijuana. Surprisingly, they also found that, when measuring addictive potential by the length of time between onset of abuse and dependence (LOTAD), marijuana was more addictive than alcohol. The NSDUH (DHHS, 2005) partially confirms the greater risk associated with various substances by reporting the dependency and abuse rates for heroin (85.9 per 1,000 users), marijuana (46.2 per 1,000), cocaine (46.0 per 1,000), and nonmedical use of prescription drugs (42.7 per 1,000).

Two conclusions appear unmistakable. First, in comparison with the prevalence of legal substance use, the use of illicit substances is quite restricted. Second, the lower prevalence of illicit substance use occurs despite the higher addictive potential of these drugs.

Federal prevalence-restraining strategies are often categorized as supply-side and demand-side controls. Supply-side controls attempt to reduce the availability of illicit drugs by crop eradication, interdiction or seizure of illicit drugs, and domestic police action. Demand-side controls focus on treatment and prevention. As Boyum and Reuter (2005) point out, this dichotomy is too simplistic and tends to overlook the variety of user sanctions that exist. Possession alone carries the potential for arrest and criminal penalties that can lead to denial of public assistance. Drug testing threatens employment. Coerced abstinence may hinder illicit drug use among the 4.9 million Americans under mandatory supervision of the criminal justice system on the state or federal level (Bureau of Justice Statistics [BJS], 2004).

The unanswered question is, which prevalence-reduction strategy is most effective? While it is safe to conclude that the overall effect of prohibition is to restrain illicit drug use, the causal mechanisms are less certain.

SUPPLY-SIDE EFFECTIVENESS

Enforcement, or domestic police action, receives the bulk of federal funding, but it is unevenly effective. Wholesale enforcement has been effective at controlling large criminal enterprises that included Myanmar's Shan United Army and Colombia's Cali cartel (Drug Enforcement Administration [DEA], 2003) in the mid-1990s (for other examples see www.dea.gov/major/major .htm). Asset seizures impose de facto taxes on distribution networks in an effective manner, but are ineffective in curtailing the multiplication of small, freelance networks for illicit drug distribution. Retail enforcement has been effective if measured by the increase in drug arrests from less than 600,000 in 1980 to over 1.7 million in 2004 (BJS, 2003), but ineffective in eliminating retail distribution and street violence.

In 2003 interdiction efforts seized almost 3 million pounds of illicit drugs (BJS, 2003). Boyum and Reuter (2005) maintain that interdiction also increases supplier costs in the delivery of illicit drugs to domestic markets. Interestingly, white interdiction is quite effective if measured by supplier costs and quantity seized, it has been ineffective at raising the street price of illicit drugs (Boyum & Reuter, 2005; MacCoun & Reuter, 2001).

In comparison, crop eradication programs have been less successful. Both coca and poppies grow in terrain poorly suited to alternative legitimate crops; other nations are disinclined to permit the environmental risks associated with aerial sprays; and alternative sources are quickly generated to compensate for crop elimination elsewhere. On one occasion a U.S.-led eradication program did have temporary success (aerial spray eradication of poppies in Mexico in the mid-1970s) (Boyer & Reuter, 2005); however, international markets compensated with increased production within two years.

The facile accommodation of international producers is explained primarily by the incredible profits generated by the retail product. The quantity of coca leaves required to produce one kilogram of 67 percent pure cocaine for the U.S. retail market costs only $300 but generates $150,000 in sales on the street in 2003. For heroin, $200 worth of poppies generated $50,000 in heroin street sales (Boyum & Reuter, 2005).

This kind of profit potential makes it virtually impossible to eliminate the supply of illicit drugs; however, every effort that results in an increase in supplier cost has an impact on prevalence reduction. In the decentralized retail distribution network for illicit drugs, the street price is effectively set as a multiple of all prior costs, but the elevation of the street price is strongly constrained by user sensitivity to price increases (MacCoun & Reuter, 2001). Boyum and Reuter (2005) suggest that cocaine consumption would double if the price were halved. Supply-side controls, by impacting the complex interplay of supply costs and demand sensitivity, have inhibited reductions in the street price.

DEMAND-SIDE EFFECTIVENESS

Treatment programs designed to assist users to abstain from continued drug use appear to be relatively effective. Almost half of heroin and cocaine users desist for 12 months following treatment; however, even if the reduction in drug use and drug-related criminal activities are limited to the period of treatment, these programs appear cost effective (Boyum & Reuter, 2005).

Ettner, Huang, Evans, Ash, Jourabchi, and Hser (2006) recently confirmed Rydell and Everingham's (1994) finding that treatment programs provide 7 dollars in social benefits for every dollar in direct cost. Due to methodological problems, it is premature to conclude that any specific treatment protocol is most effective, and there is some evidence suggesting that there is little outcome differential between coerced and voluntary programs (Boyum & Reuter, 2005). Overall, the evidence continues to support the conclusion Rydell and Everingham (1994) made 12 years ago, "if an additional dollar is to be spent on drug control, it should be spent on treatment" (p. xvi).

Prevention has been attempted primarily through school-based educational programs and media campaigns (Boyer & Reuter, 2005). To date, there is little conclusive evidence suggesting that media has been effective in reducing drug use (Boyum & Reuter, 2005); however, a recent systematic review of school-based educational programs suggests a small reduction of 1.7 percent in lifetime use for marijuana and 3 percent for cocaine (Paddock, 2005). Paddock contends that school-based prevention is cost effective over the long-term even with these low rates of reduction.

Unlike alcohol and tobacco users, who demonstrate a strong tendency toward lifetime use, 60 percent of illicit drug users discontinue using in the early to mid-twenties (MacCoun & Reuter, 2001). At this point, it is unfair to attribute desistance to any specific governmental policy, yet it appears unlikely that the discontinuance of illicit drug use and the assumption of adult employment and family roles are only coincidental. Supply-side controls mitigate initiation of illicit drug use through pricing mechanisms and the threat of legal sanctions. Demand-side controls mitigate initiation through education and continuance through treatment. User sanctions, largely untested as a causal restraint of prevalence, may have the largest impact by threatening employment.

HARM REDUCTION

Critics of the federal prohibition of illicit drugs contend that the mere use of these drugs is not the problem. The problem, they contend, is the harm that is associated with illicit drug use. Accordingly, these critics discount prevalence-reduction strategies as effective because they are not focused on the most important issue: reducing the harmfulness of drug use. Furthermore, these critics contend that the harmfulness of illicit drug use is actually exacerbated by the federal prohibition. For example, MacCoun and Reuter (2001) identify 48 drug-related harms. More than half of these harms are the direct cause of enforcement action (e.g., violence, inhibition to seek treatment, increased costs associated with the criminal justice system), and a quarter are related to the illegal status of the drugs (e.g., harm to employability and acquaintance with criminals). Only 19 of 48 harms are identified with use, and these cluster predominately on the adverse health impact and social/economic functioning of the user.

The argument is quite simple. Legalization of illicit drug use would eliminate the harms associated with enforcement and the illegal status of the drugs, thereby freeing substantial public resources to deal with mitigating the consequences of use. The reasoning underlying this argument is faulty in at least two respects. First, it assumes that prevalence and harmfulness are distinct, and second, it underestimates the potential harm associated with increased prevalence.

The harmfulness of illicit drug use is actually a complex interaction between three variables. Total harmfulness (MacCoun & Reuter, 2001) incorporates the degree of use (prevalence), the dosage (intensity of use), and the negative individual user impact (consequences of use). Critics of drug prohibition often fail to acknowledge that prevalence is associated with negative consequences. After a comprehensive review of the American and European experiences, the critics MacCoun and Reuter conclude that "allowing some form of legal access to a drug increases the prevalence and intensity of its use" (p. 326). Monshouwer, Smit, de Graaf, van Os, and Vollebergh (2005) add that the Dutch experience suggests that legal access is also likely to lower the age of onset.

Increases in prevalence are only problematic if there is harm associated with illicit drug use. Proponents of legalization are careful to distinguish between use and abuse/dependence, attributing harms to the latter. Proponents of prohibition note that increases in prevalence are causally linked to increases in abuse/dependence and conclude that prevalence-restraining strategies are inherently preventative.

Perhaps the best lens through which to gain perspective on these antithetical positions is the harmfulness associated with legal drug use. The Centers for Disease Control and Prevention (CDC), (2005) report that alcohol use is the third leading cause of death in America. Alcohol abuse has been associated with violence, crime, child and spousal abuse, unintentional injuries, and sexually transmitted disease (CDC, 2005; Gmel & Rehm, 2003; Haggard-Grann, Hallqvist, Langstrom, & Moller, 2006; Parker & Auerhahn, 1998). In comparison to the dependency and abuse rates for illicit drugs, alcohol is particularly risky. If every American over the age of 11 used alcohol, the abuse/dependence rate would be 77.5 per 1,000 (DHHS, 2005). Only heroin has a greater risk for abuse/dependence, and only tobacco has a greater incidence of mortality. Tobacco use causes over 400,000 deaths annually, making this the most deadly—and preventable—cause of death in the nation (CDC, 2004).

The National Institutes of Health estimated that the negative economic impact of drug abuse exceeded $124 billion in 1995. In comparison, smoking cost the nation $138 billion in 1995 and alcohol abuse cost $184 billion in 1998 (Executive Office of the President, 2004). Since the prevalence of illicit drug use is only 15.8 percent of alcohol use and only 27.2 percent of tobacco use, can the nation afford the potential costs associated with a proportionate increase in illicit drug use? An affirmative response seems unlikely.

The specific case of marijuana is a favorite subject of critics of prohibition because the harmfulness of this drug is often considered particularly light. Despite federal assertions of the harmfulness of marijuana (DEA, 2003), it is difficult to find conclusive evidence in the literature. Early onset of use has been linked to a variety of problematic behavioral results (Ellickson, D'Amico, Collins, & Klein, 2005), but it is quite difficult to part the drug effects from the situational and social effects. Rational-choice behavior patterns demonstrated among long-term and frequent users suggest that users perceive the relaxation and recreational benefits to exceed negative health consequences; and mental illness, violence, and negative health consequences are difficult to substantiate (Hathaway, 2003). The single exception seems to be recent evidence linking marijuana use to increased risk of schizophrenia in a longitudinal Dutch study (van Os, Bak, Hanssen, Bijl, de Graaf, & Verdoux, 2002).

It is possible that marijuana is, in fact, a candidate for legalization. The evidence suggests that the legalization of this drug is unlikely to result in the total harmfulness that is substantially different from that absorbed by society from the use of alcohol and tobacco. From a policy perspective, what is lacking is a compelling reason to justify the elevation of social risk. By some measures, marijuana is more addictive than cocaine and alcohol (DHHS, 2005; Ridenour et al., 2005). It has strong psychoactive effects that have yet to be conclusively confirmed as temporary in duration. Why should America risk creating another public health threat that might equal that posed by alcohol and tobacco?

CONCLUSION

There is really no satisfactory policy alternative to prohibition because prohibition of illicit drugs is the best means of limiting both prevalence and harmfulness. This does not mean that the effectiveness of the War on Drugs could not be substantially improved. The near universal condemnation of prohibition by policy analysts can be interpreted as a justified reaction to the substantial collateral damages associated with prohibition. Escalating incarceration rates, disproportionate adverse effects on minority males, violence-prone distribution conflicts in urban neighborhoods, and the exploding fiscal demands of the state and federal criminal justice systems are just some of these collateral damages.

Without attempting to replicate the plethora of extant policy recommendations, changes should be made. The criminal justice system should be radically altered to focus on rehabilitation, restitution, and substance-abuse treatment rather than punishment and retribution. Enforcement should be directed at the elimination of violence rather than use. Depenalization of select illicit substances need not void the beneficial restraints of prohibition and can be implemented in a manner that has negligible effects on prevalence (MacCoun & Reuter, 2001). Since a substantial portion of current drug use is by those under supervision of the criminal justice system, mandatory treatment should replace incarceration as the preferred response.

What should not happen is a complete reversal of prohibition. "Illegal drugs are illegal because they are harmful" (DEA, 2003, p. 8). The War on Drugs has been effective, if not fully efficient, in restraining the prevalence and thereby the total harmfulness contained within these substances. Social workers should be among the last to advocate for legalization because they will be the first called to help rebuild the damaged lives that result.

NO

Diana M. DiNitto

Although it can be used in a milder sense, the term *war* brings to mind armed conflict. The U.S. War on Drugs involves both armed conflict that can occur during interdiction and other law enforcement efforts to intercept supplies of illicit drugs, and milder coercive efforts such as offering defendants in possession cases treatment in lieu of incarceration (DiNitto, 2002). The U.S. War on Drugs began with the Harrison Narcotics Act of 1914, but the Anti-Drug Abuse Act of 1986 set the stage for many aspects of the current war. Today, the War on Drugs is also embodied in the President's *Drug Control Strategy*.[1]

Since it is drug *use,* not the mere presence of drugs, that can harm individuals, families, and communities, the War on Drugs is defined in this essay as efforts to stop Americans from using substances defined as illicit under the Controlled Substances Act of 1970. Among these substances are heroin, cocaine, methamphetamine, and cannabis.[2]

This essay concentrates mostly on the futility of interdiction and law enforcement to halt drug addiction. *Addiction* is a term the public often uses to denote a serious drug problem rather than experimentation with drugs. Instead of *addiction,* the American Psychiatric Association (APA) (2000) uses the term *substance use disorders* and divides these disorders into *substance abuse* and *substance dependence.* The APA defines both abuse and dependence as "maladaptive pattern[s] of substance use, leading to clinically significant impairment or distress" (pp. 197, 199). Dependence requires meeting at least three of seven criteria. Among these criteria are tolerance (needing more of the substance to achieve the same effect); withdrawal symptoms; using more of the drug than intended; unsuccessful efforts to cut down or quit; and physical, social, or legal problems. Abuse requires meeting one or more of four criteria over a period of time, such as recurrent drug use in hazardous situations (e.g., driving a car) or use that results in failure to meet responsibilities at home, work, or school. Abuse may seem like the lesser of the two evils, but it can also result in serious consequences, such as traffic fatalities.

There are other ways to define or conceptualize the problems that human beings develop with regard to illicit drug use. Rather than the two somewhat discrete entities that the APA presents, some think of drug problems on a continuum from no problem to severe problems, as Pattison,

---

[1]The current and previous editions of President George W. Bush's *Drug Control Strategy* can be found at www.whitehousedrugpolicy.gov.

[2]There is no war on alcohol use, except perhaps with regard to stricter drunk-driving laws. Alcohol can be used legally by those aged 21 and over, and is, therefore, not a subject of this essay. Like alcohol, tobacco is a highly addictive drug. It is also available legally and is not addressed here. It should be noted, however, that alcohol abuse and dependence and nicotine dependence are much more prevalent than illicit drug abuse and dependence and exact much greater costs from society.

Sobell, and Sobell (1977) suggest with regard to alcohol use. One concise def-inition of drug disorders is repeated use of substances that causes serious life problems. Definitions are important to discussions of the drug war because the way "the drug problem" and its causes are defined should lead logically to the solutions chosen to address it.

I present five reasons why the drug war, comprised more of interdiction and law enforcement efforts than prevention and treatment efforts, has not succeeded in halting addiction. First, drug dependence (if not abuse) likely has a neurobiological basis that interdiction and law enforcement cannot remedy. Second, the War on Drugs has had little effect on the number of Americans who experiment with illicit drugs or meet criteria for drug abuse or dependence. Third, it is treatment and not incarceration that helps people with drug disorders refrain from use. Fourth, interdiction and law enforce-ment efforts do not stop the flow of illicit drugs. Fifth, the high rates of drug arrests and incarcerations that have resulted from the drug war do more pri-vate and public harm than good.

Since Drug Dependence Likely Has a Neurobiological Basis, It Is Illogical to Think That Interdiction and Law Enforcement Can Remedy It

No one knows exactly what biological, psychological, and/or social forces must come to bear for an individual to develop a drug disorder. The APA defines abuse and dependence in terms of its manifestations but is mum on potential causes of these problems.

Erickson and Wilcox (2001) describe growing evidence of the neurobi-ological basis of addiction. In fact, Alan Leshner (2001), former head of the National Institute on Drug Abuse (NIDA), calls addiction a "brain disease." Leshner believes that addiction begins with voluntary use, but that drug use causes changes in the brain that promote the disease, which manifests itself in the form of compulsive use.

There is also evidence of a genetic predisposition to dependence that has been indicated in studies of alcoholism (alcoholism has been studied more than drug disorders) and might also be true of dependence on illicit substances. For example, research shows a heightened propensity for adopted individuals born to a parent or parents with alcoholism to develop alcoholism themselves, even when adopted very early in life by individuals who are not alcoholics (see, for example, Cloninger, 1983; NIDA, 2000). Other studies indicate that susceptibility to alcohol dependence is related to partic-ular chromosomes (Reich et al., 1998; NIDA, 2000). Given these types of evi-dence, drug dependence may best be thought of as a "chronic medical illness" similar to diabetes and heart disease, and with similar rates of treat-ment compliance (McLellan, Lewis, O'Brien, & Kleber, 2000), rather than a problem for the criminal justice system. The neurobiology of addiction may explain why some individuals who have been incarcerated for long periods of time return to drug use soon after reentry into the community and why such punishment is ineffective in halting drug dependence. It may also explain why some people are drawn to illicit drug use even with knowledge of the harmful effects of these substances, and why some people describe their initial use of drugs as feeling "normal" for the first time.

Substance abuse may be another matter. Erickson and Wilcox (2001) suggest that rather than a neurobiological problem, abuse is a behavioral problem amendable to environmental interventions such as stricter drunk-driving laws, educational campaigns, and serving alternative beverages. If so, the drug war might persuade some people not to experiment because of the possibility of arrest, or having experienced the consequences of arrest and incarceration, an individual might stop using. However, as the next section demonstrates, drug experimentation remains at high levels.

The War on Drugs Has Had Little Effect on the Number of Americans Who Experiment with Drugs or Meet Criteria for Abuse and Dependence

The number of Americans who have ever used drugs or who develop drug disorders has been affected little by the drug war. Since 1975, NIDA has sponsored a study to track drug use among secondary school students. In 2005, the study authors concluded that "in the last third of the twentieth century, young Americans reached extraordinarily high levels of illicit drug use either by historical comparisons in this country or by international comparisons" (Johnston, O'Malley, Bachman, & Schulenberg, 2006, p. 10). For example, in 2005, 38 percent of 12th graders said they had used one or more illicit drugs in the last year, slightly lower than the 42 percent of 12th graders who reported using in 1997, but considerably higher than the 27 percent who reported doing so in 1992. Though prevalence rates have dropped for college students, in 2004, an estimated 36 percent of college students had used an illicit drug in the last year, and 52 percent reported having used an illicit drug in their lifetime (Johnston et al., 2005). These figures are not a ringing endorsement for the War on Drugs, including many well-intentioned prevention efforts. A "floor effect" may be operating. In other words, there may be a level of drug experimentation that will occur almost regardless of prevent efforts. Efforts may be better directed at preventing harm to those who do experiment.

Fortunately, most drug experimentation does not result in serious or long-lasting harm. Drug abuse and dependence exact a more serious toll. Tracking the percentage of the population that meet criteria for substance abuse or dependence over time is difficult due to differences in study methodologies and the figures they produce. One analysis, which relied on data from a large, methodologically rigorous, federally funded study, conducted at two periods in time, focused on the most widely used illicit drug by far—marijuana. It found that "the prevalence of DSM-IV marijuana abuse or dependence significantly (p = 0.01) increased between 1991 and 1992 (1.2 percent) and between 2001 and 2002 (1.5 percent)" (Compton, Grant, Colliver, Glantz, & Stinson, 2004, p. 2114). In the last few years, the federal government's Substance Abuse and Mental Health Services Administration (SAMHSA) (2006) has also reported rather consistent figures on the percent of the population that currently meet criteria for drug abuse or dependence: 2.7 in 2002, 2.6 in 2003, and 2.8 in 2004. These figures may seen surprisingly low. Lifetime rates are higher, but most substance use disorders result from problems with alcohol and not illicit drugs.

Also noteworthy is SAMHSA's (2005) report that "the number of persons that needed treatment for an illicit drug use problem in 2004 (8.1 million) was higher than the number that needed treatment in 2003 (7.3 million)" (p. 8). If the drug war were effective in reducing drug problems, we would expect the number needing treatment to decrease, not increase, over time. Apparently, this has not happened.

Treatment, Not Interdiction and Punishment, Helps People with Drug Disorders Refrain from Use

According to President Bush's 2006 drug strategy, "When drug supply does not fully meet drug demand, changes in drug price and purity . . . contribute to treatment efforts by eroding the abilities of users to sustain their habits" (Office of National Drug Control Policy, 2006, p. 17). It is true that when drug supplies are interrupted, individuals may be motivated to detoxify in treatment facilities where medications are prescribed to ease withdrawal symptoms. However, as NIDA (1999) emphasizes, "medical detoxification . . . by itself does little change to long-term drug use," and "remaining in treatment for an adequate period of time is critical for treatment effectiveness" (p. 1).

Also important is that involuntary treatment, e.g., treatment mandated by the courts or by the terms of an offender's probation agreement, can be effective (NIDA, 1999). But it is treatment and not incarceration or coercion alone that helps people stay clean after they get clean. The saving graces of the War on Drugs are that more individuals are being diverted to drug courts where they receive treatment in lieu of incarceration and more correctional facilities have offered some form of drug treatment, or at least make space available for meetings of mutual help groups like Alcoholics Anonymous and Narcotics Anonymous. Unfortunately, many offenders with alcohol and/or drug problems still do not receive drug treatment while incarcerated. For example, in 2002, only 15 percent of jail inmates who reported being regular users in the past year said they received help during their current incarceration (James, 2004). The most frequently reported types of help these inmates reported were "self-help" and "education." Though 58 percent had received help at some time in their lives, substance use disorders are chronic, relapsing conditions that often require ongoing attention. Treatment saves $12 for every $1 spent on it (National Institute on Alcohol Abuse and Alcoholism [NIAAA], 2000). Since interdiction and incarceration in and of themselves do nothing to reduce drug dependence, there is a negative return on those investments.

Interdiction and Law Enforcement Efforts Do Little to Stop the Flow of Illicit Drugs into and within the United States

It is impressive to hear reports of drug busts in which tons of marijuana or kilos of cocaine worth millions of dollars are seized. No one wants to live in a neighborhood infested with illicit drugs. Those who run big-stakes drug enterprises should be punished to the extent of the law, but the illicit drug supply is infinite. Even with the technological advances that make it possible to conduct air surveillance and sophisticated searches, the supply of drugs never dries up, and new "designer drugs" appear on the market. Many individuals continue to risk involvement with the criminal justice system to profit from the drug trade; others take the risk to support their drug habit.

The High Rates of Drug Arrests and Incarcerations Do More Private and Public Harm Than Good

Rather than curb drug-related crime, arrests and incarcerations have swelled. In 1982, there were about 676,000 drug arrests—538,000 for possession and 138,000 for sale or manufacture (Bureau of Justice Statistics [BJA], 2005b). In 2004, of the 14 million arrests reported by law enforcement agencies, the largest group, 1.7 million, was for drug violations. Of these 1.7 million, 1.4 million were for possession and 300,000 were for sale or manufacture. The dramatic increase in incarcerations for drug violations is also indisputable (McNeece & DiNitto, 2005). For example, between 1985 and 1995, almost three-quarters of the increase in federal prison population was due to drug offenses, and the state prison population incarcerated for drug-law violations increased by 478 percent (Office of National Drug Control Policy, 1998). In 2000, 57 percent of federal inmates and 21 percent of state inmates were incarcerated for drug offenses (BJS, 2005a). In 2002, 156,000 local jail inmates were being held on drug charges, an increase of 42,000 inmates or 37 percent since 1996 (James, 2004).

In 2002, two-thirds of all 665,475 local jail inmates described themselves as "regular drug users" (James, 2004, p. 1). This provides another reason to focus on reducing the "treatment gap," because the vast majority of Americans residing in the community who need drug treatment do not get it (SAMHSA, 2005). Of mothers in state prisons, 32 percent said they committed the crime for which they were serving a sentence to obtain drugs or money to buy drugs (Mumola, 2000). Separation of parents from children has a major impact on all parties concerned. It further burdens state child-welfare systems, which can hardly keep up with the demand for foster care services, and often puts children at risk for poor outcomes.

The "overincarceration" of the U.S. population takes an especially high toll on individuals and communities of color. In particular, African Americans are overrepresented in U.S. prison and jail populations. One explanation for this overrepresentation involves crack cocaine, a drug most likely to be available in poor communities inhabited disproportionately by people of color. For example, due to erroneous assumptions about how much more detrimental crack is compared to powdered cocaine, a first-time offense of trafficking 5 grams of crack cocaine gets the same mandatory 5-year minimum penalty as trafficking 500 grams of powdered cocaine (United States Sentencing Commission [USSC], 2002). According to the USSC, about 85 percent of offenders sentenced under the stiffer crack cocaine penalties are black. A majority of USSC members have practically begged Congress and the president to do something about the inequity, but no action has been taken.

CONCLUSION

When a problem is poorly understood, and the behavior that results from it is offensive to communities and the larger society, the tendency is to criminalize it. Nearly 62 percent of President Bush's 2006 drug control budget is dedicated to reducing drug supplies and 38 percent is dedicated to treatment and prevention. The President's 2007 budget request drops treatment and prevention funding to 35.5 percent. In order to win the War on Drugs, Americans must recognize that drug supplies will continue to flow and drug experimentation will continue to occur. Americans need to make peace with the fact that substance dependence is a chronic, relapsing condition with a neurobiological basis. Once we do, more emphasis will be placed on developing more efficacious treatments and meeting treatment needs.

REFERENCES

American Psychiatric Association. (2000). *Diagnostic and statistical manual of mental disorders* (4th ed., text rev). Washington, DC: Author.

Boyum, D., & Reuter, P. (2005). *An analytic assessment of U.S. drug policy.* Washington, DC: The AEI Press.

Bureau of Justice Statistics. (2003). *Enforcement.* Retrieved May 11, 2006, from www.ojp.usdoj.gov/bjs/dcf/enforce.htm#seizures.

Bureau of Justice Statistics. (2004). *Probation and parole statistics.* Retrieved May 11, 2006, from www.ojp.usdoj.gov/bjs/pandp.htm.

Bureau of Justice Statistics. (2005a). *Criminal offender statistics.* November 13. Washington, DC: U.S. Department of Justice. Retrieved March 14, 2006, from www.ojp.usdoj.gov/bjs/crimoff.htm.

Bureau of Justice Statistics. (2005b). *Drugs and crime facts: Drug law violations, Enforcement.* October 17. Retrieved March 14, 2006, from www.ojp.usdoj.gov/bjs/dcf/enforce.htm.

Centers for Disease Control and Prevention. (2005). *General alcohol information.* Retrieved May 1, 2006, from Centers for Disease Control, National Center for Chronic Disease Prevention and Health Promotion website: www.cdc.gov/alcohol/factsheets/general_information.htm.

Centers for Disease Control and Prevention. (2004). *Tobacco-related mortality: Fact sheet.* Retrieved May 1, 2006, from Centers for Disease Control, national Center for Chronic Disease prevention and Health Promotion website: www.cdc.gov/tobacco/factsheets/Tobacco_Related_Mortality_factsheet.htm.

Cloninger, C. R. (1983). Genetic and environmental factors in the development of alcoholism. *Journal of Psychiatric Treatment and Evaluation, 5,* 487–496.

Compton, W. M., Grant, B. F., Colliver, J. D., Glantz, M. D., & Stinson, F. S. (2004). Prevalence of marijuana use disorders in the United States: 1991–1992 and 2001–2002. *Journal of the American Medical Association, 291,* 2114–2121.

Department of Health and Human Services. (2005). *Overview of findings from the 2004 National Survey on Drug Use and Health.* Retrieved May 3, 2006, from Department of Health and Human Services, Substance Abuse and Mental Health Services Administration, Office of Applied Studies: http://oas.samhsa.gov/NSDUH/2k4NSDUH/2k4Overview/2k4Overview.pdf.

DiNitto, D. M. (2002). War and peace: Social work and the state of chemical dependency treatment in the United States. *Social Work Practice in the Addictions, 2*(3/4), 7–29.

Drug Enforcement Administration. (2003). *Speaking out against drug legalization.* U.S. Department of Justice, Drug Enforcement Administration. Retrieved May 3, 2006, from www.usdoj.gov/dea/demand/speakout/index.html.

Ellickson, P. L., D'Amico, E. J., Collins, R. L., & Klein, D. J. (2005). Marijuana use and later problems: When frequency of recent use explains age of initiation effects (and when it does not). *Substance Use & Misuse, 40,* 343–359.

Erickson, C. K., & Wilcox, R. E. (2001). Neurobiological causes of addiction. In R. T. Spence, D. M. DiNitto, & S. L. A. Straussner, (Eds.), *Neurobiology of addictions: Implications for clinical practice* (pp. 7–22). Binghamton, NY: Haworth Press.

Ettner, S. L., Huang, D., Evans, E., Ash, D. R., Jourabchi, M., Hser, Y. (2006). Benefit–cost in the California Treatment Outcome Project: Does substance abuse treatment "pay for itself"? *Health Services Research, 41,* 192–213.

Executive Office of the President. (2004). *The economic costs of drug abuse in the United States: 1992–2002.* Office of National Drug Control Policy. Retrieved May 3, 2006, from www.whitehousedrugpolicy.gov/publications/economic_costs/.

Gmel, G., & Rehm, J. (2003). Harmful alcohol use. *Alcohol Research & Health, 27,* 52–62.

Haggard-Grann, U., Hallqvist, J., Langstrom, N., & Moller, J. (2006). The role of alcohol and drugs in triggering criminal violence: A case-crossover study. *Addiction, 101.* 100–108.

Hathaway, A. D. (2003). Cannabis effects and dependency concerns in long-term frequent users: A missing piece of the public health puzzle. *Addiction Research and Theory, 11,* 441–458.

James, S. J. (2004, July). *Profile of jail inmates, 2002.* Washington, DC: U.S. Department of Justice. Retrieved March 14, 2006, from www.ojp.usdoj.gov/bjs/abstract/pji02.htm.

Johnston, L. D., O'Malley, P. M., Bachman, J. G., & Schulenberg, J. E. (2005). *Monitoring the future national results drug use, 1975–2004: Volume II, College students and adults ages 19–45*. (NIH Publication No. 05-5728). Bethesda: MD: National Institute on Drug Abuse.

Johnston, L. D., O'Malley, P. M., Bachman, J. G., & Schulenberg, J. E. (2006). *Monitoring the future national results on adolescent drug use: Overview of key findings, 2005*. (NIH Publication No. 06-5882). Bethesda: MD: National Institute on Drug Abuse.

Leshner, A. I. (2001, Spring). Addiction is a brain disease. *Issues in Science and Technology*. Retrieved March 5, 2006, from www.nap.edu/issues/17.3/leshner.htm.

MacCoun, R. J., & Reuter, P. (2001). *Drug war heresies: Learning from other vices, times, and places*. New York: Cambridge University Press.

McLellan, A. T., Lewis, D. C., O'Brien, C. P., & Kleber, H. D. (2000). Drug dependence, a chronic medical illness: Implications for treatment, insurance, and outcomes evaluation. *JAMA, 284*, 1689–1695.

McNeece, A., & DiNitto, D. M. (2003). *Chemical dependency: A systems approach* (3rd ed.). Boston: Allyn & Bacon.

Monshouwer, K., Smit, F., de Graaf, R., van Os, J., & Vollebergh, W. (2005). First cannabis use: Does onset shift to younger ages? Findings from 1988 to 2003 from the Dutch National School Survey on Substance Use. *Addiction, 100*, 963–970.

Mumola, C. J. (2000, August). *Incarcerated parents and their children*. Washington, DC: U.S. Department of Justice.

National Institute on Drug Abuse. (1999). *Principles of addiction treatment: A research-based guide*. Bethesda, MD: U.S. Department of Health and Human Services.

National Institute on Alcohol Abuse and Alcoholism. (2000). *Tenth special report to the U.S. Congress on alcohol and health*. Washington, DC: U.S. Department of Health and Human Services.

Office of National Drug Control Policy. (1998). *The national drug control strategy, 1998*. Washington, DC: Executive Office of the President.

Office of National Drug Control Policy. (2006, February). *The president's national drug control strategy*. Washington, DC: Executive Office of the President. Retrieved March 18, 2006, from www.whitehousedrugpolicy.gov/.

Paddock. S. M. (2005). *School-based drug prevention and other strategies for reducing drug use*. Santa Monica, CA: RAND Corporation. Retrieved May 15, 2006, from www.rand.org/pubs/testimonies/2005/RAND_CT237.pdf.

Parker, R. N., & Auerhahn, K. (1998). Alcohol, drugs, and violence. *Annual Review of Sociology, 24*, 291–311.

Pattison, E. M., Sobell, M. B., & Sobell, L. C. (1977). *Emerging concepts of alcohol dependence*. New York: Springer.

Pew Research Center for the People and the Press. (2001). *Interdiction and incarceration still top remedies*. Retrieved March 19, 2006, from http://peoplepress.org/reports/display.php3?ReportID=16.

Reich, T., Edenberg, H. J., Goate, A., Williams, J. T., Rice, J. Pl, Van Eerdewegh, P., et al. (1998). Genome-wide search for genes affecting the risk for alcohol dependence. *American Journal of Medical Genetics, 81*, 207–215.

Ridenour, T. A., Maldonado-Molina, M., Compton, W. M., Spitznagel, E. L., & Cottler, L. B. (2005). Factors associated with the transition from abuse to dependence among substance abusers: Implications for a measure of addictive liability. *Drug and Alcohol Dependence, 80*, 1–14.

Rydell, C. P., & Everingham, S. S. (1994). *Controlling cocaine: Supply versus demand programs.* Santa Monica, CA: RAND Corporation. Retrieved May 15, 2006, from www.rand.org/pubs/monograph_reports/2006/RAND_MR331.sum.pdf.

Substance Abuse and Mental Health Services Administration. (2005). *2004 National Survey on Drug Use & Health: Overview.* September 8. Retrieved March 12, 2006, from www.oas.samhsa.gov/nsduh/2k4nsduh/2k4overview/2k4overview.htm#1.4.

Substance Abuse and Mental Health Services Administration. (2006). *2004 National Survey on Drug Use and Health: Results,* Appendix E: Other Sources of Data. March 2. Retrieved March 16, 2006, from www.oas.samhsa.gov/nsduh/2k4nsduh/2k4Results/appe.htm.

United States Sentencing Commission. (2002). *Report to the Congress: Cocaine and federal sentencing policy.* Washington, DC: author.

van Os, J., Bak, M., Hanssen, M., Bijl, r. V., de Graaf, R., & Verdoux, H. (2002). Cannabis use and psychosis: A longitudinal population-based study. *American Journal of Epidemiology, 156,* 319–327.

CAN ASSET-BASED WELFARE POLICY REALLY HELP THE POOR?

Editor's Note:
Governmental programs for the alleviation of poverty have traditionally provided resources for consumption. While it is clearly necessary to address the consumption needs of the poor, proponents of asset-based social policies believe that the poverty problem can be more effectively addressed by helping them accumulate both the economic and human capital that can lift them out of their condition. Programs that encourage the poor to save by matching their deposits with government resources are far more useful than income-support programs, which merely maintain the poor at basic consumption levels. Critics of this approach are not so sure. While they agree that an asset-development program is worthwhile, they are doubtful that it offers a ready solution to the problem of poverty. Poverty, they contend, is so widespread, serious, and intractable that large-scale government intervention, rather than individualized programs, is needed. Solving the problem of poverty requires economic planning, the creation of new jobs, enhanced education and training, massive social investments, and similar measures rather than the subsidization of individual savings.

Michael Sherraden, Ph.D., is the Benjamin E. Youngdahl Professor of Social Development at the George Warren Brown School of Social Work, Washington University. He is also the director and founder of the Center for Social Development. Prof. Sherraden is the co-author of *Kitchen Capitalism* (SUNY Press, 2004), and author of *Assets and the Poor: A New American Welfare Policy* (M. E. Sharpe, 1991).

James Midgley, Ph.D., is Harry and Riva Specht Professor of Public Social Services and Dean of the School of Social Welfare at the University of California at Berkeley. He has published widely on issues of social policy, social work, and international social welfare. His books include: *Social Welfare in Global*

Context (Sage, 1997), *Alternatives to Social Security* (with Michael Sherraden, Greenwood Press, 1997) and *The Handbook of Social Policy* (Sage, 2000).

YES
Michael Sherraden

My great-grandparents were immigrants who homesteaded in Kansas in the 1870s. They were given 160 acres of land by the federal government. They worked hard, raised 12 children, held barn dances on Saturday nights, and left the community and the country a little better off. The Homestead Act, a massive asset-giveaway program, was one of the most successful domestic policies in U.S. history. It was based on the Jeffersonian idea that people become better citizens in a democracy when they have a stake, assets, and ownership. Although the United States is no longer a nation of small farmers, the concept of stakeholding is just as relevant today as it was at the beginning of the republic.

Despite the prominence of asset ownership in U.S. values and history, social policy in the modern welfare state—and especially means-tested policy for the poor—has been focused almost exclusively on the distribution of income for consumption. Indeed, means-tested policy usually prohibits savings and the accumulation of assets.

Of course, income and consumption are essential—many Americans do not have enough to eat, many are without basic shelter, and many do not have medical insurance of any kind—but income-based policy, by itself, does not help poor households develop economically. Income-based policy traps families in a cycle of spending that goes from check to check. Yet, the simple reality is that not many families manage to spend their way out of poverty. After more than 50 years of income-maintenance policy, we have confirmed that it is correctly named—it provides only maintenance, not development.

ASSETS: A DIFFERENT PERSPECTIVE

We should consider a different approach. Social policy, including welfare policy, should promote asset accumulation. In addition to the income and consumption policy of the current welfare state, asset-based policy would focus on savings and investment.

The rationale for this new direction can be stated in two parts. First, for the vast majority of households, the pathway out of poverty is through savings and accumulation. Reaching important economic development goals almost always requires the prior accumulation of assets. Assets are needed to move to a better neighborhood, to send a child to college, to purchase a home, to start a small business, or to achieve other economic goals. Second, when people begin to accumulate assets, their thinking and behavior changes as well. One way to say this is that while incomes feed people's stomachs, assets change their heads. Accumulating assets leads to important psychological and social effects that are not achieved in the same degree by receiving and spending an equivalent amount of regular income. In contrast to mainstream economic thinking, I am suggesting that assets do more than provide a storehouse for future consumption, and these psychological and social effects of asset accumulation are very important for household "welfare" or well-being. Why do assets matter?

- Assets lead to greater household stability.
- Assets create long-term thinking and planning.
- Assets lead to development of knowledge and skills (creation of human capital).
- Assets provide a foundation for risk taking.
- Assets increase personal efficacy and self-esteem.
- Assets increase social status and influence.
- Assets increase political involvement and community participation.

Altogether, these effects of assets can contribute substantially to the well-being and development of poor households.[1]

THE DISTRIBUTION OF ASSETS

Assets are much more unevenly distributed than income. Looking at income, the top 5 percent of the population receives about as much annual income as the bottom 40 percent. But looking at assets, the top 1 percent holds about as much assets as the bottom 90 percent.[2]

Asset statistics also tell us a great deal about racial inequality. African Americans have virtually never had—and still don't have today—the same access to asset accumulation as have European Americans. For example, at the time my great-grandparents were receiving free land from the government, the promise of "40 acres and a mule" for freed slaves was not kept (Oubre, 1978). Today, the continuing discriminatory record of banks and savings-and-loan associations in making real-estate loans to African Americans is a national disgrace. Statistics show that even when they have the same income, blacks are much less likely to be granted a loan than are

---

[1]These suggested effects of asset accumulation are discussed in *Assets and the Poor* (Sherraden, 1991). They are offered as propositions that have considerable intuitive appeal and certain theoretical and empirical support, although specific tests with poverty populations will be desirable.

[2]Asset distribution data are from the Federal Reserve's *Survey of Consumer Finances* for 1989. Asset distribution in the United States grew considerably more unequal during the 1980s.

whites.[3] What is the result? African American households have only about one-eleventh the assets of white households (U.S. Census Bureau, 1990).

ASSETS AND DOMESTIC POLICY

The importance of asset accumulation has been virtually ignored in the antipoverty policies of the welfare state. However, through the tax system, we do support asset accumulation for the non-poor, primarily in two categories: tax expenditures for home equity and tax expenditures for retirement pension accounts. In these two categories, the federal government spends well over $100 billion each year—and the total is rising rapidly.[4] These two categories make up the bulk of asset accumulation in most American households, heavily subsidized by federal government. Almost everyone would agree that these policies of asset accumulation have been highly successful and good for the country. Thus, we have asset-based policy for the non-poor, and we spend quite a lot of money on it. But we do not have asset-based policy for the poor.

Poor people, by and large, do not benefit from asset-accumulation tax policies because they have tax rates that are either zero or too low to receive substantial tax benefits. Perhaps worse, welfare transfer recipients, under current law, are restricted from accumulating ordinary savings and even business assets. Welfare policy, as currently structured, is anti-savings policy.

This policy does not make sense. As a nation, we should not be telling welfare recipients that they cannot save for a business, a home, or their children's education. An asset-based policy would, in contrast, structure, encourage, and provide incentives for asset accumulation.

INDIVIDUAL DEVELOPMENT ACCOUNTS

One way to achieve this goal is to create a system of Individual Development Accounts (IDAs). IDAs would be a relatively simple and universal system of accounts similar to Individual Retirement Accounts (IRAs). IDAs would be optional, earnings-bearing, tax-benefited accounts in the name of each

---

[3]Evidence of discrimination by race in home purchase and mortgage lending is overwhelming and pervasive. Studies consistently report steering of clients by real-estate agents, redlining of neighborhoods, and systematic loan denials by race. The Community Reinvestment Act of 1977 requires the Federal Reserve Board to keep statistics on mortgage lending, and these statistics indicate strong racial bias, particularly against African Americans.

[4]A good source for estimates of tax expenditures is U.S. Congress, Joint Committee on Taxation (1989). *Estimates of federal tax expenditures for fiscal years 1990–1994.* Washington, DC: U.S. Government Printing Office.

individual, initiated as early as birth and restricted to designated purposes. Regardless of the category of social policy (housing, education, self-
employment, retirement, or other) assets would be accumulated in these
long-term restricted accounts. The federal government would match deposits
for the poor, and there would be potential for creative financing through the
private sector.

In developing a single IDA policy structure, the government would
limit complexity and better integrate various asset-based initiatives into an
overall national strategy. Also, the policy would be essentially direct-to-the-
beneficiary, with very limited intervention by a welfare bureaucracy. The
following general guidelines should be considered for IDAs:

- IDAs should complement income-based policy.
- The policy should be simple—both conceptually and administratively.
- The accounts should be voluntary.
- The accounts should receive favorable tax treatment.
- Federal and state governments should provide deposit matches for the
  poor.
- Creative participation by the corporate and nonprofit sectors should be
  actively encouraged.

Once the structure of Individual Development Accounts is in place,
even with minimal direct funding from the federal government, there would
be opportunities for a wide variety of creative funding projects from the
private and nonprofit sectors. To build IDA accounts, one can imagine
corporations "adopting" a school or a neighborhood, church fundraisers,
contributions from civic organizations, bake sales, car washes, carnivals,
student-run businesses, and so forth. The key is to establish a policy structure
that could leverage private money with tax benefits, spark creative ideas and
partnerships, attract diverse funding, and gradually expand as the policy
demonstrates its worth.

A NEW DIRECTION: SOCIAL POLICY AS INVESTMENT

Social policy should invest in the American people—and encourage them to
invest in themselves—so they become stakeholders and active citizens. The
key is to combine social policy with economic development through a program of asset-building and stakeholding.

As a closing thought, Individual Development Accounts, or some other
form of asset-based domestic policy, could become for the 21st century what
the Homestead Act was for the 19th—an investment-oriented policy to
develop individual capacity, strengthen families and communities, promote
active citizenship, and contribute to economic growth.

NO

James Midgley

Of various alternatives to conventional policies for the alleviation of poverty, the asset approach is the most original and radical. As formulated by Sherraden (1991), this approach re-orients existing antipoverty policies by encouraging the accumulation of wealth rather than the payment of benefits for consumption. By helping the poor to save, the asset approach purports to really help the poor.

THE ASSET-BASED APPROACH

The asset-based approach is critical of conventional antipoverty programs. Many existing programs such as Aid to Families with Dependent Children (AFDC), Food Stamps and Medicaid promote the consumption of goods and services. They fail, however, to encourage savings and engender behaviors that make the poor responsible, independent, and self-reliant. While it is obvious that basic needs can only be met through consumption, critics contend that the continual provision of consumption goods to the poor simply maintains them at minimal levels of living. If the goal of social policy is the eradication of poverty, the poor must be offered an opportunity to escape poverty. Proponents argue that the asset approach helps poor people accumulate the resources to lift themselves out of poverty, and it allows them to become self-reliant and self-respecting citizens.

At the core of the asset approach is the Individual Development Account (IDA), which, like the Individual Retirement Account (IRA), encourages savings. These accounts would be established for all individuals, and would be tax benefited to foster asset accumulation. Depending on the financial circumstances of the depositor, individual savings would be matched by state contributions at varying rates. For example, a person in severe financial need would have a match as high as 90 percent while someone who is working and enjoying a relatively good income would receive no match at all. The matching system would be highly flexible and permit the government to supplement savings as the economic circumstances of individuals change. The accounts would be managed by individuals themselves so that they would become familiar with investment options and learn to use their money wisely. However, the account would be restricted so that withdrawals could be made only for approved purposes, such as the purchase of a home, education, retirement, or the establishment of a business. Accumulated IDA assets could be transferred to children at death or prior to death if desired.

Although the asset approach would not replace the Temporary Assistance for Needy Families (TANF) program, or other programs that assist the poor meet their basic needs, it would encourage recipients to deposit a part of their benefits into IDAs and generously match their contributions. In this way, poor people would derive concrete financial benefits, and their predilection to be dependent on the state would be reduced. Asset accumulation through IDAs would be a long-term process but would foster thrift and responsibility among the poor who have little propensity to save.

Consonant with the tenets of Jeffersonian liberalism, the political philosophy underlying the asset approach is essentially individualist in character and firmly rooted in the American experience. Indeed, this approach was first used in the United States in the form of the Homestead Act of 1862, which delivered about 200 million acres of land to settlers. However, similar approaches have been adopted in other countries. Of interest are the provident funds established in many former British colonial territories to provide an alternative to social security (Midgley, 1984). An asset approach was also introduced by General Pinochet's regime in Chile to replace the country's long-standing social security system (Borzutsky, 1992).

CAN ASSETS REALLY HELP THE POOR?

The mobilization of capital through personal savings is regarded by most economists as highly desirable. Whether operated on command, corporatist, or free-market principles, modern economies require investment to renew infrastructure and establish productive enterprises. By encouraging ordinary citizens to save, the economy benefits, and those who save benefit as well. Through savings, people accumulate the resources needed to purchase goods and services and, in this way, contribute to the aggregate demand, generating more production and employment.

While the advocacy of asset accumulation is noncontentious, the role of assets in solving the problem of poverty is more problematic. Few would disagree with the idea that the poor should be encouraged, and even helped, to save, but it is unlikely that the implementation of an assets approach through the creation of IDAs will, of itself, really help the poor.

It is obvious that the poorest sections of the population, such as TANF recipients, do not have the financial resources to save at appreciable levels. Even if supplemented by the government, it is difficult to believe that their meager savings can help them to escape poverty within a reasonable period of time. TANF benefit levels are appallingly low, and despite propagandistic claims that recipients enjoy a comfortable level of living at taxpayers expense, they endure a daily struggle to survive. The poorest sections of the population subsist on incomes that are below minimal physical-survival levels, and below the minimum standards of decency that a civilized society should tolerate. It is unlikely that these people could somehow find the resources to contribute to IDAs, and that their meager savings, even if supplemented by the state, could eventually propel them out of poverty. The prospects of saving to escape poverty are even more remote for those who have lost their homes and who live on the streets, surviving through begging, scavenging, or scrounging.

The asset approach is designed to encourage responsibility and self-sufficiency among the poor. Indeed, its potential as a means for inculcating puritan attitudes is far greater than that of generating the material resources needed to escape poverty. But while it has become fashionable to indict the moral behavior of the poor, it is doubtful whether poverty can be solved through the cultivation of middle-class values. Those who work with welfare mothers know that they manage their meager budgets with the hard-nosed acumen of small-town bankers. Their need for material resources, realistic employment opportunities, day care for children, and adequate housing is far greater than their need for lessons on the virtues of thrift, sobriety, and self-reliance.

In addition to the problem of inadequate resources, the asset approach presents difficult economic, organizational, and political challenges. The costs of subsidizing IDAs would be considerable, especially if the government supplements them to a significant degree. Also, there are formidable organizational issues to be resolved if the IDA program is to be implemented on the national level and if it is to be sufficiently flexible to adjust quickly to people's changing economic circumstances. However, proponents of IDAs have no doubt that these problems can be overcome, and they believe that political obstacles can be surmounted. Although the asset approach has secured bipartisan political support, it is not certain whether this support will endure when the political ramifications of the program's funding requirements are fully understood. To finance IDAs for the poor, it is proposed to abolish a variety of tax benefits which the non-poor currently enjoy. Given the realities of the political process, it is by no mean certain that political support for these proposals will be sustained as well-organized constituents react negatively to plans for reducing the benefits they currently enjoy.

More fundamentally, the asset approach, like most other attempts to deal with poverty on an individual level, fails to address the basic causes of poverty and deprivation in society. Poverty is rooted in economic and social structural factors, and not in the declining propensity of individuals to save. Economic decline associated with de-industrialization and global economic changes, reduced employment opportunities in traditional blue-collar occupations, falling wages for those in regular employment, deteriorated urban areas, declining educational standards, cutbacks in the human services, and entrenched inequalities are far more relevant in understanding the nature of poverty today. If the problem of poverty is to be effectively addressed, these realities must be addressed at the national level through comprehensive economic and social policies. Like other programs that attribute poverty to individual misfortune and assign primary responsibility for escaping poverty to the individual, attempts to encourage the poor to save, however worthwhile, cannot eradicate poverty.

Programs for the alleviation of poverty that have had the greatest degree of success in the past have implemented macroeconomic and social policies and mobilized the resources of the state on a large scale. Despite its many shortcomings, the Johnson administration's attempts to address the poverty problem resulted in a significant decline in the incidence of poverty (Marmor, Mashaw, & Harvey, 1990). The experiences of Western Europe and the newly industrializing East Asian nations, which have highly interventionist governments, offer further evidence of the effectiveness of collectivist solutions that combine economic and social policies through the powerful agency of the centralized, interventionist state (Esping-Anderson, 1985; Midgley, 1986).

Of course, such strategies are unlikely to garner much political support in United States' highly individualistic enterprise culture, where the power of the central government is used to promote the accumulation of wealth among those who are already wealthy, rather than deal with pressing social ills. In this political climate, the asset approach may make a contribution. However, despite its advantages, it is unlikely that the asset-based approach can *really* help the poor.

REFERENCES

Borzutsky, S. (1992). The Chicago boys, social security and welfare in Chile. In H. Glennerster, & J. Midgley (Eds.), *The radical right and the welfare state: An international assessment* (pp. 79–99). Savage, MD: Barnes and Noble.

Esping-Anderson, G. (1985). *Politics against markets: The social democratic road to power.* Cambridge, MA: Harvard University Press.

Glennerster, H., & Midgley, J. (Eds.). (1991). *The radical right and the welfare state.* Hertfordshire, England: Harvester Wheatsheaf; and Savage, MD: Barnes and Noble.

Marmor, T. R., Mashaw, J. L., & Harvey, P. L. (1990). *America's misunderstood welfare state: Persistent myths, enduring realities.* New York: Basic Books.

Midgley, J. (1984). *Social security, Inequality and the third world.* New York: John Wiley and Sons.

Midgley, J. (1986). Welfare and industrialization: The case of the four little tigers. *Social Policy and Administration, 20,* 225–238.

Midgley, J. (1992). Development theory, the state, and social development in Asia. *Social Development Issues, 14*(1), 22–36.

Oubre, C. F. (1978). *Forty acres and a mule: The Freedman's Bureau and black land ownership.* Baton Rouge: Louisiana State University Press.

Sherraden, M. (1991). *Assets and the poor: A new American welfare policy.* Armonk, NY: M. E. Sharpe.

U.S. Census Bureau. (1990). *Household wealth and asset ownership: 1988.* Washington, DC: U.S. Government Printing Office.

PART II

THE CULTURE WARS: DISCRIMINATION, STIGMA, AND SOCIAL POLICY

■ ■ ■ ■ ■

SHOULD SAME-SEX
MARRIAGES BE LEGALIZED?

Editor's Note:
Pundits attempting to interpret the exit polls in 2004 were quick to conclude that opposition to gay and lesbian marriage was a values issue that drove many conservative voters to the polls and, thereby, indirectly accounted for Bush's second term in office. Regardless of the accuracy of this assessment, the American public is radically polarized on this issue. Despite census data suggesting that the traditional nuclear family has become a relative rarity, with less than 25 percent of American households fitting this model, traditionalists and a broad array of religious leaders oppose same-sex marriage. Progressives, recognizing that new models of family structure dominate contemporary American society, view same-sex marriage through a lens suggesting that opposition is an unjust impediment to full citizenship of gay and lesbian people.

Less than 35 years ago, homosexuality was still listed as a mental illness in the American Psychiatric Association's *Diagnostic and Statistical Manual of Mental Disorders* (3rd ed.). Same-sex sexual relations were still criminalized in many states as recently as 3 years ago. In many respects, the issue of same-sex marriage is much more than a political question. Same-sex marriage has become a litmus test for the inclusive limits of American society.

Lori Messinger, Ph.D., is an assistant professor and director of the BSW Program at the University of Kansas School of Social Welfare. Her primary areas of research include social work with lesbian and gay populations, comprehensive community-planning processes, cultural competence in social-work education, and feminist theories and research methodologies. She is coeditor (with Dr. Deana Morrow) of the books, *Sexual Orientation and Gender Expression in Social Work Practice* (Columbia, 2006) and *Case Studies on Sexual Orientation and Gender Identity in Social Work Practice* (Columbia University Press, 2006). She is chair of Educators and Friends of Lesbians, Gays, Bisexuals, and

Transgender Persons, a committee of the social work Baccalaureate Program Directors Association, and she serves on the state board of Kansans for Equality, an organization working to advance full equality and civil rights for all the people of Kansas through education and action. She and her same-sex partner have been in a committed relationship for 15 years.

Glenn T. Stanton is the director of Global Insights and Trends and senior analyst for Marriage and Sexuality at Focus on the Family. He is also the author of *Why Marriage Matters* (Naupress, 1997) and *Marriage on Trial: The Case Against Same-Sex Marriage and Parenting* (with Bill Maier, Intervarsity Press, 2004).

YES
Lori Messinger

The question for this debate is in some ways an anachronism. Same-sex marriages were legalized in Massachusetts in 2004, and, by September 2005, more than 6,500 same-sex couples had taken advantage of this opportunity to be married (Lewis, 2005). These marriages are recognized by the state as legitimate, conferring on the same-sex couples all the same rights and responsibilities that heterosexual married couples have. So, while some people still argue about the appropriateness of the Massachusetts Supreme Court's decision and the resulting changes in state law, same-sex couples in Massachusetts now have marriage as a potential option. The question then becomes: Should same-sex marriages be legalized in every state in the United States?

DEFINING MARRIAGE AND ITS TRUE HISTORY

Marriage, as we know it in the United States, is both a religious institution—structured by the beliefs and doctrine of religious bodies—and a civil institution—governed by the state. Religious bodies regulate marriage as a sacrament or religious practice, and the state regulates the provision of legal rights and the enforcement of legal responsibilities on members of the married couple.

The clear distinction between these two types of marriage has been blurred by state governments' approval of religious leaders as "representatives of the state," with the right to solemnize marriages in such a way that the state will legally recognize them, as long as the religious leaders follow the laws of their state. Nonetheless, it is important to note that marriages do not need to be performed by religious leaders to be legal. Heterosexual couples throughout the United States can be legally married by a judge or other non–religiously affiliated person recognized by the state. Additionally, no one must hold a religiously based understanding of marriage in order for their civil marriage to be recognized; atheists, agnostics, and people of various faith traditions can all be legally married. Thus, it is important to recognize that the question being asked in this essay regards extending only the civil institution of marriage to include same-sex couples throughout the United States.

The American Christian political group Focus on the Family proclaims that no less than "history, nature, social science, anthropology, religion, and theology all coalesce in vigorous support of marriage *as it has always been understood:* a life-long union of male and female for the purpose of creating stable families" (emphasis mine) (Stanton, 2004b). Stephanie Coontz (1998, 2000, 2005, 2006), a scholar of marriage and family history, refutes this claim about the static nature of marriage in her books and essays, where she explodes many myths about marriage. She explains that polygamy is actually the most common form of marriage throughout human history; in fact, polygamy "is the family form most often mentioned in the first five books of the Old Testament" (Coontz, 2006). As a religious state, marriage was not always considered sacred; the Catholic Church first declared marriage a sacrament in 1215 and only required religious marriage ceremonies in 1563. In addition, most marriages throughout time and in different cultures have been based on securing property and political interests rather than familial love and desired intimacy (Coontz, 2005). We must recognize that marriage, as both a religious and a civil institution, has changed over time, and that the expansion of civil marriage to include same-sex couples is actually part of a larger tradition of change.

ARGUMENTS FOR SAME-SEX MARRIAGE

Equal rights protections are an important component of the argument for same-sex marriage, due to the many rights and privileges attached to marriage in the United States. The U.S. Government Accounting Office (2004) listed 1,138 ways in which marital relationships are given special treatment by the federal government. There are also hundreds of rights, benefits, and responsibilities automatically conferred upon married couples that have implications at the local and state levels of government. In a report for the National Gay and Lesbian Task Force, Cahill Ellen, and Tobias (2002) list some of the most important benefits granted to partners in a marriage:

- the ability to access coverage of partners under Medicare and Social Security
- the ability to file joint tax returns
- the ability to obtain death benefits when a partner dies
- the ability to obtain health and retirement benefits from an employer
- the right to sponsor his or her spouse for immigration to the United States

- the ability to take sick leave or bereavement leave to care for a partner or a partner's child
- the right to make medical decisions for a partner who falls ill
- the assumption that children born to a marriage are the children of both partners, regardless of biological relationship
- access to stepparent adoption of a partner's children
- the right to use the courts for divorce
- the right to sue for wrongful death
- the right to choose the method to dispose of a partner's remains when a partner has died. (pp. 23–24)

The authors also find that children born to a marriage or adopted by their parent's opposite-sex partner obtain the following benefits:

- the right to live with a nonbiological parent after a biological parent dies
- access to health benefits and the right to inherit death benefits from either parent
- the right to Social Security benefits if either parent dies
- the right to financial support and a continued relationship with both parents should their parents separate. (pp. 23–24)

None of these benefits is automatically conferred on unmarried partners in same-sex relationships. It costs thousands of dollars to create legal contracts to achieve minimal protections for same-sex relationships, a price tag that puts this option out of reach for low-income couples. Moreover, many legal protections are conferred by law and cannot be secured by drafting documents or other private arrangements. Even heterosexual relatives suffer as a result of discriminatory marriage laws—for example, parents of a lesbian have no legal status as grandparents to any nonbiological children their daughter is raising (Cahill et al., 2002).

The current lack of protections affects thousands of lesbian and gay couples and their children. The 2000 census found approximately 600,000 self-identified same-sex couples who share a residence, with a large number of those same-sex couples raising children: 22.3 percent of male couples and 34.3 percent of female couples had children under 18 years old in their household (Gay demographics, 2003). It is more common for lesbian and gay persons of color to be parents. One survey found that "while only 23 percent of the white women living with a same-sex partner had given birth to one or more children, 30 percent of Asian/Pacific Islander women, 43 percent of Hispanic women, and 60 percent of African American women in same-sex cohabiting relationships had given birth" (Cahill et al., 2002, p. 14). Allowing same-sex marriage would provide real protections for lesbian and gay parents and their children.

Allowing same-sex marriage would also proactively address the legal confusions facing transgender persons who seek to be married. Currently, it is unclear whether a couple who were differently gendered when married but where one partner has sex reassignment surgery and becomes legally recognized as a person of the same gender as the spouse can still have a legally valid marriage. It is similarly unclear whether a typically gendered person can marry a transgendered person who is legally recognized as differently gendered than the partner and have that marriage recognized in a court of law. Legal precedents are mixed—sometimes the marriages are upheld, and other times they are invalidated (Cahill et al., 2002). If persons could marry someone of the same or different gender, all marriages including a transgendered person would be legally valid and the rights of both partners (transgendered and traditionally gendered) would be protected.

COUNTERING ARGUMENTS AGAINST SAME-SEX MARRIAGE

Many who oppose same-sex marriage oppose it on religious grounds. Yet it is important to note that not all religious groups currently oppose same-sex religious marriages. American religious leaders in reform Judaism, United Church of Christ, Unitarian Universalism, and some Quaker meetings and Baptist congregations already openly conduct same-sex marriage rituals. One could argue that current laws prohibiting same-sex marriage actually inhibit the exercise of their religious freedom. Additionally, there are ongoing arguments in most other major religions and Christian denominations about solemnizing same-sex relationships, with people of faith on both sides of the issue. Perhaps it is most important that we remember that the First Amendment requires that religious groups get to determine their own doctrine and practice their beliefs without the interference of the government. Therefore, if same-sex marriage was legalized in every state, religious leaders who did not support same-sex marriage would never be required to marry a same-sex couple, while those who did support same-sex marriages could perform legally recognized marriages for same-sex couples.

Others argue that same-sex marriage will be the "undoing" of heterosexual relationships, harming the states and countries in which it is allowed. Yet evidence from Massachusetts, as well as from countries that allow same-sex marriage, such as Belgium, Canada, the Netherlands, and Spain, offers proof that same-sex marriage is not detrimental. Marriage and divorce rates have not changed substantially in European countries that allow same-sex marriages, while out-of-wedlock birth rates are much the same in European countries that do not allow same-sex marriage as those who do (Badgett, 2004). In fact, in Massachusetts, public opinion has turned in favor of same-sex marriage (Lewis, 2005).

Nor is there any credible evidence that children of same-sex parents suffer from growing up with two parents of the same gender, another argument offered by opponents of same-sex marriage (Stanton, 2004a). While a review of previous studies of children of same-sex parents have shown small differences in children raised with same-sex parents, pertaining to their comfort with sexual diversity and their rejection of strict gender roles (Stacey & Biblarz, 2001), these children had few differences related to other aspects of personal development, including personality, academic performance, self-concept, and conduct (Perrin, 2002b; Stacey & Biblarz, 2001; Tasker, 1999). Many arguments against gay and lesbian parents that are used by those opposing same-sex marriage (e.g., Stanton, 2004a) cite studies of divorced parents and single parents, not studies of same-sex couples who reside and raise children together. The American Psychological Association, the National Association of Social Workers, the Child Welfare League of America, and the American Association of Pediatrics all support the rights of same-sex couples to be parents.

Some who oppose same-sex marriage argue that civil unions, such as those in Vermont and Connecticut, or domestic partner registries, such as those in California and New Jersey, offer more measured and appropriate policy responses to meeting the needs of same-sex couples and their children. These policy options do not carry the same emotional, religious, and political implications as marriage, and they could be easier to legislate. Yet they do not offer the same benefits as marriage. If a same-sex couple who had a civil union or a registered domestic partnership moved away from their home state to another state that did not have these legal options, the couple (and their children) would lose all protections granted by that home state. Further, neither civil unions nor domestic partnerships have any legal standing in the eyes of the federal government.

Opponents often base their argument on tradition. Yet even if marriage between one man and one woman had always been the norm, the statement "this is the way it has always been" is not a very strong legal or political argument. Many discriminatory laws throughout history have been defended this same way. Every group that has had to fight for their rights in the United States—including African Americans and other people of color, children, people with disabilities, women, and lesbians and gay men—has had to upset the status quo. In the area of marriage, laws and legal precedents had to be challenged to allow marriages among people who were enslaved, poor people (Coontz, 2006), and between African Americans and whites. In each case, changes in the marriage laws required lawmakers and justices to overlook legal precedent and social mores supporting discrimination and recognize the humanity and equal rights protections of those individuals seeking marriage rights.

Finally, Congresswoman Marilyn Musgrave (2003) has critiqued same-sex marriage as an attempt by gay activists to "legitimize their lifestyle." In some ways, Musgrave is correct. Advocates of same-sex marriage are work-ing not only to secure rights for same-sex couples and their children; they are also trying to gain respect for these families. If same-sex couples could be rec-ognized as legitimate, worthy, married couples, they might be treated more fairly, with less discrimination, and their children might experience less homophobia as well. Recognizing the dignity and worth of same-sex couples is a challenging concept for many who oppose same-sex marriage, but it is a requirement for competent social workers. As social workers, whose code of ethics requires respect for the human dignity and self-determination of all persons, we must support the legalization of same-sex marriage throughout the United States.

CONCLUSION

In the award-winning play *Angels in America* (Kushner, 1993), a gay man named Prior and a Mormon woman named Harper have a conversation. Upon realizing that the Prior is gay, Harper says, "In my church, we don't believe in homosexuals." Prior responds, "In my church, we don't believe in Mormons." Prior's teasing response shows the underlying problem with Harper's assertion about homosexuality; it does not matter whether you "believe in" or support homosexuality or Mormonism—they are both reali-ties, representing the lives of real people. Gay men and lesbians exist. A good number of gay men and lesbians are in committed relationships and want to be legally recognized as married, so that they can utilize the many rights and privileges that attend to the state of marriage. In a country that supports diversity of thought and practice, the separation of religion and government, and the protection of the minority against domination by the majority; in a profession that requires respect for human dignity and self-determination—how can we ethically argue any position other than supporting same-sex marriage laws?

NO

Glenn T. Stanton

Marriage, appearing in various forms in all human cultures, is a consistently and inherently heterosexual norm, transcending time, culture, politics, and religion. And it is such for very good reasons. In this essay, I explore the main questions consistently brought up in the many same-sex marriage debates I engage in on college campuses around the country every year. When refer-ring to *marriage,* I am speaking about a heterosexual institution.

But first, let me say from the outset that well-being for individuals and community is what motivates me in this debate. I am not motivated by hate, homophobia, bigotry, or sheer moralizing. I am interested in what is good for people and the community.

And lazy assumptions like these are constantly made about people who oppose same-sex marriage. Perhaps some are motivated by such things. While I cannot speak for others, it should be recognized that many gay and lesbian people oppose the legalization of same-sex marriage as well—ranging from those who believe that marriage, as a heterosexual institution, serves a vital public good that androgynous marriage would not to those who feel that marriage in any form is a restricting institution and would hinder the values and dreams of gay culture (Levine, 2003; Rinnert, 2003). Let us address some of the major topics and questions in the same-sex marriage debate.

QUESTION 1: HOW WILL MY SAME-SEX MARRIAGE HURT YOUR MARRIAGE?

I am asked this question in nearly every public debate, and my opponent usually brings it up while pointing to his or her partner, whom I met just before the debate. The answer is simple. "If this were *only* about *your* marriage," I respond, "then maybe we could work something out. If we're talking about only the two of you, then no real harm will be done. But we are not talking about only you two."

Efforts to legalize same-sex marriage is about asking *everyone—all* of society—to dramatically and permanently alter their definition of family to say that male and female are not essential for marriage, family, and society. It demands we accept male and female as merely optional for the family.

The same-sex family proposition reduces the essence of being male or female to merely sperm or egg—reproductive material—for that, the same-sex-marriage-and-family proposition says, is all that one gender needs from the other. And to say that half of humanity—either male or female—is not essential to the family is to radically deconstruct humanity.

QUESTION 2: IS BANNING SAME-SEX MARRIAGE LIKE BANNING INTERRACIAL MARRIAGE?

Banning same-sex marriage is nothing like banning interracial marriage. Segregation was an evil social problem. Marriage as an exclusively heterosexual union is a profound social good. Racism is about power and suppression, about keeping the races apart, and that is *wrong*. Marriage is about bringing the two parts of humanity together, male and female, and that is *good*. Marriage has nothing to do with race. It has everything to do with a husband and wife working together to create and care for the next generation.

Striking down bans on interracial marriage *affirmes* marriage by saying that any woman has a right to marry any man. Same-sex marriage *redefines* marriage by saying that men and women are optional for the family. And what is more, it is very different for a child to say, "I have a black mother and a white father than to say, "I have two moms and no father."

There is no research showing that interracial parenting is developmentally harmful to children, but literally thousands of studies indicating that children are hindered developmentally when they are denied their mothers or fathers (Blankenhorn, 1994; Popenoe, 1997; Pruett, 2000; Stanton, 1997).

What is most troubling about this argument is the implication that people who value the necessary contributions men and women bring to marriage are bigots. This is a vile implication and has no place in civil discourse!

QUESTION 3: WHERE DOES IT STOP?

If we say marriage is not about husband and wife, mother and father, where do we stop in our redefinition? Andrew Sullivan (2004), a homosexual writer, says, "The right to marry whomever you wish is a fundamental civil right."

Is Marriage Only Two?

What would Sullivan say to Jonathan Yarbrough and Cody Rogahn? They were the first couple to get a same-sex marriage license on May 17, 2004, in Provincetown, Massachusetts. When the media asked Yarbrough about their relationship, he said, "I think it's possible to love more than one person and have more than one partner. . . . In our case, it is. We have an open marriage" (Richardson, 2004). What do we tell these men if they want to bring their new love interests into their marriage? What rationale do we have for telling them marriage is only about two?

When Cheryl Jacques, former director of the homosexual lobbying group Human Rights Campaign, was asked why same-sex marriage would not lead to multiple-party marriages, she said, "Because I don't approve of that" (Crossfire, 2004). Here's our question for Cheryl: "Why is your disapproval of polygamy more reasonable than my disapproval of same-sex marriage?"

Jonathan Turley, a professor of law at George Washington Law School, has opined in *USA Today* that the only real difference between homosexuals and polygamists seeking to change marriage laws in their favor is that the former group is more socially fashionable than the latter. He is correct in recognizing that no network is going to air *The Polygamist Eye for the Monogamist Guy.* He says to make such a change for a "hip" group and *not* for a polyester-clad group would be unequal treatment under the law and hypocritical (Turley, 2004).

Thought Control?

Same-sex marriage is not about tolerance; same-sex homes are tolerated in society. This is about forcing everyone to accept these experimental families. Here is another question: If same-sex marriage is legalized, could the statement, "Children need a mother and father" be deemed hate speech? It is becoming exactly that in Massachusetts, where same-sex marriage has been legalized. *The Boston Globe* complained, "Governor Romney is denigrating gay families, practicing divisive, mean-spirited politics . . . by insisting that every child 'has a right to a mother and a father' " (Not fair, 2005).

Swedish pastor Ake Green was threatened with prison and entangled legal problems for many years, not for physically threatening anyone, but simply for preaching from the Bible about homosexuality. Say the wrong thing, go to jail. Only months after same-sex marriage became legal in some parts of Canada, legislators there passed a law that carries a maximum two-year jail sentence for *saying* certain things about homosexuals that could be deemed hateful. Now, we might not like what others say, but we should protect their right to say it.

Heather Has Two Mommies, K–12

How will same-sex marriage affect what our children learn in schools at a young age? All textbooks will change, not just sociology books in highschool. Imagine your children's reading books showing Suzie going to feed the ducks, hand-in-hand with her two dads. But the ducks—because we cannot get away from nature—will be in male/female pairs!

Seem far-fetched? Consider a recent National Public Radio story from Boston aired after same-sex marriage was legalized there. It reports efforts underway to create a "new gay-friendly curriculum for kindergarten and up." It also tells of Deb Allen, an eighth-grade teacher who teaches her students about gay sex "thoroughly and explicitly with a chart." When asked if parents complained about their children learning such explicit material, this teacher retorts, "Give me a break. It's legal now" (Block & Smith, 2004).

Religious Freedom

Many times, I am told that this debate is about civil marriage, not religious marriage, so religious people should not be concerned. Does anyone really believe that the ACLU will not challenge churches when they refuse to honor their "constitutionally protected" same-sex marriage? Proponents say, that the Catholic Church is not forced to perform divorces, because divorce is against church beliefs and the same will be true for same-sex marriages. But divorce is not a constitutionally protected right like same-sex marriage will become if proponents are successful in the courts.

In fact, in Canada the Catholic Church is being challenged because a local parish refused to rent out the church hall for a lesbian couple's reception, even though church officials incredible good-faith by making arrangements for the reception to be moved to another, neutral venue (O'Connor, 2005).

QUESTION 4: CAN'T WE ALL JUST GET ALONG BY HAVING SEPARATE RELIGIOUS AND CIVIL MARRIAGES?

Marriage is more than a religious institution. It shows up in *all* societies, not just Christian or religious ones. It is a human institution that involves both church and state. Churches are interested in making sure marriages are healthy and strong, and city hall—as well as state and federal governments—is interested in what marriage provides society. Maggie Gallagher (2003), a columnist who writes often about marriage, explains.

> There is scarcely a dollar that state and federal government spends on social programs that is not driven in large part by family fragmentation: crime, poverty, drug abuse, teen pregnancy, school failure, mental and physical health problems.

Every society needs men and women to cooperate in founding homes and raising children, and marriage is the way *all* societies accomplish this.

QUESTION 5: WHAT PUBLIC GOOD DOES MARRIAGE PROVIDE?

Through marriage, people produce and raise the next generation of humanity, which every society needs. If you do not believe this is a need, look at the current depopulation trends in much of Europe. Governments there are realizing that a dearth of childbearing couples raises serious social and economic issues.

Spin a globe, pick any place on earth, and visit that place at any time in human history; you will find that marriage is always *between men and women*. There may be some diversity in the number of spouses or in the division of labor, but marriage is *always* heterosexual. Why do we find this global and historic universality of marriage? Is it because Jerry Falwell or James Dobson have gone everywhere, throughout all time, and forced marriage on all cultures? Is it a political trick of the Republican Party? Did the Catholic Church enforce it on everyone, everywhere? No. It is because nature enforces and imposes heterosexual coupling on all human societies, and it does so with no tolerance. We *need* heterosexual families.

Conversely, there is no public need for the same-sex family. If there were, societies would have created such families before now. But they have not, because same-sex "marriage" meets the personal desire of a few adults, not society as a whole.

Anthropologists tell us that marriage, as a heterosexual institution, performs four primary functions. It is the only institution that provides these things, and *every* society needs marriage to achieve them.

1. *Marriage socializes men.* Anthropologists tell us that a society's most serious problem is the unattached male. Marriage is the answer. Natural marriage socializes men by channeling male sexuality and aggression in socially productive ways. And it is women who do this through marriage.

Gail Collins, editor of the *New York Times* editorial page, wrote a wonderful book titled *America's Women*, which examines the role of women in American culture. In an interview on National Public Radio, Collins explained her primary finding, "The most important implicit role women play in society is to make men behave" (Collins, 2003). Other scholars have recognized the same thing (Akerlof, 1998; Gilder, 1987).

But same-sex marriage will not socialize males, because males do not socialize other males, however close they might be. The lack of monogamy and relational durability in gay male relationships is evidence of this. Same-sex marriage fails in this first purpose of marriage.

2. *Marriage regulates sexuality.* By socializing men, marriage regulates sexuality. Marriage establishes sexual guardrails, which are a requirement for successful societies. We cannot survive with everybody doing whatever they want sexually. Every society must have rules, mores, and standards about sexual behavior; and marriage is how societies manage human sexuality. The research is very clear: Societies that weaken these sexual standards end up with serious and unexpected social problems. There is no evidence that same-sex marriage would serve society in regulating sexuality; and as such, it fails this second public purpose of marriage.

3. *Marriage protects women from exploitive males.* When we do not have the social norm of monogamy, women become commodities—things to be collected, used, and then discarded. Marriage helps protect women by regulating sex. When women socialize men through marriage and parenthood, men are more likely to care for and respect their wives and other women. When fewer men are married to women, fewer men care for and respect women. A wealth of research shows that abuse of women by their partners or strangers is lowest in married homes and highest in cohabiting and dating situations. Same-sex marriage fails the third purpose of marriage in its inability to protect women.

4. *Marriage provides mothers and fathers for children.* Healthy children define a growing society. And marriage is the way we ensure that the next generation grows up with the irreplaceable benefit of a mother and father on the scene every day. A loving and compassionate society comes to the aid of motherless and fatherless children, but no compassionate society *intentionally* subjects children to motherless or fatherless families. *But this is what every same-sex home does and for no other reason but to satisfy adult desire.* So, same-sex marriage fails in fulfilling the fourth public purpose of marriage.

No society anywhere has been able to sustain itself with a buffet-like mentality of family, where you simply go through the line and pick and choose what suits you, with one choice just as good as another.

QUESTION 6: IS IT HEALTHY TO SUBJECT CHILDREN TO EXPERIMENTAL FAMILIES?

Not all married couples have children, but most do. And not all married same-sex couples will want children, but many will. So the argument for same-sex marriage *is* the argument for the same-sex family.

No society at any time—primitive or developed, ancient or modern—has ever raised a generation of children in same-sex homes. Same-sex marriage will subject a generation of children to the status of lab rats in a vast, untested, social experiment. In *The Lesbian Parenting Book,* the authors admit that in founding lesbian homes, "Our children are not the only ones who may find themselves in uncharted territory" (Clunis & Green, 2003). The words "uncharted territory" sound similar to "experiment." And here is what they say about what it would mean to raise boys in lesbian homes: "It will be interesting to see over time whether lesbians' sons have an easier or harder time developing their gender identity than do boys with live-in fathers" (p. 243). The key phrase: "It will be interesting to see."

We live in a warning-label society—warning labels tell us no animals were harmed in the testing of this or that particular product. The warning label on the same-sex family is, "It will be interesting to see." Do you think it will be "interesting" to subject millions of children to these experimental families for no other reason than that adults desire them?

QUESTION 7: BUT HAVEN'T MEDICAL AND PSYCHOLOGICAL GROUPS SAID SAME-SEX PARENTING IS FINE?

The American Academy of Pediatrics (AAP) has a statement supporting same-sex parenting. And so do the American Psychological Association, the American Psychiatric Association, and the American Medical Association. But there are a number of reasons to question the conclusions of these organizations. Here's the American Academy of Pediatrics' statement (2002):

> [T]here is a considerable body of professional literature that suggests that children with parents who are homosexual have the same advantages and the same expectations for health, adjustment and development as children whose parents are heterosexual.

First of all, very few researchers are questioning that the quality of a person's parenting is related to their sexual orientation. This is an important point. It would be just as wrong to subject a child to a two-mom or two-dad home if those two adults are heterosexual. But we must consider how the AAP came to this decision. Did they gather all the best pediatricians together and carefully study the literature, or did they do it another way?

They did it another way.

They made this decision with a select committee of nine people. And once they made this statement, the reaction of the larger membership of the Academy was phenomenal! Consider this e-mail, written by the lead author of the AAP's study, and what it says about the larger membership's response:

> The AAP has received more messages—almost all of them CRITICAL—from members about the recent policy statement on [same-sex adoption] than it has EVER received on any other topic. This is a serious problem, as it means that it will become harder to continue the work that we have been doing to use the AAP as a vehicle for positive change. (emphasis in original) (Perrin, 2002a)

Consider that last statement: ". . . use the AAP as a vehicle for positive change." *Is this careful science or plain activism?* The AAP and these other professional medical organizations cannot make statements about how same-sex families serve the well-being of children because we have not performed the experiment yet! Sociologists need two things to make such conclusions about the health of new family forms: large, diverse populations to study and long periods of time—decades—to observe them. The AAP admits there are no large populations of children raised in same-sex homes to study:

> The small and non-representational samples studied and the relatively young age of most of the children suggest some reserve. . . . Research exploring the

diversity of parental relationships among gay and lesbian parents is just beginning. (Perrin, 2002b)

Yet within sentences of these recognized cautions, the Academy claims:

[T]he weight of evidence gathered during several decades using diverse samples and methodologies is persuasive in demonstrating that there is no systematic difference between gay and non-gay parents in emotional health, parenting skills, and attitudes toward parenting. (Perrin, 2002b)

In stating that kids who grow up in same-sex homes look pretty much like children who grow up in heterosexual homes, the AAP is both right and wrong. The fine print of study tells the full story. The Academy report's that children who grew up in same-sex homes had outcomes similar to children who grew up in heterosexual *divorced* and *stepfamily* homes (Perrin, 2002b). That is another way of saying kids who grew up in same-sex homes *did not* look like kids who grew up with their own mother and father!

But consider what another major study on same-sex marriage says. The Stacey/Biblarz study is used widely by same-sex marriage proponents to show that such families are not harmful to children. And this is indeed the conclusion the authors offer. But regarding research done on children raised in same-sex homes, they admit "Thus far, *no work* has compared children's long-term achievements in education, occupation, income, and other domains of life" (emphasis mine) (Stacey & Biblarz, 2001).

How can we draw a conclusion about the long-term impact of same-sex parenting if the research is "just beginning," if no long-term research has been done?

QUESTION 8: HOW DO WE KNOW WHAT KIND OF FAMILIES CHILDREN NEED?

All the family experimentation over the past 30 years—no-fault divorce, the sexual revolution, cohabitation, and widespread fatherlessness—have been documented failures, harming adults and children in far deeper ways, for longer periods of time, than even the most conservative among us ever imagined. How can we think this radical new experiment will somehow bring good things?

Every child-development theory tells us that kids do best when they are raised by their own mothers and fathers. And it is interesting that even liberal organizations are starting to understand this. In a recent research brief, Child Trends explains that "An extensive body of research tells us that children do best when they grow up with both biological parents. . . . Thus, it is not simply the presence of two parents, as some have assumed, but the presence of *two biological parents* that seems to support children's development" (Moore, Jekielek, & Emig, 2002). The Center for Law and Social Policy also finds that "most researchers now agree that . . . on average, children do best when raised by their two married, biological parents" (Parke, 2003).

By definition, no child living in a two-parent, same-sex home is living with both biological parents. As a result, every child living in such a home is living in a home that is less than best.

QUESTION 9: IS THE SAME-SEX FAMILY ABOUT THE NEEDS OF CHILDREN OR THE WANTS OF ADULTS?

We can learn a lot from the world's most famous lesbian mom. In an interview on ABC's *Primetime Live* a few years ago, Diane Sawyer asked Rosie O'Donnell, "Would it break your heart if he [Rosie's 6-year-old son, Parker] said, 'I want a mommy and a daddy'?" Rosie said, "No. And he has said that."

Diane said, "He has?"

Rosie answered, "Of course he has. But as I said to my son, Parker, 'If you were to have a daddy, you wouldn't have me as a mommy because I'm the kind of mommy who wants another mommy' " (O'Donnell, 2004).

Can anyone say that is a good parenting ethic? The child *needs* a daddy, but he is told "no" because the parent has *wants,* and those wants come before the child's needs.

Why does Parker want a daddy? Not because Rosie enrolled him in a fundamentalist day school where they indoctrinated him with that idea.

When he looks in the mirror, he wonders if he looks like his dad, and not because masculinity is merely a social construct. He will wonder if he has his father's eyes or chin. He will ask, *Where is my father, who is like me, whom I can emulate, whom I can follow after?* But he will have to keep wondering, like most children in same-sex homes, simply because their parents are the kind of parents who want "another mommy."

Today's experiment in same-sex marriage is similar to our nation's experiment with divorce 40 years ago. Then, we did not think marriage should be about "till death do us part." Today, we do not think it should be about husband and wife. Judith Wallerstein (Wallerstein, Lewis, & Blakelee, 2000), one of the world's leading researchers on how divorce impacts children, observes:

> We made radical changes in the family without realizing how it would change the experience of growing up. We embarked on a gigantic social experiment without any idea about how the next generation would be affected. If the truth be told, and if we are able to face it, the history of divorce in our society is replete with unwarranted assumptions that adults have made about children simply because such assumptions are congenial to adult needs and wishes. (p. xxii)

Today, we are still making unwarranted assumptions about children simply because such assumptions are congenial to adult needs and wishes. We must realize how this new gigantic social experiment will change the experience of growing up.

QUESTION 10: DOES GENDER REALLY MATTER?

The question of whether gender really matters is the crux of this whole issue. If same-sex and male–female families are interchangeable—like vanilla or chocolate ice cream, mere preference—which is exactly what the same-sex family proposition asserts, then . . .

- male or female,
- mother and father, or
- husband and wife

as such do not really matter to the family or society. We are told, "You can have a man and a woman in your family if you want, but neither is necessary." Consider the new marriage licenses in Massachusetts. You will not find the words "husband" "wife," "man," or "woman," but merely "party A" or "party B." That is what we have come to. Perhaps it will not be long until we see the same genderless categories on birth certificates.

Same-sex marriage proponents hold what I call a "Mr. Potato Head" view of humanity: there is no real difference between Mr. and Mrs. Potato Head. They have the same central core, and interchangeable external parts. There is no real difference. But gender is not merely social construction. Gender is an essential, primary part of our humanity. Our maleness and femaleness go to the very core of our being. Every person matters as a male or female. Each has what the other needs but lacks.

Proponents of same-sex marriage say children need love. But children need more than love, for love will not be enough to help two dads guide a scared, young girl through her first period or help her pick out her first bra. These men will have very little to say because they have never experienced such things. Likewise, what kind of message can two lesbian moms give a little girl about loving a man or a little boy about growing into a man?

The same-sex family celebrates sameness; The natural family celebrates the diversity that is humanity. Any family that intentionally rejects either the male or female gender—saying either is not necessary—cannot be viewed as good and virtuous in a society that esteems the unique value of both male and female. The idea that male and female are replaceable and optional is really an antihuman message, and that is the primary reason why same-sex marriage is a dangerous public policy.

REFERENCES

Akerlof, G. A. (1998, March). Men without children. *Economic Journal.*

American Academy of Pediatrics. (2002, February 4). *News Release: AAP says children of same-sex couples deserve two legally recognized parents.* Retrieved April 7, 2005, from www.aap.org/advocacy/archives/febsamesex.htm.

Badgett, M. V. (2004). *Will providing marriage rights to same-sex couples undermine heterosexual marriage? Evidence from Scandinavia and the Netherlands.* Amherst, MA: Institute for Gay and Lesbian Strategic Studies.

Blankenhorn, D. (1994). *Fatherless America: Confronting our most urgent social problem.* New York: Basic Books.

Block, M., & Smith, T. (2004, September 13). Massachusetts schools weigh gay topics. National Public Radio (NPR).

Cahill, S., Ellen, M., & Tobias, S. (2002). *Family policy: Issues affecting gay, lesbian, bisexual, and transgendered families.* New York: The National Gay and Lesbian Task Force Policy Institute.

Clunis, D. M., & Green, G. D. (2003). *The lesbian parenting book: A guide to creating families and raising kids* (2nd ed.). New York: Seal Press.

Collins, G. (2003, October 9). Interview with Jean Williams. *Morning Edition,* NPR. Audio available at www.npr.org/templates.story.story.php?storyId=1459945.

Coontz, S. (1998). *The way we really are: Coming to terms with America's changing families.* New York: Basic Books.

Coontz, S. (2000). *The way we never were: American families and the nostalgia trap.* New York: Basic Books.

Coontz, S. (2005). *Marriage, a history: From obedience to intimacy, or how love conquered marriage.* New York: Viking.

Coontz, S. (2006, February 23). "Traditional" marriage has changed a lot. *Seattle Post-Intelligencer.* Available online at http://seattlepi.nwsource.com/opinion/260456_marriage.ht.

Crossfire. (2004, February 24). CNN. Transcript #022401CN.V20.ml.

Gallagher, M. (2003). The stakes: Why we need marriage. *National Review.* Retrieved April 7, 2005, from www.nationalreview.com/comment/comment-gallagher071403.asp.

Gay demographics. (2003). *Percent of households with children under 18 years.* Retrieved August 14, 2003, from www.gaydemographics.org/USA/SF1_children.html.

Gilder, G. (1987). *Men and marriage.* Gretna, LA: Pelican.

Kushner, T. (1993). *Angels in America: Part one, Millenium approaches.* New York: Theater Communications Group.

Levine, J. (2003, July 23–29). Stop the wedding! Why gay marriage isn't radical enough. *The Village Voice.* Online at www.villagevoice.com/issues/0330/levine.php.

Lewis, R. (2005, September 12). Gay marriage ban expected to fail. *The Boston Globe.* Retrieved March 11, 2006, from www.boston.com/news/local/articles/2005/09/12/gay_marriage_ban_expected_to_fail.

Moore, K. A., Jekielek, S. M., & Emig, C. (2002). *Marriage from a child's perspective: How does family structure affect children, and what can we do about it?* (Child Trends Research Brief). Washington, DC: Author.

Musgrave, M. (2003, Fall). Defending the sanctity of marriage in America. *Campaign for Working Families Newsletter.* Arlington, VA: Campaign for Working Families. Retrieved March 9, 2006, from www.cwfpac.com/newsletter.php?id=020403.

Not fair, governor. (2005, March 3). *The Boston Globe.*

O'Connor, E. (2005, January 25). Lesbians who tried to book wedding at Catholic hall claim discrimination. *Canadian NewsWire.*

O'Donnell, R. (2004, March 14). Rosie's story. For the sake of the children: Rosie O'Donnell's crusade on behalf of gay parents seeking to adopt children. Interview with Diane Sawyer. ABC News, *Primetime.*

Parke, M. (2003). Are married parents really better for children? Center for Law and Social Policy. Washington, DC: Author.

Perrin, E. (2002a, February 15). E-mail to select AAP members from Ellen Perrin.

Perrin, E. (2002b). Technical report: Coparent and second-parent adoption by same-sex parents. *Pediatrics, 109,* 341–344.

Popenoe, D. (1997). *Life without father: Compelling evidence that fatherhood and marriage are indispensable for the good of children.* New York: Free Press.

Pruett, K. D. (2000). *Fatherneed: Why father care is as essential as mother care for your child.* New York: Free Press.

Richardson, F. (2004, May 17). Bay State gays ring in new era: P'town ready for the "big day." *The Boston Herald.*

Rinnert, J. (2003, December 30). The trouble with gay marriage. *In These Times.*

Stacey, J., & Biblarz, T. (2001). (How) does the sexual orientation of parents matter? *American Sociological Review, 66,* 159–183.

Stanton, G. T. (1997). *Why marriage matters: Reasons to believe in marriage in postmodern society.* Colorado Springs, CO: Pinon Press.

Stanton, G. T. (2004a). *Are same-sex families good for children? What the social sciences say (and don't say) about family experimentation.* Available online at www.family.org/ cforum/pdfs/fosi/marriage/Citizen_Health_of_SSF.pdf.

Stanton, G. T. (2004b). *Focus on the Family's position statement on same-sex "marriage" and civil unions.* Available online at www.family.org/cforum/fosi/marriage/ssuap/ a0029773.cfm.

Sullivan, A. (2004, April 3). Shelby Steele, separatist: A fisking. Retrieved June 23, 2004, from www.AndrewSullivan.com.

Tasker, F. (1999). Children in lesbian-led families: A review. *Clinical Child Psychology and Psychiatry, 4,* 153–166.

Turley, J. (2004, October 3). Polygamy laws expose our own hypocrisy: Rights should be based on principle, not popularity. *USA Today,* p. 13A.

U.S. Government Accounting Office. (2004). *Defense of Marriage Act: Update to prior report* (GAO-04-353R). Washington, DC: Author.

Wallerstein, J., Lewis, J. M., & Blakeslee, S. (2000). *The unexpected legacy of divorce: A 25-year landmark study.* New York: Hyperion Books.

■ ■ ■ ■ ■ ▬▬▬▬▬▬▬▬▬▬▬▬▬▬▬▬▬▬▬▬▬▬▬▬▬▬▬▬▬▬▬▬▬▬

HAS AFFIRMATIVE ACTION GONE TOO FAR?

Editor's Note:
Public sentiment has turned against affirmative action in recent years. Preferential treatment toward underrepresented and disproportionately disadvantaged groups was once favored as a just reaction to generations of legal discrimination, segregation, and systematic exclusion from full participation in American citizenship. As globalization has exacerbated the economic pressures on the white American middle class, domestic competition has escalated. The view that affirmative action is just recompense has given way to charges of reverse discrimination. Proponents of affirmative action contend that equal opportunity cannot be achieved without reversing the historical consequences of discrimination. Opponents contend that affirmative action violates equal protection provisions of the Fourteenth Amendment. Both sides in this issue passionately argue for fairness and equity.

José Enrique Idler is a fellow in the National Research Initiative program at the American Enterprise Institute for Public Policy Research in Washington, 1150 17th St. NW, Washington, D.C. 20036.

Jolyn Mikow, Ph.D., is an assistant professor in the Department of Social Work, University of Texas at San Antonio. Dr. Mikow has held numerous positions in child welfare, and has published in the area of ethnicity, acculturation, and substance use among Mexican American adolescent females.

YES

José Enrique Idler

The question of whether affirmative-action policies have gone too far has to be constrained by what we mean by affirmative action, how the policy is applied, and what it is supposed to achieve. Additionally, consider that different settings (e.g., contracting, education, political representation) generate different policies that go by the name affirmative action. Even if we decide that the common denominator for all those policies—race, or some other group attribute—is taken into account, we need to remember that the policy is applied differently in various settings. Affirmative action in hiring practices (Eastland, 1997) looks different from affirmative action in voting practices (Guinier, 1995; Thernstrom, 1987) and education (Gurin et al., 2004). Also, affirmative action takes different shapes in various countries (Sowell, 2004). Given that this essay is an introductory one, we will not be able to look at all the factors, historical reasons, and complexities that characterize the debate (Anderson, 2004; Cohen & Sterba, 2003; Nobles, 2000; Omi & Winant, 1994). Only after characterizing what affirmative action is and what it is supposed to achieve, even in general terms, will we be able to assess whether it is good policy.

I will argue that affirmative-action policies have gone too far as a measure with integrative purposes for certain groups because they do not identify the right groups or do not do so in a way that attempts to achieve the right outcomes. After briefly mentioning two faulty claims commonly confused with the topic of affirmative action, I will provide a general characterization of what affirmative action is and apply this characterization to two distinct groups: Hispanics and blacks. By looking at two different groups, we will see that affirmative action cannot be applied to minorities without understanding who the minority groups are—and the ways in which they are different from one another (Glazer, 1998).

Let me begin by clarifying claims related to affirmative action that do not reflect reality. First, some people think that affirmative action requires group representation by way of filling in quotas. This view is false. Under constitutional norms, quotas and rigid schemes of racial classification are illegal (Edley, 1998)—a point first made by the famous case on race-based admission policies *Regents of University of California v. Bakke* (1978) and reiterated by the Michigan Law school case *Grutter v. Bollinger* (2003).

Second, the claim is sometimes made that taking race into account, as a factor among a set of other factors, equals affirmative action. It is important, however, to distinguish between affirmative action and particular instances in which race counts as one factor among others—for instance, in hiring determinations. Affirmative action is a policy of systematic treatment toward a group—or, more precisely, members of the group. A company may not have a policy of affirmative action and yet take race, or some other attribute, into account in a particular hiring situation for a certain reason. Whether the reason is legitimate or not, or whether it constitutes discrimination, may be a question at stake—one that I will not try to answer here. The particular point here is that *systematic* treatment differs from *particular* instances in which a certain attribute makes a difference in deciding which candidate will get the job.

Let us now characterize affirmative action as the policy that occurs under the following condition: disadvantaged groups of a certain kind—or more precisely, group members—are the object of preferential treatment in order to achieve particular outcomes. Note that under this condition there is an identifiable group to which a certain measure is directed for a specific purpose. In the cases we have in mind, groups are generally identified on the basis of an attribute such as race, ethnicity, or gender; the measure taken toward the group is preferential treatment in reference to people who are not members of the group; and the sought outcome is group representation on the grounds of equity, reparation, or diversity (Corlett, 2003; Kymlicka, 2001; Gurin et al., 2004). Any of those grounds would modify the arguments for and against affirmative action; but, given space constraints, I will bypass a careful consideration of the cases built on different grounds.

With this characterization in mind, we can now turn to Hispanics and examine whether affirmative action toward the group is good policy. Much of what will be said about Hispanics also applies to other groups, such as Asian Americans (Reeves & Bennett, 2004), who are also sometimes the object of affirmative action. My claim is that affirmative action is not a coherent policy with regard to Hispanics because it does not identify a coherent group. Consider for a moment who are Hispanics. According to the Standards for the Classification of Federal Data on Race and Ethnicity, a Hispanic or Latino is someone of Mexican, Puerto Rican, Cuban, South or Central American, "or other Spanish culture, or origin, regardless of race." (Revisions to the Standards, 1997, p. 58789).

Presumably, a particular group known as Hispanic or Latino—or members of the group—should be the object of preferential treatment. The problem is that the Hispanic category is too broad and encompasses too many groups at once, so that we cannot really speak of a group that is identifiable on the basis of common attributes. Some authors have argued that Hispanics do have a common identity (Gracia, 2000), but the reality is that Hispanics are an extremely varied group with sometimes very little in common. For first-generation Hispanics—namely, those who have migrated from Latin American countries—national identities often remain strong. As an illustration, Cubans, Colombians, and Mexicans belong to different nations and take pride in their different identities (Portes & Rumbaut, 1996, p. 135). Thus, there is no reason to believe that they will give up their Latin American national identities in order to start thinking of themselves as a common group, namely Latinos, when they come to the United States Puerto Ricans in New York are different from Mexicans in the Southwest and Cubans in Miami. We also find significant differences across generations. Based on a report on the 2002 National Survey of Latinos, generational differences are crucial for understanding how varied the Hispanic group is with regard to views, attitudes, and experiences (Pew Hispanic Center, 2004).

Now suppose, for the sake of argument, that a strong case can be made for affirmative action. The difficulty is that even if we assume that a strong case can be made, we would not be able to identify a coherent group toward which the policy could apply. Affirmative action was previously characterized as a policy that makes disadvantaged groups, which can be identified on the basis of certain attributes, the object of preferential treatment in order to achieve particular outcomes. But what is the disadvantaged group that will be the object of preferential treatment? What is the defining attribute of Hispanics? As I have pointed out, we cannot identify Hispanics as a coherent group; hence, it follows that we are not exactly sure which group will be the object of preferential treatment.

Someone could reply, for instance, that we should not focus on the Latino category as such, but rather on the different groups within the category, namely, Mexicans, Cubans, or Salvadorians. The problem with this approach is that groups that have not been discriminated against will end up being included under the umbrella of affirmative action. So, for instance, Spaniards and Cubans would technically be part of the Hispanic group. According to U.S. Census Bureau data from the most recent decennial census in 2000, the national median income for all American families was $50,046. But the median income of Spaniards was $53,002; and for Cubans it was $43,642—lower than the national median income, but higher than for Dominicans, whose median income was $28,729 (Ramirez, 2004, p. 14).

The point is that subgroups that are presumably united under the common Latino category are very different from each other, and not all subgroups are plainly disadvantaged with regard to the general population. Hence, even assuming that affirmative action is good policy, it is not clear that it should apply to *all* Hispanics. Some important distinctions would have to be made among subgroups. Otherwise, groups or people who are not intended to be protected could end up free-riding on the system, hurting those who are truly disadvantaged (Gimenez, 1992).

So far we have assumed for the sake of argument that affirmative action is good policy, only that it cannot apply to Hispanics because they are not a coherently identifiable group. Now, however, what about African Americans? African Americans, in contrast with Hispanics, are clearly a more coherent group, although the makeup of the group might change as more first-generation African immigrants come to the United States. It is clear that the group has been historically discriminated against, as shown, for instance, by the 1947 report by Lawson (2004), and is also generally disadvantaged with regard to the general population. As an illustration, according to U.S. Census Bureau data from the last census, a black family's median income was $33,255, against a general median income of $50,046 (McKinnon & Bennett, 2005). These figures mask important differences, such as the fact that black women tend to do educationally better than black men; the gap between black women and other women is narrower than the one between black men in comparison with other men; and black married couples tend to be better off than single-parent families (McKinnon & Bennett, 2005). But for the current purpose, I will ignore some of these differences and simply assume, in broad terms, that blacks are generally disadvantaged with regard to the rest of the population. Based on our considerations so far, it would seem that we could make a case for affirmative action as it applies to African Americans. We have an identifiable disadvantaged group that should be the object of preferential treatment in order to achieve particular outcomes. But there are several problems with this view, such as the assumption that all blacks think and behave alike, which stigmatizes people.

Let us now focus primarily on the problem of outcomes. What outcomes are affirmative actions supposed to achieve? The most plausible answer to this question is that affirmative action intends to assure group representation. And so people who are members of certain groups will receive preferential treatment by virtue of group membership, with the intended result that the group will be represented in, say, a student body or a company.

Nonetheless, the focus on representational outcome by virtue of group membership has the wrong approach. The problems we face here have to do with the nature of qualified candidates. Bodies and organizations that implement affirmative action normally require entrance qualifications. So, for instance, in order to be hired in a company or admitted into a student body, the candidate needs to have the right kind of qualifications; otherwise the person will not be eligible for the job or student slot. What affirmative action does is alter this condition by giving some candidates, who may be equally or less qualified than other candidates, a certain advantage.

Note now that there is nothing in group attributes as such that makes someone eligible for a job. So, in other words, just because someone has a particular group characteristic does not mean that he or she will be an adequate candidate for the job. The person needs the right *qualifications.* Under most circumstances, when looking at job candidates for a company, we do not consider whether they have an attribute such as believing in God, since this attribute is generally irrelevant for job performance. What matters is the attributes that are directly related to the job, namely qualifications.

If the point on qualifications is true, candidates should not be systematically hired, or given advantage in the hiring process, simply because they belong to a particular racial or ethnic group—or because they possess any kind of attribute that is not directly related to the qualifications necessary for the task. Achieving group representation, then, by virtue of a certain characteristic that is not directly related to qualifications or performance is the wrong goal.

The goal ought to be to have more strongly qualified candidates from currently disadvantaged groups in order for them to compete for jobs and educational slots. Notice that the result will still be that more blacks, or members from other disadvantaged groups, move into certain positions. But this outcome will not be achieved by the kind of preferential treatment, systematically implemented, that seeks simply to guarantee representation for some people by virtue of group membership—a prospect that might even hurt qualified candidates from disadvantaged groups (Eastland, 1997). The outcome will be achieved by making people more competitive. Instead of group representation due to group attributes as such, the focus for disadvantaged groups should be placed on making sure that disadvantaged group members have *higher and stronger qualifications* in order to be able to compete on an equal footing with other people.

CONCLUSION

Someone might reply here that we would still need affirmative action because certain groups are discriminated against. Nonetheless, we need to make an important distinction between making sure that no qualified candidate is discriminated against and according such candidate preferential treatment. Making sure that people are not discriminated against by virtue of sex, color, race, or nationality is an extremely significant legislative goal (Civil Rights Act, 1991). Nonetheless, giving people preferential treatment due to some group attribute goes beyond civil rights legislation. As I have argued, affirmative action does not always apply to coherent groups and, when it does, it does not focus on the right outcomes. Instead of policies that give preferential treatment, what disadvantaged groups need is policies that make them more qualified and competitive. In this sense, affirmative action has gone beyond what civil rights legislation dictates and what the conditions of fairness and minority advancement require.

NO

Jolyn Mikow

The first step in any consideration of affirmative-action policies is to understand the history, aim, and intention of such policies. As a social and political policy, affirmative action has undergone an evolution, from a policy aimed at workforce recruitment and upward mobility to one of statistical goals and timetables. While designed to reinforce the American values of equality and equal opportunity, few other social and political issues have had such a polarizing effect on the American populace (Urofsky, 1991).

Initially, affirmative-action policies, beginning in the 1960s and continuing through the 1970s, appeared to be on sound political footing with both Democratic and Republican administrations. Contrary to public misconceptions, affirmative action is not a single policy or law, but a combination of executive orders, congressional laws, and court rulings. In conjunction with the Civil Rights Act of 1964, the amended Civil Rights Act of 1991, the creation and empowerment of the Equal Employment Opportunity Commission, and various rulings of the Supreme Court, policies prohibiting discrimination based on race, color, national origin, religion, age, disability, and gender have been created as a remedy to the inequitable distribution of social goods. Laws and policies addressing equal opportunity in employment, education, and housing were extended by both the Congress and Republican and Democratic presidential Executive Orders, creating the affirmative action policies we know today.

As a policy, affirmative action (as contained in President Johnson's Executive Order 1146) is fairly brief and straightforward: discrimination is prohibited and affirmative steps are required to achieve equal treatment of all individuals. This perspective rejects the idea that policies are sufficient if they simply do not discriminate against individuals. There must be positive steps made, both active and proactive, to eliminate systemic discrimination and achieve equality in admission to higher education institutions, in hiring and promotion in employment, and in other arenas, including housing and finance (DiNitto, 2000; Gibelman, 2000). Equality in the distribution of public and social goods is a means to achieve equal opportunity, and equal opportunity is a precondition for the exercise of freedom (Kwok & Tam, 2003). The broad goals of these programs were to increase the numbers of underrepresented groups in business, education, and professional positions to reflect their numbers in American society. However, what began as a policy aimed at righting past wrongs among groups of people has become one of timetables, quotas, and plans to control the enforcement of equal-opportunity initiatives.

Despite the equality protections in the Constitution and regardless of Executive Orders, Congressional laws, and Supreme Court rulings, equal and just treatment has not been achieved in the United States (Darity & Mason, 1998; Karger & Stoesz, 2006; Kim & Tamborini, 2006; Kwok & Tam, 2003; Takahashi, 2005). This fact has been borne out in research studies, government reports, and census statistics over the last 20 years and provides the basis for my argument that affirmative action policies have not gone too far. They have, in fact, neither gone far enough nor been effective enough in creating real change. Over the last 20 years both public and political resolve to address the impact of unequal treatment and discrimination in our society has eroded. Even with the impact of these well-intentioned policies and their frequently ill-conceived plans of implementation, there remains concrete evidence that the very groups targeted by this policy have not fully benefited and, in recent decades, have lost many of the early gains that were achieved.

To understand how this has happened in a country that consistently voices a commitment to the principles of democracy and equal opportunity in both foreign and domestic policy, one must examine how the political and public opinion has changed toward affirmative action programs over the last 40 years. Elliot and Ewoh (2000) and Gibelman (2000) have examined the evolution of affirmative action and the rise and decline in both its impact on discrimination and support from the public and political arenas. Taken in a broader historic view, affirmative action as a policy and public reality has evolved from initiating majority support for measures that provide for equal opportunity to presenting broad resistance on key elements of this antidiscrimination effort.

The early success of affirmative action can be traced to the support of the populace, the courts, the executive branch, and Congress. Through the early 1980s, executive orders remained in force, Congress exhibited little polarization on the issue, and the courts and general public were, as a rule, sympathetic to affirmative-action policies (Gibelman, 2000). It was the 1984 election of Ronald Reagan to a second term and the ensuing eroding of support from the executive branch that marked a beginning of the decline in the effectiveness of affirmative action (Elliot & Ewoh, 2000).

This decline of support continued in the courts as can be see in: (1) The 1989 Supreme Court ruling in *City of Richmond v. J.A. Croson Company*, striking down Richmond's minority contracting program as unconstitutional, requiring that an affirmative-action program be supported by a "compelling interest" and be narrowly tailored to ensure that the program furthers that interest; (2) The 1996 U.S. Supreme Court's letting stand a Circuit Court ruling that the University of Maryland's Benjamin Banneker Scholarship, intended for black students, was unconstitutional; (3) The 1996 U.S. Supreme Court's letting stand the Court of Appeals for the Fifth Circuit ruling against the University of Texas Law School's admissions program designed to achieve diversity in the student body, suggesting that diversity does not constitute a compelling state interest; (4) The 1997 U.S. Supreme Court's refusal to hear a challenge to California's Proposition 209, which abolished all public-sector affirmative-action programs in the state in employment, education, and contracting, there by allowing it to go into effect; and (5) The 2003 U.S. Supreme Court ruling against a point system used by the University of Michigan's undergraduate admissions programs but approving a separate policy used by the University of Michigan law school that gives race less prominence in the admissions decision-making process. This last ruling is remarkable because the Court, in the majority opinion written by Justice O'Conner, stated that "We expect that 25 years from now, the use of racial preferences will no longer be necessary to further the interest approved today" (*Grutter v. Bollinger*, 2003, p. 31).

With the election of George Bush to the presidency in 1989 and the 1994 election of a Republican majority in both the House and Senate, the continuing erosion of support for affirmative action was seen in the voting public and in national and local government, as evidenced by the following events: (1) Senator Dole and Representative Canady, in 1995, introduced the Equal

Opportunity Act, which prohibits race or gender-based affirmative action in all federal programs; (2) in 1995 the Regents of the University of California voted to end affirmative action programs at all University of California campuses; (3) California Proposition 209 was passed by the voters in 1996, abolishing all public-sector affirmative action programs in the state in employment, education, and contracting and permitting gender discrimination that is "reasonably necessary" to the "normal operation" of public education, employment, and contracting; (4) in 1998 the voters in Washington State passed Initiative 200, banning affirmative action in higher education, public contracting, and hiring; (5) the Florida legislature passed the "One Florida" Plan in 2000, banning affirmative action and racial preferences in university admissions and state contracting.

In light of this public and political shift in support for and commitment to affirmative action, the question remains, what should be done? First (and foremost) a national dialogue is needed to examine and clarify the country's commitment to supporting equal treatment.

Antidiscrimination efforts need to be defined in terms of the public good, rather than a competition between individual and group interests (Gibelman, 2000). The growth of the underclass, who are primarily minorities and poor, and the underrepresentation of African Americans, Hispanics, and other minority groups in the labor market and higher education does not serve the public good. Large numbers of any group in our society that do not contribute to the economy and culture impact the society as a whole and contribute to a drain on our productivity and social intuitions. While a national dialogue on discrimination, race, poverty, and unequal opportunity may sound like a lofty (and therefore unattainable) goal and unlikely to be embraced by the current Republican administration, the president has already introduced this discussion into the public arena. In the aftermath of Hurricane Katrina, Mr. Bush, in September 2005, spoke to the American public from Jackson Square in New Orleans, stating:

> As all of us saw on television, there's also some deep, persistent poverty in this region, as well. That poverty has its roots in the history of racial discrimination, which cut off generations from the opportunities of America. We have a duty to confront this poverty with bold action. So let us restore all that we have cherished from yesterday, and let us rise above the legacy of inequality. (Bush, 2005)

Second, the social and political focus needs to shift from a dismantling of these policies altogether to a focus on addressing the flaws in the implementation. Programs based solely on group classification (race, color, national origin, religion, age, disability, and gender) are inadequate to deal with the complex problems of the most disadvantaged members of these groups, who suffer the cumulative effects of subjugation and are denied the necessary resources to compete effectively in a free society (Wilson, 1990). In reviewing the professional literature on affirmative action and its effects on employment and educational outcomes, the reader will notice that a discussion of specific mechanisms that obtain measurable effects is largely absent. Much of the empirical analysis of affirmative action treats these programs as a "black box," generating reduced-form estimates on outcomes (usually by race and gender). It does not control for—nor explore—the varying impact that the different practices employed in recruitment, hiring, promotion, and university admissions have on affirmative-action program outcomes and employee or student success or failure (Holzer & Neumark, 2000). This lack of knowledge and information on what works, what is successful, and what is not hampers any implementation of a meaningful and effective affirmative-action program and is critical in implementing any public policy. Much of the substantial backlash to affirmative action stems from unintended consequences of the policy and the failure to consider alternative means to accomplish equal opportunity in employment, education, and housing (Elliot & Ewoh, 2000).

CONCLUSION

The conditions that led to the need for the creation of affirmative action have been unrelenting in their persistence in American society (Gibelman, 2000). Despite the initial success of affirmative-action policies, equal and just treatment in education and employment is not a reality for most minority groups and women. Affirmative action has not gone far enough in creating the just and equal society that was initially envisioned. Without a renewed commitment in the American public and political arenas to address this inequity and to look at alternative, creative ways to achieve it, the disparity between those who enjoy the benefits of social, political, and economic power and those who are marginalized will widen. This raises basic questions about the future prosperity of our society and our true commitment to the principles of democracy and equal opportunity.

REFERENCES

Anderson, T. (2004). *The pursuit of fairness: A history of affirmative action.* New York: Oxford University Press.

Bush, G. (2005). President discusses hurricane relief in address to the nation. Retrieved March 1, 2006, from www.whitehouse.gov/news/releases/2005/09/20050915-8.html.

Civil Rights Act of 1991. (1991). Retrieved March 21, 2006, from www.eeoc.gov/policy/cra91.html.

Cohen, C., & Sterba, J. (2003). *Affirmative action and racial preference: A debate.* New York: Oxford University Press.

Corlett, A. (2003). *Race, racism and reparations*. Ithaca, NY: Cornell University Press.

Darity, W., & Mason, P. (1998). Evidence on discrimination in employment: Codes of color, codes of gender. *Journal of Economic Perspectives, 12*(2), 63–90.

DiNitto, D. (2000). *Social welfare: Politics and public policy* (5th ed.). Boston: Allyn & Bacon.

Eastland, T. (1997). *Ending affirmative action: The case for colorblind justice*. New York: Basic Books.

Edley, C. (1998). *Not all black and white: Affirmative action and American values*. New York: Hill and Wang.

Elliot, E., & Ewoh, A. (2000). The evolution of an issue: The rise and decline of affirmative action. *Policy Studies Review, 17*(2/3), 212–238.

Gibelman, M. (2000). Affirmative action at a crossroads: A social justice perspective. *Journal of Sociology and Social Welfare, 27*(1), 153–174.

Gimenez, M. (1992). U.S. Ethnic Politics: Implications for Latin Americans. *Latin American Perspectives, 19* (4), 7–17.

Glazer, N. (1998). *We are all multiculturalists now*. Cambridge, MA: Harvard University Press.

Gracia, J. (2000). *Hispanic/Latino identity: A philosophical perspective*. Oxford, England: Blackwell.

Grutter v. Bollinger, 539 U.S. 306. (2003).

Guinier, L. (1995). *The tyranny of the majority: Fundamental fairness in representative democracy*. New York: Free Press.

Gurin, P., Lewis, E., Gurin, G., Dey, E., Hurtado, S., & Lehman, J. (2004). *Defending diversity: Affirmative action at the University of Michigan*. Ann Arbor: University of Michigan Press.

Holzer, H., & Neumark, D. (2000). What does affirmative action do? *Industrial and Labor Relations Review, 53*(2), 240–271.

Karger, H. J., & Stoesz, D. (2006). *American social welfare policy: A pluralist approach* (5th ed.). New York: Allyn & Bacon.

Kim, C., & Tamborini, C. (2006). The continuing significance of race in the occupational attainment of whites and blacks: A segmented labor market analysis. *Sociological Inquiry, 76*(6), 23–51.

Kwok, S., & Tam, D. (2003). The affirmative action debate and the implications for social work education. *The Social Policy Journal, 2*(1), 57–74.

Kymlicka, W. (2001). *Politics in the vernacular: Nationalism, multiculturalism, and citizenship*. New York: Oxford University Press.

Lawson, S. (Ed.). (2004). *To secure these rights: The report of President Harry S. Truman Committee on Civil Rights*. Boston: Bedford/St. Martin's.

McKinnon, J., & Bennett, C. (2005). *We the people: Blacks in the United States* (Census 2000 special reports). Washington DC: U.S. Census Bureau.

Nobles, M. (2000). *Shades of citizenship: Race and the census in modern politics*. Stanford, CA: Stanford University Press.

Omi, M., & Winant, H. (1994). *Racial formation in the United States: From the 1960s to the 1990s* (2nd ed). New York: Routledge.

Pew Hispanic Center & The Henry J. Kaiser Family Foundation. (2004). *Survey brief: Generational differences*. Retrieved from http://pewhispanic.org.

Portes, A., & Rumbaut, R. (1996). *Immigrant America: A portrait* (2nd ed.). Berkeley, CA: University of California Press.

Ramirez, R. (2004). *We the people: Hispanics in the United States* (Census 2000 special reports). Washington DC: U.S. Census Bureau.

Reeves, T., & Bennett, C. (2004). *We the people: Asians in the United States* (Census 2000 special reports). Washington DC: U.S. Census Bureau.

Regents of University of California v. Bakke, 438 U.S. 265. (1978).

Revisions to the Standards for the Classification of Federal Data on Race and Ethnicity (1997, October 30). *Federal register, 62*(210).

Sowell, T. (2004). *Affirmative action around the world: An empirical study.* New Haven, CT: Yale University Press.

Takahashi, R. (2005). *NASW policy on affirmative action: Proposed revisions.* Retrieved March 1, 2006, from www.socialworkers.org/da/da2005/2005comments/documents/affirmativeaction.pdf.

Thernstrom, A. (1987). *Whose vote counts? Affirmative action and minority rights voting.* Cambridge, MA: Harvard University Press.

Urofsky, M. (1991). *A conflict of rights: The Supreme Court and affirmative action.* New York: Charles Scribner and Sons.

Wilson, J. (1990). *The truly disadvantaged: The inner city, the underclass and public policy.* Chicago: University of Chicago Press.

■ ■ ■ ■ ■

HAS THE AMERICANS WITH DISABILITIES ACT (ADA) GONE TOO FAR?

Editor's Note:
About 8 to 17 percent of the population between the ages of 20 and 64 have disabilities that limit their ability to work, and about half that number have disabilities to the point that either they cannot work or can work only irregularly. Although the range of disabilities is great, people with disabilities share a central experience rooted in stigmatization, discrimination, and oppression. The greatest stride in addressing discrimination against the disabled was made in 1990 when former president George Bush signed the Americans with Disabilities Act (ADA) (PL 101-336) into law. This act is the most comprehensive legislation for people with disabilities ever passed in the United States. The extension of civil rights to the disabled satisfied some supporters, alienated those who believed they were hurt by the act (especially some small-business employers), and left some members of the disabled community wondering what had actually been accomplished and for whom.

Howard Jacob Karger, Ph.D., is a professor at the University of Houston. He is the author of *Shortchanged: Life and Debt in the Fringe Economy* (Berrett-Koehler, 2005) and, along with David Stoesz, of *American Social Welfare Policy* (5th ed.) (Allyn & Bacon, 2006). Karger has published widely in the field of social-welfare policy, including community economics, income maintenance policy, poverty policy, and social development.

John C. Bricout, Ph.D., is an associate professor at the George Warren Brown School of Social Work. He also holds an appointment in occupational therapy at Washington University School of Medicine. Bricout's professional specialty is assessing and improving organization–worker fit for employees with a disability. His current research focuses on the impacts of work and community environments on the rehabilitation and independence of people with physical or psychiatric disabilities. He has published articles on work-environment strain, supported employment, telecommuting and computer-mediated classroom accommodations.

YES

Howard Jacob Karger

The Americans with Disabilities Act (ADA) was signed into law by former president George Bush on July 26, 1990. The goal of the ADA was to further the full participation of people with disabilities by giving them civil-rights protections similar to those provided to individuals on the basis of race, sex, national origin, and religion. The ADA guarantees equal opportunity to individuals with disabilities in employment, public accommodation, transportation, state and local government services, and telecommunications. This law applies to companies with more than 15 employees, and forbids them to discriminate against a person with a disability in hiring or promotion if the person is otherwise qualified for the job (U.S. Department of Justice, 1995).

On some levels, the ADA is working extremely well. Structural barriers are being removed, much of the new building construction is designed to accommodate the disabled, public transportation is becoming more responsive, and there is an increasing awareness of the contribution of the disabled. On other levels, especially employment and education, the ADA is not faring as well. This debate will focus on those areas.

IS THE ADA WORKING?

There are several questions that should be asked of any social policy. First, who is the target population, and are they being adequately served by the policy? According to the ADA, a person is considered to have a disability if he or she has difficulty performing certain life functions (seeing, hearing, talking, walking, climbing stairs, and lifting and carrying) or has difficulty with certain social roles (doing schoolwork, working at a job, etc.). A person who is unable to perform one or more of these activities, or who uses an assistive device to get around, or who needs assistance from another person to perform basic activities is considered to have a severe disability. The U.S. Census Bureau reports that 1 in 5 Americans (54 million) have some kind of disability; with 1 in 10 having a severe disability. Under this broad definition of the ADA, more than half of all those 65 and older have a disability (U.S. Department of Commerce, 1997). Of the 54 million Americans with disabilities, fewer than 4 million are legally blind, deaf, or in wheelchairs. As such, one of the key problems in the ADA is the vague interpretation of the term *disabilities,* which allows large numbers of people with varying levels of broadly defined disabilities to seek protection under the law.

The second question is whether a particular policy is accomplishing its intended goal. A major goal of the ADA is to promote employment opportunities for people with disabilities. According to the Census Bureau, between 1994 (after the passage of the ADA) and 1999, the overall unemployment rate fell from 6.6 to 4.1 percent. The rate of unemployment for persons with disabilities actually rose from 71.8 to 78 percent (U.S. Department of Commerce, 1997). Moreover, only 32 percent of people of working age (18 to 64) with disabilities, work full- or part-time compared to 81 percent of the nondisabled population. According to the National Organization on Disability (2000), more than two-thirds of those unemployed said they would prefer to be working. Of those who report that they are able to work despite their disability, only 56 percent are actually working (National Organization on Disabilities, 2000). More than 10 years after the passage of the ADA, people with disabilities are almost three times as likely as the nondisabled to live in households with total yearly incomes of $15,000 or less. Twenty-one percent of those with a disability and 28 percent of those with a severe disability live in poverty, compared to 8 percent of those with no disability (Diversity, Inc., 1999) Based on these statistics, the ADA has not only failed to increase employment opportunities for people with disabilities, but may have actually worsened them.

PROBLEMS WITH THE ADA

The ADA was obviously based on good intentions. It was an open-ended act predicated on letting the courts decide the particulars of the law. This vagueness was also an invitation to lawsuits. In 1999, the U.S. Supreme Court curtailed the scope of the law in two separate decisions. In *Sutton v. United Airlines, Inc.,* United Airlines refused to hire twin sisters who were regional airline pilots because they had uncorrected vision of 20/400. The sisters maintained that their vision was correctable to 20/20 and argued that United Airlines violated the ADA when they refused them employment. In *Murphy v. United Parcel Service, Inc.,* UPS fired a mechanic because he had high blood pressure. He claimed that his medication made him able to work and therefore his firing was unlawful under the ADA. In both cases, the Supreme Court ruled that the ADA does not cover people whose disabilities can be sufficiently corrected with medicine, eyeglasses, or other measures. These cases could profoundly affect the rights of individuals with a range of impairments, from diabetes and hypertension to severe nearsightedness, hearing loss, prostheses, and even cancer. Those able to function in the employment arena with the help of medicine or auxiliary aids may not be able to challenge employers who refuse to hire them, fail to accommodate or promote them, or discharge them based on the belief that their disabilities make them ineligible for certain jobs.

Although the ADA has resulted in the removal of important physical barriers from employment, it has erected newer and even more potent ones. Employers and most institutions are lawsuit averse. In a litigious society, many employers view hiring the disabled as an invitation to trouble. They fear that hiring employees with disabilities is a lawsuit waiting to happen. Others fear that ADA provisions insulate employees with disabilities from being fired, lest the employers risk an expensive lawsuit. Still others argue that the vague language of the ADA makes it difficult for employers to comply with the provisions of the act, thereby inviting lawsuits.

Complying with the ADA structures employer–applicant interaction by limiting questions about an applicant's disability. Hence, many employers are not certain what questions can be asked of an applicant with disabilities. Instead of encouraging an open dialogue around work expectations and allowing applicants with disabilities to address their strengths, employers frequently circumvent the problem by simply not interviewing them.

Employers' fear of ADA-related lawsuits or complaints has a basis in reality. There were almost 17,000 ADA-related complaints or lawsuits filed in 1999. While employers prevailed 95 percent of the time in ADA lawsuits and 85 percent of the time in administrative complaints handled by the Equal Opportunity Commission, the disposition was costly. Some analysts claim that employer costs in grievances and lawsuits average $10,000 and can go as high as $75,000 (Hudgins, 1999). Regardless of whether an employer is on firm ground, it is often more cost-effective to settle out of court.

Like most forms of social-policy legislation, the ADA has been subject to abuse. Some employees want to get into a protected class to grab the bludgeon and use it against their employer. On average, more than one-third of ADA complaints are filed because of bad backs (19.5 percent), emotional problems (11.4 percent), and alcoholism and drug abuse (3.6 percent). No more than 6 percent of complainants have impaired vision or hearing. Only 12.1 percent of complaints were filed by people with spinal cord injuries and other neurological problems—the conditions pointed to when the ADA was being written (Matthews, 1995).

In general, the most disadvantaged are frequently the last ones to reap the benefits of being in a protected social class. The ADA is no different. A Harris poll done in the mid-1990s reported that only 40 percent of people with disabilities had any substantial knowledge of the ADA (Matthews, 1995). On the other hand, many ADA complaints involve exploring the limits of the act, including complaints around "boutique" disabilities such as Adult Attention Deficit Disorder (ADD) or personality disorders.

SCHOOLS OF SOCIAL WORK AND THE ADA

Not surprisingly, the inherent problems in the ADA are also evident in schools of social work. These disability issues play out primarily in two areas: mental health and learning disabilities.

A small but important number of applicants to social-work programs experience mental-health problems, some of which are severe. These problems can range from clinical depression to anxiety disorders and even to schizophrenia. Are schools of social work obligated to accept these applicants because they are covered under the ADA? Is it ethical or socially responsible to credential social-work graduates who have significant mental-health problems in order to comply with the ADA? Are there higher obligations than those reflected in the ADA? Should schools of social work try to circumvent problematic parts of the ADA? According to the National Association of Social Workers' (NASW) Code of Ethics: "Social workers should not practice, condone, facilitate, or collaborate with any form of discrimination on the basis of race, ethnicity, national origin, color, sex, sexual orientation, age, marital status, political belief, religion, or mental or physical disability" (National Association of Social Workers, 1999). While most instructors in schools of social work have encountered at least a few severely mentally ill students in their classes, it is unclear how many of them have actually done something about it.

The specter of the ADA also arises in terms of grading and class performance. Most helping professionals know that it is relatively easy to obtain a diagnosis of a learning disability. Increasingly, students are turning to the excuse of a learning disability to justify inadequate class work or test performance. Occasionally, these students will request special assignments, special test-taking procedures, the use of editors or grammatical software programs, and special tutors. Some even argue that writing is not a necessary prerequisite for professional competence and therefore should not factor in the class grade.

Learning disabilities are a real problem, and in legitimate cases they should be accommodated in classroom settings. However, what constitutes a legitimate disability, especially since these diagnoses are relatively easy to come by? Are students who failed to master writing skills learning disabled, or have they just not mastered these skills? Is it appropriate for students who have a conceptual learning disability to enter a profession that requires a high level of conceptual thought? One of the dangers of the ADA is that it creates loopholes that allow certain individuals to exploit the intent of the law. While, admittedly, only a small percentage of students exploit the ADA, it nevertheless creates an uneven playing field that penalizes diligent students and at the same time rewards students who have found an angle to make their social-work education easier. The net result is the demoralization of students (and faculty) who choose to play by the rules.

The exploitation of well-intentioned social policies also applies to a small number of social-work educators. Tenure is becoming increasingly difficult to secure in most American universities, and some faculty are turning to desperate measures in response to this challenge. Not surprisingly, more diagnoses of disabilities such as Adult ADD, lower back pain, Carpal Tunnel Syndrome, mental-health problems, and so forth are being offered as a justification why some faculty are unable to sustain research and publish. Although these disabilities may be legitimate for some faculty, for others it is a convenient ruse to cover up incompetence or the lack of self-discipline. Moreover, it begs an important question. Namely, if one has Adult ADD, then a profession that requires a high level of self-discipline, focus, and concentration may not be the appropriate career choice. It is patently wrong to assume that a particular career or vocational choice is an entitlement. If I have a writing or conceptual disability, should I demand that a university evaluate me on criteria other than research and scholarship, even though these are the currency of the academic realm?

The tension around the ADA and social-work education exists on multiple levels. Schools of social work have the implicit gatekeeping function of credentialing trained and professionally competent social-work practitioners. There is an inherent societal expectation that any student who receives an M.S.W. or B.S.W. degree is capable of helping rather than hurting clients. On the other hand, the social-work profession is committed to promoting a society free of discrimination, including discrimination toward the disabled. In the case of a student with a long history of mental illness (but who is currently in remission), which side do we err on? This is the slippery slope of the ADA.

The gatekeeping function of social-work education is frustrated by an institutional aversion to litigation. In an increasingly litigious society, greater numbers of students and faculty are willing to retain legal counsel and sue over what they consider a breach of their rights. The implicit assumption is that most of these cases will be settled out of court, since universities are averse to prolonged legal battles. Unfortunately, this assumption is too frequently correct because universities will often settle before a court hearing (even if their case is strong) to save money and avoid bad publicity. The resolve of universities and schools of social work when faced with spurious disability grievances or lawsuits is particularly weak because neither wants to be thought of as being antagonistic toward people with disabilities. As a result, many university and school of social work administrators are reluctant to question the disability claims of students, even if those claims appear bogus.

CONCLUSION

The inherent problems in the ADA manifest themselves in various ways. First, the vague language of the ADA allows for a definition of disabilities that often stretches the imagination. Boutique disorders such as Adult ADD, environmental stress, and so forth, denigrate not only the intent of the act but also the integrity of a disability. These boutique disabilities create a loophole whereby those who refuse to take responsibility for their behavior can comfortably hide under the umbrella of a protected class. It is part of a societal mind-set that excuses unacceptable behavior and deflects responsibility from the actor. The most egregious part of exploiting the ADA is that it trivializes real disabilities. Those people for whom the ADA was originally designed (the physically and mentally disabled) are lumped together with those who have more suspect disabilities. Morever, as nuisance claims and lawsuits proliferate, it is likely that new legislation or judicial actions will be implemented to curtail the intent and spirit of the ADA. The unfortunate victims in this backlash will be those people who need the protection of the ADA the most.

Second, unclear expectations regarding appropriate accommodations for people with disabilities when coupled with the vague language of the ADA, are having a chilling effect on the employment prospects of workers with disabilities. These factors, in conjunction with the growth of ADA-related lawsuits and grievances, are leading a growing number of employers to be suspect, if not downright hostile, when hiring workers with disabilities. In an all-too-common irony in social policy, the ADA may be having the exact opposite effect of the intent of the law.

Third, the creation of yet another protected class has its drawbacks. By creating and implementing the ADA, we have defined people with disabilities as another group of victims in need of social protection. While the list of victims grows in our society, so too does the backlash. Moreover, the ADA makes the assumption that all people with disabilities want to be part of a protected class. This is unfair to those who choose not to enjoy the protection (and stigma) of being part of a protected class.

American social policy is predicated on the piecemeal approach of putting vulnerable populations into an almost infinite number of little "protected class" boxes. It then proceeds to protect each little box from the other. If the purpose of the ADA is to mainstream the disabled, how can putting people into yet another box facilitate that goal? By segregating the disabled into a protected class, we are further isolating rather than incorporating them into mainstream American society. Given the policy blunders of the past 50 years, one would think that American policymakers would finally realize that they can not legislate morality, responsible behavior, good citizenship, tolerance, or compassion. The goal of social policy should not be to further balkanize American society, but to create conditions that allow all people to participate as equal citizens with equal protections under the law. Piecemeal approaches to equality and fairness (such as the ADA) do not work.

NO

John C. Bricout

Today, more than a decade since it was signed into law in 1990, the Americans with Disabilities Act (ADA) has become something of a lightning rod for debates around the adequacy and appropriateness of federal legislation for protecting the rights of individuals with a disability. The ADA is neither the first major piece of federal legislation to address the needs of individuals with a disability (viz., the Architectural Barriers Act of 1968), nor the most recent (viz., the Technology-Related Assistance for Individuals with Disabilities Act Amendments of 1994). Yet, the five titles of the ADA provide the most comprehensive and far-reaching legislative guidelines for protecting the rights of individuals with a disability. In an effort to remove physical and attitudinal barriers to the participation of individuals with disabilities in American society, the ADA has reshaped the practices of private and public entities in the realms of employment, transportation, construction of the built environment, and telecommunications. Given such ambitious goals, and the broad scope of affected organizations, ranging from small businesses to metropolitan transportation authorities, state governments, and major software manufactures, it is little wonder that the necessity as well as the efficacy of the ADA has come into question. For this reason, the question of whether the ADA has gone too far cannot be settled by facts alone, but must include explicit considerations of values, perspectives, and power relations.

QUESTIONS RAISED BY THE ADA

At its heart, the question of whether the ADA has gone too far is a question of legitimacy, which itself hangs on at least three suppositions. The first supposition is that people with disabilities face barriers that require a legislative remedy at the federal level. The second supposition is that the costs entailed in the broad civil-rights mandate of the ADA is warranted in the current social, economic, and political context. The third supposition is that the ADA has made sufficient progress in realizing some of its goals to warrant its continuation. In examining the merit of each supposition in turn, it is necessary to articulate the value positions, perspectives, and power issues that undergird arguments for and against the legitimacy of the ADA.

THE ACT

The Americans with Disabilities Act (P.L. 101-336) has five titles covering: (I) employment, (II) public services, (III) public accommodations and services operated by private entities, and (IV) telecommunications services, followed by (V) miscellaneous provisions, including insurance issues, integration, state immunity, and relations to other laws and bodies. The ADA is enforced through designated federal agencies and covers most private and public entities, including all businesses with 15 or more employees. Despite the claim that the ADA is too exigent of covered entities, the Act allows exceptions to accommodation requirements in the face of significant implementation difficulties. Title I and Title II allow exceptions to the requirement of providing either reasonable (Title I), or public (Title II) accommodations. In Title I reasonable accommodations are not required where they would impose undue hardship on an employer, or pose a direct threat to the health or safety of others in the workplace. In Title II removal of architectural or communication barriers in existing buildings must only be carried out if readily achievable; otherwise, alternative methods of making goods, services, and accommodations must be provided.

   The definition of disability in the ADA is very broad, but explicitly so, in order to avoid excluding anyone with a legitimate claim. An individual must meet one or more of the following three criteria: (1) substantial limitation in one or more major life activities (such as work) due to a physical or mental impairment, (2) a record of such impairment, or (3) the recognition by others as having such an impairment. A wide range of conditions have been included within this rubric, including substance abuse; HIV infection; and physical, psychiatric, mental, neurological, sensory, and learning impairments.

IS THE ADA WARRANTED?

Do the barriers to social participation that people with disabilities face require a legislative remedy at the federal level? A 2001, Supreme Court ruling (*University of Alabama v. Garrett*) found that state governments are immune from lawsuits for job discrimination claims. This decision would seem to suggest that in the eyes of the Court, the employment protections owed individuals with a disability are not on a par with those owed individuals identified as belonging to a racial or ethnic minority. This in turn seems to question the minority model of disability implicit in the ADA's civil-rights protections patterned on the Civil Rights Act of 1964.

A MINORITY OR MINORITIES?

Do people with disabilities fail to meet the standards of an oppressed minority population that merits civil-rights protections at the federal level? Some have argued that by covering the estimated 54 million Americans with disabilities of varying severity and nature, from quadriplegia and schizophrenia to learning disabilities and asymptomatic HIV, the notion of an oppressed minority is lost, and with it, the right to special civil-rights protections (e.g., Baldwin, 1997; Elvin, 2000). This argument fails to take into account several facts that serve to narrow the range and number of persons benefiting from a disability designation. First, there is a trend in the U.S. Supreme Court toward excluding as disabilities impairments or conditions that can be managed or compensated (Griffin & Brown, 2000; Hall & Hatch, 1999). Second, there is evidence to suggest that people claiming employment protections under the ADA tend overwhelmingly to lose their cases, whether decided by a judge (92 percent) or administratively (86 percent) according to a 1998 study (Porter, 1998). Others have argued that there exist two distinct groups of people with disabilities: a more severely impaired group perhaps deserving special protections, and a less severely impaired group undeserving of such protections (e.g., Johnson, 1997).

DISCRIMINATION AND JUST DESERTS

Typically, two arguments emerge to support this declension between deserving and undeserving individuals with disabilities. First, critics argue that the framers of the ADA had in mind only individuals with the most severe disabilities. This argument fails to take into account the role of accommodations and assistive technologies in enhancing the functional abilities of individuals with quite severe, congenital, or chronic conditions. Surely the framers of the legislation did not believe that level of functional impairment was the only criterion for ADA protections. Indeed, the Act's focus on discrimination would suggest that they (accurately) foresaw continued stigmatization and prejudice against even high-functioning individuals, whether people with asymptomatic HIV, or individuals managing their mental illness with medications. Second, it is argued that the addition of difficult-to-diagnose conditions (such as soft-tissue impairments), or mild disabilities (such as chronic back pain) encourage specious claims by individuals who are either malingering or, if actually impaired, not in need of special protections. Again, the 1998 study of Equal Employment Opportunity Commission (EEOC) records revealed that the reason so few employees won their cases was due to the obstacles to proving substantial limitations to functioning (Porter, 1998), casting doubt on the efficacy, if not the prevalence, of malingering and gold digging.

The available evidence seems to suggest that, as a group, people with a disability live disproportionately with unemployment, poor education, poor housing, poor health care, and low incomes (Kopeks, 1995; McNeil, 2000, N.O.D./Harris, 2000). Even college-educated individuals with a disability appear to earn less money over the course of their careers than their non-disabled peers (Hendricks, Schiro-Geist, & Broadbent, 1997). This is not to suggest that there are not important in-group differences; in particular, racial and ethnic minorities seem to find less favorable employment and encounter more discrimination than white individuals with a disability (Blanck, 1996; Kim, 1996).

It would be disingenuous to claim that all individuals with a disability live under equally oppressive social, political, and economic conditions. Clearly, individuals with more education and resources to begin with, most commonly individuals with an adventitious disability who are able to return to work, will enjoy better economic success than those with developmental disabilities who typically have poor work histories and less-developed inter-personal skills. However, all will be vulnerable to discrimination. Even if a Stephen Hawking or a Christopher Reeve continues to produce creative and lasting work in their fields, the discrimination faced by others with similar disabilities is likely to be undiminished.

From the standpoint of civil rights, to deny people with disabilities minority status on exclusionary arguments grounded in notions of deserv-ingness is not only to divide and conquer, but also to remove discrimination from societal, institutional, and organizational contexts and place it in the context of individual bad behavior. In this framework, only the most impaired individuals would be worthy of special consideration, presumably because of their infirmity. Discrimination would be limited to the truculence of unkind or ignorant people who do not respond appropriately to someone in the sick role. The impact of disablement on individual functioning and productivity reintroduces the second supposition to be explored in deter-mining the legitimacy of the ADA: namely, the costs of such a broad civil-rights mandate.

WEIGHING COSTS AND BENEFITS

The question of whether the costs associated with the ADA are warranted in the current social, political, and economic context must include a discussion of what costs are, in fact, investments, and what benefits may engender unforeseen costs. The ADA has been widely but unfairly criticized as an unfunded federal mandate, when in fact there is evidence that the cost of most workplace accommodations is low (Batavia, 1997; Bruyere, 2000). Estimates of the average costs of job accommodations have ranged from $100 (Morely & Hyatt, 1996) to $500 (Jonse, Watzlaf, Hobson, & Mazzoni, 1996). Another study similarly found the cost of new ADA-related construction to be quite low—a modest 4.9 percent of total costs for a significant portion of respondents (Jonse et al., 1996). At the same time, even job accommodations that do not incur a direct cost, such as flexible scheduling, might nonetheless be perceived as having a cost because of additional supervisor or coworker responsibilities, and coworker resentment about accommodations as special treatment (Frierson, 1992; Pati & Bailey, 1995).

Fortunately, employers have found reason to provide accommodations despite such concerns. Several workplace studies have reported accommodation costs either to be small or a good investment, allowing workers to retain their jobs longer (Bruyere, 2000; Burkhauser, 1997). In fact, the greatest cost burden of the ADA seems to be borne by U.S. Equal Employment Opportunity Commission (EEOC), which enforces Title I. The EEOC has had to absorb the costs of burgeoning caseloads and ADA training without a corresponding budget increase (Bruyere, 2000). The costs to the federal government and to public and private entities seem worthwhile in a context in which an estimated 68 percent of individuals with disabilities are unemployed, 22 percent fail to complete high school, and 29 percent live in poverty (N.O.D./Harris, 2000).

Some authors have argued that the ADA has improved employer attitudes by altering basic assumptions about people with disabilities, recasting people with disabilities as productive agents, when previously they had been viewed as social-service recipients (Baldwin, 1997; Wehman, 1993). In fact, the employment picture for individuals with a disability may have improved slightly of late. In the recent 2000 N.O.D./Harris survey of people with disabilities, 32 percent of respondents indicated that they were employed, a 3 percent increase over the previous survey of 1998. Moreover, 56 percent of respondents with a disability who say they are able to work reported they were working as compared to only 46 percent in the 1986 N.O.D./Harris Survey.

However, there may be unforeseen attitudinal costs in terms of employer backlash against the ADA. Although the great preponderance of employers surveyed in recent national N.O.D./Harris disability surveys (1998, 2000) have expressed their approval of the ADA, the employment barriers faced by individuals with a disability, including high unemployment rates and job stagnation, persist. This strongly implies unexpressed reservations by employers about the ADA (Schall, 1998). In her review of the Title I EEOC complaint data from 1992 to 1996 Schall (1998) found only 9.8 percent of the complaints addressed the hiring process, compared to 51.9 percent discharge-related complaints. The disparity between hiring and discharge-related complaints suggests that some employment discrimination may escape detection (Schall, 1998). The ADA may have made employers only more cautious, rather than more conscientious, due to fears about the costs of employing individuals with a disability. This resistance actually creates an argument for perpetuating the ADA, rather than desisting, because systemic change often engenders resistance (Senge, 1990). Such resistance directs the attention of change agents (i.e., disability activists and their allies) to the underlying power relations and supportive norms (Senge, 1990). Thus, the challenge to the ADA is to foster the development of a community and allied coalitions that can actively address the power inequities arising from institutional and societal structures and practices that favor nondisabled persons to the disadvantage of people with disabilities. This leads to an examination of the third supposition: Whether the ADA has made sufficient progress toward its goals.

PROGRESS THROUGH COMMUNITY

One way of appraising the progress of the ADA is to assess the satisfaction of individuals with disabilities themselves. In the most recent N.O.D./Harris survey, 63 percent of all respondents with a disability indicated that life has improved for people with disabilities in the past decade, which the investigators claim may be due in part to the ADA.

However, in the previous N.O.D./Harris (1998) survey, when respondents were asked directly about the impact of the ADA, 58 percent said that it had not made a significant impact on their lives. Ambivalence about the difference made by the ADA is understandable given the mixed reactions of those providing accommodations and the persistence of negative beliefs about the capacity of people with disabilities. Negative attitudes toward people with disabilities by nondisabled people endure even in the climate of civil rights fostered by the ADA. Recent studies have found negative attitudes and attributions coexisting with more positive views among employers, neighbors, student peers, teachers, and others. (Bruce, Harman, & Baker, 2000; Clark, 1997; Hernandez & Keys, 2000; Silverman & Segal, 1996).

In some sense then, the ADA may have served as a catalyst to raise the expectations of individuals with a disability, ironically leading them to express skepticism about the very legislation that articulated a new vision of relationships between people with disabilities and their environments: social, physical, and electronic. Is there evidence that the ADA has been a catalyst to positive community building among people with disabilities in the same way that it has raised expectations? Although this is difficult to assess, it is interesting to note that disability advocates have been successful in expanding the scope of ADA protections to people with a psychiatric disability, people with a learning disability, and people with HIV.

The federal government, some private and public institutions, and private litigants are making strong efforts to make the World Wide Web accessible by arguing an effective communication rationale using the ADA (Waddell, 2000a, 2000b). The ADA can also contribute to a rights-based framework for providing online accessibility to people with disabilities (Bricout, 2001). By expanding the boundaries of the community of people with disabilities, the ADA can claim to have laid a foundation for coalition building and political action to combat inequities. However, the role of the ADA in bringing about progress—not only on an individual or aggregated basis, but also on the basis of fostering a community of shared interest—is unclear at present. Thus, the question of whether the ADA has made sufficient progress to warrant its continuation cannot be satisfactorily answered. Certainly, the ADA offers the promise of fostering new relations between the community of people with disabilities and the institutional and societal structures that have denied access to opportunities for participation and development. Whether such a community will develop is an issue larger than the ADA, although one in which the ADA could play an important role. The role of the ADA in fostering positive change for people with disabilities will hinge to large degree on its evolution.

CONCLUSION

The ADA, like all legislation, is evolving over time, with changes in enforcement; relevant jurisprudence; and social, political, and economic circumstances. At the time of this writing the political context has taken a decidedly conservative turn. The obvious portents of this change is the emphasis on states' rights, which has already led to the granting of immunity to states from ADA-based lawsuits for job discrimination. An outcome of the state-focused approach that is more supportive of the aims of the ADA is the New Freedom Initiative for People with Disabilities. The New Freedom Initiative allocates money to states for assistive technologies, education, home ownership, transportation, work, and community access. Nonetheless, the slowdown of the U.S. economy may have a pernicious effect on the ADA as employers, builders, and others become more cost-conscious and scale back their plans.

It is unclear what impact a states' rights orientation will have on federal enforcement of the ADA, but given the need for more proactive enforcement approaches and more funding for additional staff and resources (Reichert, 2000), the portents may not be good. The tendency of the Supreme Court to strike down lawsuits in which the plaintiffs compensate for their disability or can take medications or other treatments that mitigate the impact of the disability has the potential to remove many individuals from the umbrella of the ADA (Griffin & Brown, 2000). Employees with a disability who fail to take their medications or who can attain a high level of functioning without assistive technologies for whatever reasons may be forsaking their rights to claim ADA protections. On the other hand, it appears that employees with a disability have reason to be more optimistic about receiving precisely the job accommodations they need, thanks to a recent ADA-based lawsuit. Recently, a federal Appeals Court (*Vollmort v. Wisconsin DOT*) found that employers must provide accommodations fitted to the exact needs of the job and the employee's disability (Hatch & Hall, 2000). However, costly accommodations for individuals with more severe disabilities who are employed by small businesses may still be beyond the scope of ADA protections, if the cost of the accommodation would cause undue hardship to the employer.

There are perhaps, on balance, more reasons to be concerned about the efficacy of the ADA and its sustainability, than there are reasons to be sanguine. However, this is not tantamount to saying that the ADA ought to be abandoned as unsalvageable. The alternative to the ADA—reliance on a score of disparate federal laws and the devolution of ADA functions and intentions to state or local legislatures—would severely undermine any real hope of ending the discrimination against people with disabilities. This is the judgment that has already been made for other minority groups for whom federal civil-rights protections are the source not only of legal protections but also of societal sanctions, public legitimacy, and distributive justice. Rather than dismantle the ADA as a failed experiment, the aspirations of people with disabilities for equality require a reinvigoration of its purpose, mandate, and resources.

REFERENCES

Baldwin, M. L. (1997). Can the ADA achieve its employment goals? *Annals of the American Academy, AAPS,* 37–52.

Batavia, I. A. (1997). Ideology and independent living: Will conservatism harm people with disabilities? *Annals of the American Academy, AAPS,* 53–70.

Blanck, P. D. (1996). Empirical study of the ADA (1990–1994). *Behavioral Science and the Law,* 14(1), 5–27.

Bricout, J. C. (2001). Making computer-mediated education responsive to the accommodation needs of students with disabilities. *Journal of Social Work Education,* 37(2), 15–30.

Bruce, A. J., Harman, M. J., & Baker, N. A. (2000). Anticipated social contact with persons in wheelchairs: Age and gender differences. In F. Columbus (Ed.), *Advances in Psychology Research, Vol. 1* (pp. 219–228). Huntington, NY: Nova Science.

Bruyere, S. M. (2000). Civil rights and employment issues of disability policy. *The Journal of Disability Policy Studies,* 11(1), 18–28.

Burkhauser, R. V. (1997). Post-ADA: Are people with disabilities expected to work? *Annals of the American Academy, AAPS, 549,* 71–83.

Clark, M. D. (1997). Teacher response to learning disability: A test of attributional principals. *Journal of Learning Disabilities, 30*(1), 69–79.

Diversity, Inc. (1999). The bureaucrats keep count. Retrieved June 3, 2001, from www .diversityinc.com.

Elvin, J. (2000). ADA's good intentions have unintended consequences. *Insight on the News, 16*(7), 18.

Freedom Network. (2000). *Good intentions and the ADA.* Retrieved June 7, 2001, from www.free-market.net/spotlight/ada.

Frierson, J. G. (1992). An employer's dilemma: The ADA's provisions on reasonable accommodations. *Labor Law Journal, 43*(1), 309–312.

Griffin, J. W., & Brown, B. D. (2000). Chipping away at the ADA. *Trial, 36*(13), 48.

Hall, J. E., & Hatch, D. D. (1999). Supreme Court decisions require ADA revision. *Workforce, 78*(8), 60–66.

Hatch, D., & Hall, J. E. (2000). ADA requires disability-specific accommodations. *Workforce, 79*(2), 92.

Hendricks, W., Schiro-Geist, C., & Broadbent, E. (1997). Long-term disabilities and college education. *Industrial Relations, 36*(1), 46–60.

Hernandez, B., & Keys, C. (2000). Employer attitudes toward workers with disabilities and their ADA employment rights: A literature review. *Journal of Rehabilitation, 66*(4), 4–16.

Hudgins, Edward L. (1999, May 24). Counterpoint on ADA and HIV. *Physician's Weekly,* 1–5.

Johnson, W. G. (1997). The future of disability policy: Benefit payments or civil rights? *Annals of the American Academy, AAPS, 549,* 160–172.

Jonse, D. L., Watzlaf, V. J., Hobson, D., & Mazzoni, J. (1996). Responses within nonfederal hospitals in Pennsylvania to the Americans with Disabilities Act of 1990. *Physical Therapy, 76*(1), 49–60.

Kim, P. S. (1996). Disability policy: An analysis of the employment of people with disabilities in the American federal government. *Public Personnel Management, 25*(1), 73–88.

Kopeks, S. (1995). The Americans with Disabilities Act: A tool to combat poverty. *Journal of Social Work Education, 31*(3), 337–346.

Matthews, J. (1995, April 16). Disabilities act failing to achieve workplace goals: Landmark law rarely helps disabled people seeking jobs. *The Washington Post,* 3A.

McNeil, J. M. (2000, June–July). *Employment, earnings and disability.* Seventy-fifth Annual Conference of the Western Economic Association International. Vancouver, British Columbia.

Morely, G., & Hyatt, D. (1996). Do injured workers pay for reasonable accommodating? *Industrial and Labor Relations Review, 50*(1), 92–98.

National Association of Social Workers. (1999). *Code of ethics of the National Association of Social Workers, approved by the 1996 NASW Delegate Assembly and revised by the 1999 NASW Delegate Assembly.* Silver Spring, MD: Author.

National Organization on Disabilities. (2000, July 9). *Americans with disabilities trail non-disabled in key life areas, benchmark N.O.D./Harris survey finds.* Retrieved June 3, 2001, from www.nod.org/hsevent.html.

N.O.D./Harris. (1998). *Survey program on participation and attitudes. Americans with disabilities still face sharp gaps in securing jobs, education, transportation and in many areas of daily life.* Washington, DC: National Organization on Disability.

N.O.D./Harris. (2000). *Survey program on participation and attitudes. The 2000 N.O.D./ Harris survey of Americans with disabilities.* Washington, DC: National Organization on Disability.

Pati, G. C., & Bailey, E. K. (1995). Empowering people with disabilities: Strategy and human resource issues in implementing the ADA. *Organizational Dynamics, 23*(3), 52–69.

Porter, R. (1998). Employees lose ADA suits, study shows. *Trial, 34*(9), 16–18.

Reichert, J. L. (2000). Poor federal enforcement weakens ADA, disability group asserts. *Trial, 36*(9), 93.

Schall, C. M. (1998). The Americans with Disabilities Act—Are we keeping our promise? An analysis of the effect of the ADA on the employment of persons with disabilities. *Journal of Vocational Rehabilitation, 10*(3), 191–203.

Scotch, R. K., & Schriner, K. (1997). Disability as human variation: Implications for policy. *Annals of the American Academy, AAPS, 549,* 148–154.

Senge, P. M. (1990). *The fifth discipline: The art and practice of the learning organization.* New York: Doubleday.

Silverman, C. J., & Segal, S. P. (1996). When neighborhoods complain: Correlates of neighborhood opposition to sheltered care facilities. *Adult Residential Care Journal, 10*(2), 137–148.

U.S. Department of Justice. (1995). ADA/EEOC. Retrieved June 6, 2001, from www .usdoj.gov/crt/ada/adahom1.asp.

U.S. Department of Commerce. (1997, December). *Census brief. Disabilities affect one-fifth of all Americans: Proportion could increase in coming decades.* U.S. Department of Commerce, Economics and Statistics Division, CENBR/97-5.

Waddell, C. D. (2000a). *Electronic curbcuts: The ADA in cyberspace.* Retrieved June 11, 2001, from www.abnet.org/irr/hr/winter00humanrights/waddle.htm.

Waddell, C. D. (2000b). *The National Federation of the Blind sues AOL.* Retrieved June 11, 2001, from www.abnet.org/irr/hr/winter00humanrights/waddle2.html.

Wehman, P. (1993). Employment opportunities and career development. In P. Wehman (Ed.), *The ADA mandate for social change* (pp. 45–68). Baltimore: Paul H. Brookes.

DOES SOCIAL WORK DISCRIMINATE AGAINST EVANGELICAL CHRISTIANS?

Editor's Note:

Since Abraham Flexner's denial of professional status to social work in 1915, the profession has struggled to develop a self-confident professional identity. Part of the legacy of this struggle has been a tendency to disavow the Judeo-Christian religious roots of the profession. More recently, the close association of the Moral Majority and the Religious Right with a conservative political agenda and the Republican party has exacerbated the polarization of religion and the profession of social work in the viewpoints of many. Devolution of the provision of social services to the states and the redirection of public funding to faith-based organizations have directly challenged the legitimacy and future of the profession. Even the recent embrace of spirituality as essential to client-centered practice can be interpreted as an incomplete reconciliation with religion because of the careful distinctions drawn between spirituality and religiosity. The debate of the role of evangelical Christians in social work highlights the historical, and continuing, tension between religion and the profession.

David Hodge, Ph.D., is an assistant professor at Arizona State University West Campus and a senior nonresident fellow at University of Pennsylvania's Program for Research on Religion and Urban Civil Society. He is a leading social-work scholar on spirituality and religion. Included in his work in this area are a number of publications to assist helping professionals develop cultural competency with evangelical Christians, Muslims, Hindus, and Native Americans.

Gary R. Anderson, Ph.D., is the director of the Michigan State University (MSU) School of Social Work. Prior to MSU, he was a professor at Hunter College School of Social Work, City University of New York. He is the editor of the journal *Child Welfare* and has written extensively on child-welfare topics.

YES

David Hodge

Identifying oppression can be a difficult task. Oppression is commonly understood as an exercise of power—people with less power are marginalized, denigrated, or denied rights by people with greater power (Anderson & Carter, 2003; Appleby, Colon, & Hamilton, 2001; Kirst-Ashman & Hull, 2006; Lum, 2003; Netting, Kettner, & McMurtry, 2004; Zastrow, 2000). Yet, unless individuals personally experience the effects of the oppression, even the most objective outside observers often have difficulty identifying its existence (Edelman, 1990).

Segregation, for instance, is now widely acknowledged as oppression. Segregation existed for decades, however, without being seen as a problem by most people. Since European Americans did not experience its effects, it was often hard for whites to understand that segregation was, in fact, oppression. Similarly, men often fail to understand the oppression that women encounter, since they do not share their lived reality (Kirst-Ashman & Hull, 2006).

How, then, do we know when oppression exists? As the social-work profession has struggled to become more inclusive over time, it has developed a number of tools to identify previously unacknowledged oppressions. Among the more widely used are examinations of systemic power imbalances, patterns of institutional discrimination, professional publications and other content, studies using experimental manipulation and other designs, and self-report among those with little access to power. The application of these intertwined tools in areas such as race and gender has helped social work identify oppressive conditions and move toward the creation of a more tolerant, inclusive environment.

With the same aim in mind, these tools are used here to illustrate oppression in the next frontier of diversity—religion and spirituality. The largest spiritual minority in the United States—comprising perhaps 25 percent of the population—is evangelical Christians (Green, Guth, Smidt, & Kellstedt, 1996; Richards & Bergin, 2005). This population can be defined as an inclusive, transdenominational family of Christians that emphasizes traditional Protestant beliefs (Smith, 1996; Woodberry & Smith, 1998). While this essay focuses on evangelical Christians, theory suggests they function as a proxy for an array of spiritual groups that affirm the historic, mainstream tenets of their respective faith traditions (e.g., traditional Catholics, Latter-Day Saints, Muslims) (Hunter, 1991). Identifying oppression allows us to address the underlying causes so we can move closer to a more representative profession in which people of faith are treated with the same respect and dignity regularly accorded other groups (Haynes & White, 1999).

SYSTEMIC POWER IMBALANCES

Uncovering power imbalances between groups is critical to any discussion of oppression (Farley, 2005). A power differential between opposing world-views creates an environment in which oppression can occur (Hamilton & Sharma, 1997), especially if the group with power holds prejudicial views toward the subordinate group (Wambach & Van Soest, 1997).

When considering the existence of oppression in social work, it may be helpful to adopt a systems approach. Social work does not exist in isolation. Rather, it is an academic profession embedded in higher education, which in turn is part of the postindustrial knowledge industry, or what some have called the knowledge class (Berger, 1986; Gouldner, 1979; Hodge, 2003a, 2003b; Hunter, 1991; McAdams, 1987; Smith, 2003).

One of the characteristics of this occupational grouping is the dominance of a secular worldview, rooted in the European Enlightenment. The secular worldview that pervades social work and other knowledge-class professions differs from the worldview affirmed by evangelical Christians and many other people of faith. Indeed, evangelical Christians have formed their own distinct subculture outside the mainstream secular culture (Talbot, 2000). The members of this subculture are disproportionately drawn from populations with few resources and little power: the working class, the poor, people with less prestigious occupations, African Americans, and females (Davis & Robinson, 1997; Gallup & Lindsay, 1999; Hodge, 2002b; Smith & Faris, 2005).

As noted, animosity toward minority groups can fuel oppression. Among the general public, prejudice toward evangelical Christians exceeds that directed toward African Americans (Bolce & De Maio, 1999). The most elevated levels of hostility occur among the highly educated and seculars, where extreme antipathy is "pervasive" (Bolce & De Maio, 1999, p. 54).

The power differential, along with high levels of prejudice, suggests that evangelical Christians are likely to be oppressed in social work and other knowledge-class settings. One way in which such oppression may manifest is through institutional discrimination.

INSTITUTIONAL DISCRIMINATION

Institutional discrimination refers to patterns of unequal treatment that occur between groups (Healey, 2004). If a particular group represents 10 percent of the population, one would expect it to represent 10 percent of educators, social workers, and so forth. As Diller (2004) notes, if a sizable difference in percentages exists, then it is likely that broader, discriminatory forces are behind the discrepancy.

It is important to note that discrepancies are not necessarily the product of prejudice or even conscious decisions (Healey, 2004). Institutional discrimination, like the other forms of oppression discussed here, is often the product of unacknowledged structures, relationships, and paradigms that implicitly marginalize groups without power.

In keeping with the power differential, evangelical Christians are underrepresented in many of the knowledge-class settings that shape cultural discourse (Hunter, 1991). Comparatively few evangelical Christians are chief executive officers, listed in *Who's Who*, employed in movie or television industries, or work at prominent newspapers, magazines, or TV newsrooms, and few are employed in academia (Bilgrave & Deluty, 1998; Klein & Stern, in press; Redding, 2001; Rothman, Lichter, & Nevitte, 2005a; Woodberry & Smith, 1998).

Similarly, institutional discrimination is also a problem in social work. Studies indicate that evangelical Christians are underrepresented among social-work faculty (Sheridan, Wilmer, & Atcheson, 1994), practitioners (Hodge, 2002b; Neumann, Thompson, & Woolley, 1992), and students (Hodge, 2005; Newman, Dannenfeiser, & Benishek, 2002). The disparity among faculty is a particular concern given the central role they play shaping the profession's agenda in education, policy, and research. A study of 280 full-time faculty at 25 schools in 12 Southeastern states—a geographic area in which one might expect a relatively high number of evangelical Christians—found that only 3 percent were evangelical Christians (Sheridan et al., 1994). In other words, increasing the number of evangelical Christians among faculty by roughly 700 percent would result in faculty that reflected the percentage among the general population (i.e., 25 percent).

In most cases, it is likely that the institutional disparity is not the result of deliberate attempts to exclude. However, in at least one case, a major state-run social-work program implemented institutional policies that deliberately excluded evangelical Christians (Ressler, 1998). In other words, some social workers breached the separation of church and state to use the power of the state to exclude people from public schools based on their religious beliefs. Attempts have also been made to exclude the few private evangelical Christian social-work programs from the profession (Ressler, 1998). Such practices represent attempts to deny evangelical Christians their basic human rights under both the United States Constitution (French, 2002; Ressler, 1998), and the United Nations' (1948) Universal Declaration of Human Rights.

CONTENT ANALYSIS

Because content analysis can reveal the attitudes of authors, it is widely used to reveal oppressive patterns (McMahon & Allen-Meares, 1992; Tompkins, Larkin, & Rosen, 2006; Tsang, 2001). Articles, textbooks, and other media are systemically examined. The frequency and manner in which groups are depicted reveal those populations with, and without, power. Groups depicted infrequently, or framed pejoratively, are considered to be marginalized or oppressed.

In knowledge-class settings, analysis has revealed negative depictions of evangelical Christians in network news (Kerr, 2003), and fictional television programming (Skill & Robinson, 1994). Similar findings have emerged in textbooks used in grade schools (Vitz, 1985), high schools (Oppewal, 1985; Sewall, 1995; Vitz, 1998), and universities (Glenn, 1997; Lehr & Spilka, 1989; Redding, 2001). These studies are particularly significant given the role the media and educational systems play in shaping perceptions among the general public, and likely social workers as well (Hunter & Schaecher, 1995; Tower, 2000).

Indeed, analyses of leading social-work journals found that the voices of evangelical Christians (Hodge, 2002a) along with other people of faith (Tully & Greene, 1995) were essentially absent from the surveyed literature. In perhaps the most exhaustive study to date, this basic finding was replicated in an extensive examination of the profession's abstracts, textbooks, encyclopedias, yearbooks, and conference presentations (Cnaan, Wineburg, & Boddie, 1999). This study revealed that the contributions of evangelical Christians and other people of faith were basically marginalized from the professional mainstream. Likewise, an examination of required textbooks at top social-work programs found that the presence of evangelical Christians and Muslims was largely absent from the surveyed texts (Hodge, Baughman & Cummings, in press).

While replicating previous work, the latter study also expanded on prior findings by examining how evangelical Christians and Muslims were depicted. The results indicated that both evangelical Christians and Muslims were portrayed in a negative, pejorative manner. Similarly, analysis of the DSM III-R disclosed that religion, typically traditional Christianity, was unduly associated with mental illness (Larson, Milano, & Lu, 1998).

The DSM authors linked religion with pathology in spite of the fact that research indicates that religion is generally associated with mental health rather than mental illness (Koenig, McCullough, & Larson, 2001). As Sue and Sue (1999) observe, the mental-health professions have a long history of associating minorities with pathology, a practice that is often used by dominant groups to justify patterns of institutional discrimination.

STUDIES USING EXPERIMENTAL MANIPULATION AND OTHER DESIGNS

Studies using experimental manipulation and other designs are also commonly used to illustrate oppression. An example of how these studies differ from content analysis is provided by Gartner's (1986) exploration of admission rates into Ph.D. psychology programs. Faculty across the nation were randomly sent one of three applications—one was secular, one mentioned that the applicant had become an evangelical Christian during college, and one mentioned the applicants desire to integrate her spiritual beliefs into her studies. In all other respects, the applications were identical. The results revealed that both evangelical Christian candidates were more likely to be denied admission into doctoral programs than the secular candidate.

Bias in academia has also been documented in studies on measurement and advancement. Just as measures created in male-dominated settings reflect bias against women (Gilligan, 1993), measures developed in secular settings reflect bias against people of theistic faith (Richards & Davison, 1992). Similarly, an exploration of professional advancement among faculty found that women and evangelical Christians teach at lower-quality schools than their professional accomplishments would predict (Rothman, Lichter, & Nevitte, 2005b; Rothman et al., 2005a).

Studies have also found that a variety of professionals in knowledge-class occupations discriminate against evangelical Christians in their professional decisions, including psychologists (Neumann, Thompson, & Woolley, 1991), psychiatrists (Neumann, Harvill & Callahan, 1995), physicians (Neumann & Leppien, 1997a, 1997b), and social workers (Neumann et al., 1992).

The results in the latter study mirrored those obtained in the study of admission rates to Ph.D. programs, although in this case, the study was conducted with a national sample of 131 graduate-level social workers affiliated with Veterans Affairs—presumably a more conservative sampling frame. The findings indicated that social workers discriminated against evangelical Christians in the areas of inservice training, professional presentations, and publishing (Neumann et al., 1992). These results may help explain the institutional discrimination as well as the virtual absence of an evangelical Christian perspective in the profession's literature.

SELF-REPORT

One of the most important tools for ascertaining oppression is to ask those who, theoretically, might be expected to experience it. As noted earlier, those who experience discrimination understand the situation in a manner that outsiders cannot. Firsthand accounts can play a vital role in illuminating oppressive dynamics by, for example, helping to determine if patterns of institutional discrimination are the result of self-selection or oppression (Diller, 2004).

Perceptions among evangelical Christians, in both the general population and social work, are consistent with theory and research. Among a nationally representative sample of 430, 92 percent felt that "Christian values are under serious attack" in the United States (Smith, 1998, p. 139). Follow-up qualitative work revealed that respondents generally felt excluded, marginalized, and discriminated against by secular institutions and elites. Most believed they faced widespread opposition and prejudice in secular arenas (Smith, 2000).

Similar perceptions exist in social work. Among a sample of 88 social-work students drawn from the National Association of Christians in Social Work (NACSW), roughly 60 percent of evangelical Christian reported experiencing religious discrimination in their social work programs (Hodge, 2004). Compared to a reference group of graduate students who reported no religious faith, evangelical Christian students were roughly 11 times more likely to report experiencing religious discrimination. They also perceived religious discrimination to be a significantly more pervasive problem in their social-work programs.

Qualitative research corroborates these findings by suggesting that many evangelical Christians feel oppressed in social work (Ressler & Hodge, 2003, 2005). Faculty reported being denied tenure, threatened with being fired, and fired due to their spiritual beliefs. Students reported being given lower grades for writing papers on spirituality, denied the right to compose such papers, and denied admittance to graduate school, and reported both formal and informal attempts to force them out of the profession. In classrooms, some students reported being belittled and called pejorative names by faculty and students while others reported that their reality was disparaged to such an extent that they were silenced.

CONCLUSION

Hartman (1993) has stated that nothing is more oppressive than denying or silencing another's reality, yet many evangelical Christians report that this reflects their experience in social work. Indeed, patterns of institutional discrimination are replicated in the profession's written content, which either marginalizes or denigrates their perspective. In short, the voice of evangelical Christians has been essentially silenced in the social-work profession.

These empirical results are exactly what one would expect to find, based on theory. The few evangelical Christians in the profession have little power. As noted, people with less power are often marginalized, denigrated, or denied rights by people with greater power. In short, the profession's analytical tools indicate that evangelical Christians are oppressed in social work. Such has been the case with many other minority groups in the profession's history as well.

When evidence of discriminatory patterns is made visible, dominant groups often respond by attempting to rationalize the oppression (Wambach & Van Soest, 1997). Responsibility for the obvious inequalities is often shifted away from the dominant groups onto the victims. As alluded to earlier, this may be achieved by defining the values of the minority group as abnormal or deficient.

For instance, discrimination in social work is often rationalized on the grounds that evangelical Christians affirm the wrong values (e.g., complementary gender roles, pro-life). Proponents of the existing power imbalance argue that evangelical Christians should abandon their values (which are implicitly viewed as inappropriate, bad, or pathological) and adopt those of the majority (which are implicitly viewed as appropriate, good, and healthy). If evangelicals discarded their values, the argument goes, then discrimination would cease to exist as a problem.

Such rationalizations are commonly referred to as cultural discrimination or cultural racism (Diller, 2004). Dominant groups tend to define their own values as superior while framing culturally different values pejoratively. As Diller (2004) observes, cultural racism occurs when minority groups must give up their culturally different values and take on those of the majority to be accepted. Cultural racism represents the flip side of institutional discrimination. Institutional discrimination keeps evangelical Christians outside the profession while cultural discrimination makes them feel uncomfortable if they manage to gain entry. Instead of being accepted, they are forced to deny essential components of their being.

Another way to rationalize existing inequalities is by re-labeling the oppression—to frame it as serving a higher moral purpose (Wambach & Van Soest, 1997). For instance, evangelical Christians' efforts to promote their understanding of the general welfare through the democratic process are often framed as an attempt to "impose their values on others." Conversely, the efforts of secular social workers to, for example, ban smoking, restrict firearms, prohibit spanking, regulate corporations, prohibit school choice, and force Catholic hospitals to provide abortions is labeled more positively. Secular efforts to promote their understanding of the general welfare tend to be depicted as social justice, as a legitimate action, while similar efforts by evangelical Christians are depicted as "imposing their values on others," as an illegitimate action.

This selective framing serves a number of functions. It justifies existing inequalities and provides a moral rationale for further discrimination. If evangelical Christians desire to "impose their values" on clients, individuals, and the nation, then it is appropriate and even morally necessary to discriminate against such an uncivil, dangerous population. This framing also functions to implicitly convey the message that it is illegitimate for evangelical Christians to exercise their right to engage in the legislative process.

Many other rationalizations have been developed to justify the exclusion of evangelical Christians and other minority groups (Wambach & Van Soest, 1997). As students of oppression are aware, however, justifications of unequal treatment must be treated with caution (Diller, 2004; Sue & Sue,

1999). All too often, they function to solidify the power of dominant groups while further silencing minority populations. Indeed, such rationalizations serve to confirm the existence of the oppression they seek to discount.

NO

Gary R. Anderson

To assert that evangelical Christians in social work are discriminated against is to declare that our profession is unethical, illogical, and irrational. To entertain such a charge, first, it is helpful to be more precise about what is meant by "evangelical Christians," by "social work," and by "discrimination."

There are over 2 billion people worldwide who identify with the Christian religion. In the United States, approximately 79 percent of the population identifies with a Christian faith. A subset, evangelical Christians, describes an approach to faith attributed to between 28 percent (white Protestants only) and 43 percent of the population of the United States. There are multiple definitions of "evangelical Christian." Typically, evangelicals are defined by their beliefs: (1) a belief in the literal word of the Bible as the basis for faith and behavior; (2) a belief in Jesus as their personal Lord and Savior; and (c) a belief in the importance of evangelizing other persons. A 2005 Gallop report concluded "there is no hard-and-fast definition of who 'evangelicals' are in America today. For practical purposes, one approach is to define evangelicals as white, non-Catholic Christians who agree that the labels "evangelical" or "born again" describe them. (Newport & Carroll, 2005). Others would dispute failing to include African American Protestants and Latino Protestants in this definition, and some studies have also noted that a number of Roman Catholics identify as "evangelicals." (Newport & Carroll, 2005).

Attentiveness to evangelical Christians has grown in recent years as evangelicals have been identified as a significant social and political force in the United States. Sometimes equated with the Religious Right, the American Religious Identification Survey (Kosmin, Mayer, & Keysar, n.d.) noted that evangelical Christians were much more likely than members of other religious groups to identify as Republicans and to consider themselves to be "conservative." However, a number of types of evangelicals are being identified, including a proportion who tend to vote Democratic (particularly if one includes African American evangelicals), so generalizations about political stance and social views may be more difficult to support (Saroyan, 2006).

The statement that social work discriminates against evangelical Christians might be broadened to include discrimination against persons of faith, regardless of religious affiliation or belief system. However, there may be some features associated with this particular faith expression and religious tradition that either heighten or particularly identify this group as a potential object of discrimination, such as valuing evangelism, expressing strong personal faith, and frequently being connected to political stands against abortion and gay marriage. The evangelical Christians who are allegedly discriminated against could be students in schools of social work, social-work professionals, or persons with an evangelical faith who are served by social workers. Before addressing these features or vulnerabilities, it would be helpful to determine who these "social workers" are and define "discrimination."

Evangelical Christians are discriminated against by a range of persons who have a social-work education and are employed in social-work settings. Consequently, the persons with a social-work education could be professors at schools of social work and others who provide the formal education that leads to a degree in social work. The social workers could also be employers and supervisors in social-service agencies. And the social workers who persecute evangelical Christians could be leaders of, and persons with, some degree of authority in social-work professional organizations.

Discrimination is a particularly strong word. Discrimination is defined as "actions carried out by dominant groups that have a differential and harmful impact on members of subordinate groups." (Robbins, Chatterjee, & Canda, 1998) For example, discrimination could be evidenced as a range of adverse employment or educational actions: treating a student or client in a differential and negative manner; refusing to hire someone; being overly critical or condemning; not being considered for or denied certain benefits; possessing a greater likelihood of being fired; being denied admission to a school or program; being denied faculty positions or other employment, being denied tenure and promotion or other professional benefits, including a job position. Discrimination is dynamically linked with prejudice and personal bigotry, and prejudice and discrimination are viewed as mutually reinforcing.

So, are evangelical Christians treated negatively and harmed by social-work educators, social-work agency personnel, and social-work professional leaders? No, they are not. Discriminating against evangelical Christian social workers would be unethical. It violates the profession's Code of Ethics. The social-change efforts of social workers are to be directed toward alleviating discrimination and other forms of injustice. National Association of Social Workers ([NASW], 1999). In fact, the NASW *Code of Ethics* affirms: "Social workers should not practice, condone, facilitate, or collaborate with any form of discrimination on the basis of . . . religion" (pp. 22, 23). Discrimination violates a broader standard of respect for human rights, social justice, and respect for the dignity and worth of the person.

Discriminating against evangelical Christian clients or social workers would be illogical. It does not fit with the profession's emphasis on cultural competency. It is contrary to the profession's value of acceptance. It does not match the profession's historic ties to religion in general, and to Christianity in particular, in the United States. One would expect that if there were widespread discrimination against evangelical Christians, one would not find evangelical Christians in leadership roles in agencies, educational settings, or in professional leadership roles—this is not the case. One would not expect to find evangelical Christian institutions as members of the Council on Social Work Education—yet there are schools of social work that identify as evangelical institutions. Faith-based agencies and religious-affiliated agencies are integral to the network of organizations responding to human need in the United States.

Discriminating against evangelical Christians would be irrational. Why do people choose social work as a profession? For many, the motivation for social work is integral to their personal values and belief systems that include an ethic of caring and helping, a desire to serve others, and a commitment to justice, to assist and empower the poor and vulnerable, and to create a more fair and caring society. Such a profession will naturally draw on persons with spiritual values and strong and serious religious identities who value justice and service over monetary gain. From its earliest days, social work has been motivated, informed, and supported by a range of faith communities. Remove Christian students from schools of social work and see how many students, particularly students of color, remain. A social-work profession that discriminates against evangelical Christians is a profession engaged in activities that are contrary to its own self-interest.

If there is no basis for claiming widespread discrimination, why is there a sense that evangelical Christians in social work experience discrimination? There may an occasional social-work academic or administrator who attributes some past or present harm to an evangelical Christian person or organization, or whose ignorance or inexperience with religion leads to misunderstanding and to treating a Christian student or employee in a discriminatory manner. However, there may be a number of other reasons for this perceived discrimination and perceived ill treatment: The Christian student or employee may mislabel others' actions as discriminatory or persecutory: Or he may misattribute a negative action or decision to his Christian identity. Or he may experience negative reactions if religious views are a proxy for political views, as such are interpreted as contrary to social-work views.

An evangelical social worker whose beliefs and views are challenged may mislabel this challenge as discrimination. Evangelical Christians may have some of their views challenged—in fact, all students in a school of social work should experience a lively environment that encourages critical and independent thinking. The process of stepping back and observing and critiquing one's beliefs and values may feel threatening to people who have been surrounded by like-minded people, who view questioning as doubting one's faith, who believe that their viewpoint is the truth and that truth is absolute, and who think that a critical examination of long and strongly held beliefs is a slippery slope that leads to backsliding, compromise, or loss of faith. The process of "owning one's faith" and having it integrated and deepened in one's life almost requires this challenge and critical thinking. One might experience debate, disagreement, and criticism as uncomfortable, and this critique may be mislabeled as discrimination.

Discrimination may be based on factors other than faith, yet the motive is misattributed to faith. For example, a Christian student has not been admitted to a certain graduate social-work program. The student surmises that her Christian ties were most likely known to the graduate-admissions committee, either because the applicant attended a religiously affiliated college, acknowledged Christian activities and viewpoints in the application's personal statement, worked in a faith-based setting, or used references who identified the applicant's Christian affiliation directly or indirectly. The student concludes that the lack of acceptance is due to hostility toward her Christian identity by one or more members of the admissions committee members.

Why might a Christian student not be accepted to graduate school? The student might not be accepted for all of the reasons that other people are not accepted—comparatively lower grades, lack of human-service experience, lukewarm or ineffective references, or a large and competitive applicant pool. There may also be some reasons that do not constitute discrimination but are related to the student's religious affiliation: (1) The applicant may be unable to clearly communicate with persons outside of his religious culture, perhaps as evidenced by a personal statement saturated with religious metaphors, scripture verses, jargon, and frequent references to God's calling in one's life. Some applicants appear to have less practice in communicating with persons different than themselves, due either to living in a homogeneous environment or separating themselves from the world. (2) The applicant may have limited experience—expecting that zeal, deep conviction, or calling will compensate for inexperience—or experience in settings that are unfamiliar to an admissions committee; teaching Sunday school, working with a church youth group, short-term missions trips, or leadership in a campus Christian organization may not present experiences that are familiar to an admissions-committee member. (3) The applicant's worldview, which is informed by his faith, may be expressed in terms of saving souls, combating sin, calling individuals to personal responsibility, holy living, and fighting personal vice. The absence of interest and concern for social justice and at least a beginning appreciation for the complexity of forces that shape human behavior may be troubling to an admissions committee (Gauer, 2005). This might include a concern about what appears to be an applicant's judgmental attitude. (4) Similarly, the applicant may use unintentionally offensive language in the personal statement. (5) The applicant may be overly disclosing about various aspects of personal life—a conversion experience, turning to God, aspects of a life of sin now dedicated to service, and so forth. Any applicant with a lack of exposure to diverse people and perspectives, who is unable to communicate views without using jargon, or is overconfident in the rightness of her own views and lacking a commitment to social justice, may have difficulty competing in a highly selective graduate program.

Christian students who are not admitted to graduate school may attribute this to being persecuted as a Christian but, more accurately, it may be attributable to the usual reasons someone is not accepted or to particular concerns that their self-presentation triggered. Similarly, an employer may be concerned about an employee's tendency to judge clients and respond harshly to their personal vices, to invite them to church, to suggest praying and Bible reading to clients and other employees, to use work time for Bible study, to decorate the office space with religious symbols and messages, and to isolate himself from other employees.

Social-work educators or administrators may not have direct prejudice toward Christianity; however, they may be inclined to view conservative political views with disfavor. Evangelical Christians are not persecuted because they are Christians but because they are conservative Republicans. A politically liberal Christian is welcome, but this is another debate.

At the present time in the United States, the equation of evangelical Protestantism with the base of the conservative Republican party may lead to the overgeneralization that Christians support a conservative social and political agenda. A dislike for the Religious Right and its political viewpoints may result in questions and concerns about conservative Christians in social work. Particularly among social workers who are unaware of the diversity within American Protestantism and the rising political debates within evangelicalism, it may be too easy to equate Christians with a closed-minded and militant antiscience, antigay, antichoice political posture. Christian students or employees who believe that they are discriminated against due to their faith may in fact be discriminated against due to their actual or perceived political views, not their religious or spiritual identification.

CONCLUSION

This article disputes the assertion that evangelical Christians are discriminated against in social work. While not denying that there may be an occasional social worker who may discriminate against a Christian social worker, the alleged persecution of Christians is more likely understood as mislabeling disagreements and challenges, miscommunication, and the failure to appreciate how one communicates with person's who do not share the same faith or, more accurately, a dislike of one's politics rather than one's religion. The actual assertion that someone is discriminated against because of his Christianity may be viewed by others as an insensitive statement and a potential affront. It is somewhat offensive to claim "minority status" or talk about "coming out as a Christian" when one is in the American societal majority, with the legitimacy and privileges that accompany that majority status.

Although they may be challenged, and in some cases criticized, Christians do not experience a range of discriminations due to their status as Christians.

More likely, an evangelical student, employee, or client will find that issues and knowledge about religion and spirituality are not acknowledged or explored in social work. Content on religion and spirituality is missing from the classroom, from textbooks, from research projects, from classroom discussion, from the workplace, and from the service-delivery system—or at best only briefly mentioned. This will be disconcerting for Christian students who understand what a powerful force religion is in their own lives, in the lives and communities of many others, and in the face of demographic descriptions of the American population. This neglect of religion and spirituality indicates that a faculty member, fellow students, or an employer does not dare to touch this topic. The social-work profession's increasing attentiveness to spirituality in particular, but also to religion attempts to address this vacuum, but the profession's ability to discuss religion and spirituality and to incorporate this knowledge into professional practice continues to be a challenge. However, this does not automatically mean that the profession is hostile or discriminatory toward Christian clients, students, and employees.

Will there be challenges for evangelical Christians in social work? Yes; there are differences in worldview, bases for authority and truth, secularism versus religious faith, and flash points in relation to homosexuality, abortion, and choice (Ressler, 2002). But areas of disagreement, debate, and difference do not equate with discrimination. Are evangelical faith and social work incompatible? Alan Keith Lucas, a professor at the University of North Carolina School of Social Work, affirms the compatibility of religious faith and professional social work, which he attributes to the orderliness of God's creation and the shared search for knowledge. He states, "professional social work practice can also illuminate the understanding of our relationship to God and the world" (Hugen, 2004, pp. 17–18). There is a challenge for the evangelical Christian to integrate religion with social work; and for social work to learn about evangelical religion. Both affirm the values of justice, mercy, and humility.

REFERENCES

Anderson, J., & Carter, R. W. (2003). *Diversity perspectives for social work practice.* Boston: Allyn & Bacon.

Appleby, G. A., Colon, E., & Hamilton, J. (2001). *Diversity, oppression, and social functioning.* Boston: Allyn & Bacon.

Berger, P. L. (1986). *The capitalist revolution.* New York: Basic Books.

Bilgrave, D. P., & Deluty, R. H. (1998). Religious beliefs and the therapeutic orientations of clinical and counseling psychologists. *Journal for the Scientific Study of Religion, 37*(2), 329–349.

Bolce, L., & De Maio, G. (1999). Religious outlook, culture war politics, and antipathy toward Christian fundamentalists. *Public Opinion Quarterly, 63*(1), 29–61.

Cnaan, R. A., Wineburg, R. J., & Boddie, S. C. (1999). *The newer deal: Social work and religion in partnership.* New York: Columbia University Press.

Davis, N. J., & Robinson, R. V. (1997). A war for America's soul? The American religious landscape. In R. H. Williams (Ed.), *Cultural wars in American politics* (pp. 39–61). New York: Aldine De Gruyter.

Diller, J. V. (2004). *Cultural diversity* (2nd ed.). Belmont, CA: Thomson Brooks/Cole.

Edelman, M. (1990). *Constructing the political spectacle.* Chicago: University of Chicago Press.

Farley, J. E. (2005). *Majority-minority relations* (5th ed.). Upper Saddle River, NJ: Prentice-Hall.

French, D. A. (2002). *Religious liberty on campus.* Philadelphia: Foundation for Individual Rights in Education.

Gallup, G. J., & Lindsay, D. M. (1999). *Surveying the religious landscape.* Harrisburg, PA: Morehouse.

Gartner, J. D. (1986). Antireligious prejudice in admissions to doctoral programs in clinical psychology. *Professional Psychology: Research and Practice, 17*(5), 473–475.

Gauer, L. (2005, Winter). A Christian perspective on poverty and social justice: Sin is more than just flawed character. *Social Work and Christianity, 32*(4), pp. 354–365.

Gilligan, C. (1993). *In a different voice: Psychological theory and women's development.* Cambridge, MA: Harvard University Press.

Glenn, N. (1997). *Closed hearts, closed minds: The textbook story of marriage.* New York: Institute for American Values.

Gouldner, A. W. (1979). *The future of intellectuals and the rise of the new class.* New York: Seabury Press.

Green, J. C., Guth, J. L., Smidt, C. E., & Kellstedt, L. A. (1996). *Religion and the culture wars.* New York: Rowman & Littlefield.

Hamilton, T., & Sharma, S. (1997). The violence and oppression of power relations. *Peace Review, 9*(4), 555–561.

Hartman, A. (1993). Out of the closet: Revolution and backlash. *Social Work, 38*(3), 245–246, 360.

Haynes, D. T., & White, B. W. (1999). Will the "real" social work please stand up? A call to stand for professional unity. *Social Work, 44*(4), 385–391.

Healey, J. F. (2004). *Diversity and society.* Thousand Oaks, CA: Pine Forge Press.

Hodge, D. R. (2002a). Does social work oppress Evangelical Christians? A new class analysis of society and social work. *Social Work, 47*(4), 401–414.

Hodge, D. R. (2002b). Equally devout, but do they speak the same language? Comparing the religious beliefs and practices of social workers and the general public. *Families in Society, 83*(5/6), 573–584.

Hodge, D. R. (2003a). Differences in worldview between social workers and people of faith. *Families in Society, 84*(2), 285–295.

Hodge, D. R. (2003b). Value differences between social workers and members of the working and middle classes: A nationally representative study based upon New Class theory. *Social Work, 48*(1), 107–119.

Hodge, D. R. (2004). *Religious discrimination and ethical compliance: Exploring steps to create a more inclusive profession that better conforms to its ethical mandates.* Paper presented at the 54th annual program meeting of the North American Association of Christians in Social Work. Washington, DC.

Hodge, D. R. (2005). Perceptions of compliance with the profession's ethical standards that address religion: A national study. *Journal of Social Work Education, 41*(2), 279–295.

Hodge, D. R., Baughman, L. M., & Cummings, J. A. (in press). Moving toward spiritual competency: Deconstructing religious stereotypes and spiritual prejudices in social work literature. *Journal of Social Service Research.*

Hugen, B. (2004, Spring). The geography of faith: Mapping the features of faith-based practice. *Social Work and Christianity 31*(1), pp. 3–24.

Hunter, J. D. (1991). *Culture Wars.* New York: Basic Books.

Hunter, J., & Schaecher, R. (1995). Gay and lesbian adolescents. In R. L. Edwards (Ed.), *Encyclopedia of social work* (19, Vol. 2, pp. 1055–1063). Washington, DC: NASW Press.

Kerr, P. A. (2003). The framing of fundamentalist Christians: Network television news, 1980–2000. *Journal of Media and Religion, 2*(4), 203–235.

Kirst-Ashman, K. K., & Hull, G. H. (2006). *Understanding generalist practice* (4th ed.). Belmont, CA: Thomson Brooks/Cole.

Klein, D. B., & Stern, C. (in press). Narrow-tent Democrats and fringe others: The policy views of social science professors. *Critical Review.*

Koenig, H. G., McCullough, M. E., & Larson, D. B. (2001). *Handbook of religion and health.* New York: Oxford University Press.

Kosmin, B. A., Mayer, E., & Keysar, A. (n.d.). *American religious identification survey.* Retrieved May 23, 2006, from www.gc.cuny.edu/faculty/research_briefs/aris/aris_index.htm.

Larson, D., Milano, G. M., & Lu, F. (1998). Religion and mental health: The need for cultural sensitivity and synthesis. In S. O. Okpaku (Ed.), *Clinical methods in transcultural psychiatry* (pp. 191–210). Washington, DC: American Psychiatric Association.

Lehr, E., & Spilka, B. (1989). Religion in the introductory psychology textbook: A comparison of three decades. *Journal for the Scientific Study of Religion, 28*(3), 366–371.

Lum, D. (2003). *Culturally competent practice* (2nd ed.). Belmont, CA: Thomson Brooks/Cole.

McAdams, J. (1987). Testing the theory of the new class. *The Sociological Quarterly, 28*(1), 23–49.

McMahon, A., & Allen-Meares, P. (1992). Is social work racist? A content analysis of recent literature. *Social Work, 37*(6), 533–539.

National Association of Social Workers. (1999). *Code of ethics.* Washington DC: Author.

Netting, F. E., Kettner, P. M., & McMurtry, S. L. (2004). *Social work macro practice* (3d ed.). Boston: Pearson.

Neumann, J. K., Harvill, L. M., & Callahan, M. (1995). Impact of humanistic, liberal Christian, and Evangelical Christian values on the self-reported opinions of radiologists and psychiatrists. *Journal of Psychology and Theology, 23*(3), 198–207.

Neumann, J. K., & Leppien, F. V. (1997a). Impact of religious values and medical specialty on professional in-service decisions. *Journal of Psychology and Theology, 25*(4), 437–448.

Neumann, J. K., & Leppien, F. V. (1997b). Influence of physicians' religious values on inservice training decisions. *Journal of Psychology and Theology, 25*(4), 427–436.

Neumann, J. K., Thompson, W., & Woolley, T. W. (1991). Christianity versus Humanism: The influence of values on the nonclinical professional decisions of Veterans Administration psychologists. *Journal of Psychology and Theology, 19*(2), 166–177.

Neumann, J. K., Thompson, W., & Woolley, T. W. (1992). Evangelical vs. liberal Christianity: The influence of values on the nonclinical professional decisions of social workers. *Journal of Psychology and Christianity, 11*(1), 57–67.

Newman, B. S., Dannenfeiser, P. L., & Benishek, L. (2002, Spring/Summer). Assessing beginning social work and counseling students' acceptance of lesbians and gay men. *Journal of Social Work Education, 38*(2), 273–288.

Newport, F. & Carroll, J. (2005). Callup on Evangelicals. Retrieved December 2, 2005, from Princeton News Service.

Oppewal, D. (1985). *Religion in American textbooks: A review of the literature.* Washington, DC: National Institute of Education.

Redding, R. E. (2001). Sociopolitical diversity in psychology. *American Psychologist, 56*(3), 205–215.

Ressler, L. E. (1998). When social work and Christianity conflict. In L. Scales & B. Hugen (Ed.), *Christianity and social work* (pp. 165–186). Botsford, CT: North American Association of Christians in Social Work Press.

Ressler, L. (2002). When social work and Christianity conflict. In L. Scales & B. Hugen (Eds.), *Christianity and social work.* Botsford, CT: North American Association of Christians in Social Work Press.

Ressler, L. E., & Hodge, D. R. (2003). Silenced voices: Social work and the oppression of conservative narratives. *Social Thought, 22*(1), 125–142.

Ressler, L. E., & Hodge, D. R. (2005). Religious discrimination in social work: Preliminary evidence. *Journal of Religion and Spirituality in Social Work, 24*(4), 55–74.

Richards, P. S., & Bergin, A. E. (Eds.). (2000). *Handbook of psychotherapy and religious diversity.* Washington, DC: American Psychological Association.

Richards, P. S., & Bergin, A. E. (2005). *A spiritual strategy for counseling and psychotherapy* (2nd ed.). Washington, DC: American Psychological Association.

Richards, P. S., & Davison, M. L. (1992). Religious bias in moral development research: A psychometric investigation. *Journal for the Scientific Study of Religion, 31*(4), 467–485.

Robbins, S., Chatterjee, P., and Canda, E. (1998). *Contemporary human behavior theory.* Boston: Allyn & Bacon.

Rothman, S., Lichter, S. R., & Nevitte, N. (2005a). Fundamentals and fundamentalists: A reply to Ames et al. *The Forum, 3*(2), Article 8.

Rothman, S., Lichter, S. R., & Nevitte, N. (2005b). Politics and the professional advancement among college faculty. *The Forum, 3*(1), 1–16.

Soroyan, S. (2006, April 16). Christianity, the brand. *The New York Times,* Section 6, p. 46.

Scales, L., & Hugen, B. (Ed.), (1998). *Christianity and social work.* Botsford, CT: North American Association of Christians in Social Work Press.

Sewall, G. T. (1995). *Religion in the classroom: What the textbooks tell us.* New York: American Textbook Council.

Sheridan, M. J., Wilmer, C. M., & Atcheson, L. (1994). Inclusion of content on religion and spirituality in the social work curriculum: A study of faculty views. *Journal of Social Work Education, 30*(3), 363–376.

Skill, T., & Robinson, J. D. (1994). The image of Christian leaders in fictional television programs. *Sociology of Religion, 55*(1), 75–84.

Smith, C. (1998). *American evangelicalism.* Chicago: University of Chicago Press.

Smith, C. (2000). *Christian America?* Berkeley, CA: University of California Press.

Smith, C. (2003). *The secular revolution.* Berkeley, CA: University of California Press.

Smith, C., & Faris, R. (2005). Socioeconomic inequality in the American religious system: An update and assessment. *Journal for the Scientific Study of Religion, 44*(1), 95–104.

Smith, J. Z. (1996). Evangelicals. In *The Harpercollins dictionary of religion* American Academy of Religion (Ed.), (pp. 349–351). San Francisco: HarperCollins.

Sue, D. W., & Sue, D. (1999). *Counseling the culturally different* (3rd ed.). New York: John Wiley & Sons.

Talbot, M. (2000, February 27). A mighty fortress. *The New York Times Magazine, 34–41,* 66–68, 84–85.

Tompkins, C. J., Larkin, H., & Rosen, A. L. (2006). An analysis of social work textbooks for aging content: How well do social work foundation texts prepare students for our aging society? *Journal of Social Work Education, 42*(1), 3–23.

Tower, K. (2000). In our own image: Shaping attitudes about social work through television production. *Journal of Social Work Education, 36*(3), 575–585.

Tsang, A. K. T. (2001). Representation of ethnic identity in North American social work literature: A dossier of the Chinese people. *Social Work, 46*(3), 229–243.

Tully, C. T., & Greene, R. (1995). Cultural diversity comes of age: A study of coverage, 1970–1991. *Arete, 19*(1), 37–45.

United Nations. (1948/1998). Universal declaration of human rights. Retrieved February 27, 2006, from www.un.org/Overview/rights.html.

Vitz, P. C. (1985). *Religion and traditional values in public school textbooks: An empirical study.* Washington, DC: National Institute of Education.

Vitz, P. C. (1998). *The course of true love: Marriage in high school textbooks.* New York: Institute for American Values.

Wambach, K. G., & Van Soest, D. (1997). Oppression. In R. L. Edwards (Ed.), *Encyclopedia of social work* (19th ed.), (pp. 243–252). Washington, DC: North American Association of Social Workers Press.

Woodberry, R. D., & Smith, C. S. (1998). Fundamentalism et al.: Conservative Protestants in America. *Annual Review of Sociology, 24,* 25–56.

Zastrow, C. (2000). *Introduction to social work and social welfare* (7th ed.). Belmont, CA: Wadsworth.

SHOULD ABORTION RIGHTS BE AN ACCEPTED SOCIAL-WORK VALUE?

Editor's Note:
Abortion is one of the most controversial issues of our time, with strong opinions being expressed on both sides. Although efforts have been made to prohibit abortion through judicial and legislative action, the constitutional right to have an abortion remains in force. However, abortion opponents have succeeded in curtailing abortion programs and guidelines on several fronts. Supporters of these measures argue that abortion is an evil that should not be condoned by the state. As an avowedly liberal profession, it has been assumed almost a priori that the vast majority of social workers unequivocally support the right of a woman to choose abortion. However, there are dissenting elements within the profession.

The late John T. (Terry) Pardeck was a professor of social work at Southwest Missouri State University and editor of the *Journal of Social Work in Disability and Rehabilitation*. He authored *Social Work After the Americans with Disabilities Act* (Auburn House, 1998) and published widely on disabilities and related topics. Terry is missed by all who knew him.

Roland Meinert has taught in and administered social-work education programs at all levels at Michigan State University, St. Louis University, and the University of Missouri-Columbia. He was one of the founders of the Inter University Consortium for International Social Development, and for six years was coeditor of the journal *Social Development Issues.*

YES

John T. Pardeck

The field of social work is value based. These values guide the behavior of practitioners at the policy and practice levels. Given the importance of values to the profession, it is imperative for practitioners to conduct critical analysis of important social issues from a values perspective. This paper examines one important social issue, abortion, from such a perspective. Specifically, I look at the issue of abortion from religious, historic, and legal perspectives. Obviously, each of these perspectives offers a different slant on the topic of abortion, offering the conclusion that the *Roe v. Wade* ruling in 1973 concerning a woman's right to an abortion makes perfect sense in terms of the religious, historic, and legal traditions surrounding this important issue. Given this conclusion, social workers should support a woman's legal right to an abortion.

RELIGIOUS PERSPECTIVE ON ABORTION

Christian ethics and teachings have varied on the topic of abortion. If, however, one uses Christian ethics and teachings as a justification for banning a woman's right to an abortion, one is probably using a romanticized and distorted view of Christianity. The historical Christian position on abortion, not the romanticized view, suggests that the human fetus was not particularly viewed as having intrinsic worth, nor were children and women in general. A critical interpretation of historical Christianity suggests that it was more concerned with the control of sexuality, the social order, and the preservation of male prerogatives; and not necessarily morality issues related to abortion (Harrison, 1983). Thus, to use Christian teachings as a focal point for claiming abortion is immoral is less than candid concerning the evolution of Christian teachings on this issue.

Palley (1991) notes that the western European welfare states view the right to abortion as a legitimate public concern. Abortion as a right in the European welfare states is as important as the right to a family allowance, day care, education, and health care. What is notable about the evolution of abortion rights in western Europe and the United States is that both cultures have grounding in Christian ethics and teachings. Given this tradition, one can only speculate on why western Europe versus the United States gave women the right to an abortion much earlier. Palley (1991) also argues that other patriarchal religions such as Judaism, Islam, and Confucianism have antiabortion traditions. However, these religions have had variable influence on government policy in various parts of the world. For example, in an Islamic theocracy, abortion is obviously not viewed as a legitimate alternative for women, even though women continue to have abortions under this kind of rule. Mainland China, however, which is influenced by Confucianism and other Eastern religious traditions, uses abortion as a vital mechanism to control population growth (Childbirth by Choice Trust, 1995).

If one conducts an in-depth analysis of Christian teachings, the opposition to abortion is a relatively recent development. Saint Augustine, like

Aristotle, believed that the fetus did not become a live soul until 40 days after conception for boys and 80 days for girls. The medieval church was not necessarily opposed to abortion. A tolerant approach to abortion in the Roman Catholic Church ended relatively recently, approximately in the mid-19th century. Presently, within the United States, the Roman Catholic Church, as well as a number of Protestant churches, have actively attempted to influence social welfare policy dealing with abortion (Childbirth by Choice Trust, 1995).

Other major religions in the United States have various positions on abortion. For example, the Anglican Church allows abortion when a woman's physical or mental health is endangered. Lutherans are divided on abortion and typically view it as an option in rare circumstances. Presbyterians generally oppose abortion. The Baptist Church sees abortion as an option when a woman's life is in danger. Even though historic Christianity often tolerated abortion, many modern-day Christian groups, including Roman Catholics and Protestants, view abortion as unacceptable or as an option only in certain circumstances (Childbirth by Choice Trust, 1995).

The paradox, however, is that women in virtually every society, regardless of the religious practices found in these societies, use abortion as a way of dealing with unwanted pregnancies. In primitive societies, even before recorded history, women induced abortion with herbs, sharp sticks or simply by exerting heavy pressure on the abdomen causing abortion to occur (Childbirth by Choice Trust, 1995). Regardless of whether a society outlaws abortion, women will continue to have abortions as a means to deal with unwanted pregnancies. What this means is that a right to an abortion must be made available to women to help ensure the safety of this procedure.

HISTORICAL PERSPECTIVE ON ABORTION

From the 12th century to the 19th century, abortion before quickening (movement of the fetus) was not punished under English common law. Since most abortions took place prior to quickening, abortion was not particularly seen as a moral issue. When abortion was performed after quickening, it was usually treated as a misdemeanor (Childbirth by Choice Trust, 1995).

In the early 19th century, abortions performed after quickening under English common law became a serious offense; lesser penalties continued to occur prior to quickening. Legislation in the United States regulating abortion also began to emerge in the early 19th century. Much of this legislation was more concerned with protecting the health of the mother and not necessarily the rights of the fetus. It is suggested that physicians in the 19th century within the United States became heavily involved in abortion legislation, not so much to protect the mother or fetus, but rather to consolidate their professional status and power (Childbirth by Choice Trust, 1995). The criminalization of abortion in the United States is largely a 20th-century phenomenon. Abortion in the 20th century was highly restrictive through the 1960s. In the 1960s, a tremendous amount of cultural change occurred in the United States and western Europe, including the belief that women have a right to control their fertility. During the 20th century, virtually every European country legalized abortion. For example, The Netherlands legalized abortion in 1981, even though the procedure was freely available before that date. Norway did likewise in 1979. Sweden enacted its initial abortion legislation in 1938. The only countries in western Europe that have not legalized abortion in some form are the Irish Republic, Northern Ireland, and Malta. In Ireland, even with its strict antiabortion laws in place, an estimated 4,000 Irish women a year go to Britain to have a legal abortion (Childbirth by Choice Trust, 1995).

LEGAL PERSPECTIVE ON ABORTION

Abortion in the United States was not seen necessarily as a moral issue in the 19th century but arose in the 20th-century. Abortion through most of the first half of the 20th century in the United States was highly restricted. During this time period, illegal abortions were a serious health problem; many women were harmed or died because of the illegal, unsafe abortion industry.

The most important legal ruling from the United States Supreme Court was *Roe v. Wade* in 1973. Under this ruling, states cannot ban abortion during the first trimester of pregnancy. One of the important considerations by the Court was when women obtained abortions illegally under dubious medical conditions, they sometimes died or were injured. The Court thus viewed the legalization of abortion as partly a medical issue aimed at protecting women's health. The Court also recognized that it is impossible to prevent women from using abortion as a means to ending pregnancy, even when the procedure is illegal. Even with the *Roe v. Wade* ruling favoring a woman's right to an abortion, many Americans continue to be opposed to abortion.

Since *Roe v. Wade*, a number of government regulations and court rulings have restricted access to abortion. In 1988, the United States Department of Health and Human Services forbade health-care providers under Title X of the Public Health Service Act to give clients information on abortion. The Supreme Court in 1991 upheld this so-called gag rule. The result of this ruling is that many low-income women have less access to information about abortion. In *Webster v. Reproduction Health Services* (1989), the United States Supreme Court upheld a Missouri law that prohibited abortion from being performed in any publicly financed facility, even if the client is willing to pay for the procedure. This is a clear example of how one's social class determines access to abortion services.

Many states have attempted to pass other restrictive abortion laws in the 1980s and 1990s. Restrictive abortion legislation has been enacted in Pennsylvania, Utah, and Guam. The recent appointment of John Roberts and Samuel Alito to the United States Supreme Court is an example of how George W. Bush attempted to change the Court's position on abortion.

Another threat to a woman's right to an abortion has emerged with the bombing of abortion clinics and the harassing of clinic patients and staff. One might argue that the political process has even fueled these attacks on abortion clinics. For example, former president George Bush, proclaimed in 1991 that the federal judge in Wichita, Kansas, overstepped his authority when he issued a restraining order to keep antiabortionists from harassing patients and staff of abortion clinics. The history of abortion in the 20th century in the United States was one of legal turmoil; the 21st century is not turning out to be any different.

WHY ABORTION SHOULD BE LEGAL

Even though the final chapter of *Roe v. Wade* is far from written, there is little doubt that abortion must continue to be a constitutional right for women. This position is based on religious, historic, and legal traditions surrounding the issue of abortion.

The notion that Christian teachings have historically been opposed to abortion and that this is why this procedure should be illegal today is unwarranted. As mentioned earlier in this paper, there is limited evidence that historic Christianity perceived abortion as a major moral issue. The romanticized Christian teaching suggesting that abortion is morally wrong is largely a 20th-century invention.

The history of western Europe and the United States suggests that abortion was not a major moral issue until relatively recently. If anything, abortion historically has been viewed as a method of birth control often used by many women. Laws enacted in 19th-century United States were often aimed at protecting the health of women, not necessarily protecting the fetus. As mentioned earlier, women in many parts of western Europe now see abortion as a basic right that is similar to day care, family allowance, and other related welfare benefits.

Abortion did not become a constitutional right in the United States until 1973. Many women in western Europe enjoyed a right to an abortion even in the 1930s. The United States' legal system evolved much more slowly on the right to an abortion. As suggested earlier, a woman's right to an abortion in the United States may be in jeopardy with the recent election of President George W. Bush. Given the attacks on a woman's right to an abortion by a number of political and religious groups in the United States, *Roe v. Wade* may someday be overturned. However, regardless of this possibility, I believe that women must have a constitutional right to an abortion for the following reasons:

1. Many women now believe that they have a right to determine whether to bear children or not. If this right is taken away, they will turn to acts of civil disobedience; that is, they will seek out illegal abortions.
2. The political institution is not well suited to resolve deep social, moral, and religious conflict. Given this situation, the state does not have a right to regulate a woman's right to an abortion. Only women get pregnant, yet males have largely interpreted the morality surrounding abortion and have often been those who have mandated laws restricting abortion. The political institution's role in this extremely moral issue should be to allow a right to an abortion and to ensure that abortion procedures are safe.
3. Safe legal abortions have meant that women's health has been protected. If abortion is made illegal, women will continue to use this procedure for regulating family size. Illegal abortions are often unsafe and a threat to a woman's health.
4. If abortion is made illegal, the well-to-do will continue to have access to this procedure. For example, women wanting an abortion and who can afford one will simply go to another country where abortion is legal. Poor women will have to use illegal, unsafe abortion procedures because they cannot afford to travel abroad to countries where abortion is legal.

CONCLUSION

I wish to make it very clear to the reader that abortion is a less-than-desirable option for terminating a pregnancy. However, as history suggests, women will continue to limit family size through the use of abortion, regardless of whether the procedure is legal or not.

Abortion might be viewed through a perspective found in the child-welfare literature, The "Least Detrimental Available Alternative" Standard. This Standard means an alternative is used on behalf of a child that does the least amount of harm to the child. For example, the choice between providing a sexually active adolescent with birth control versus the prospect of the child's becoming pregnant appears to have a clear resolution under this Standard—providing access to birth control.

Since women will continue to have abortions whether they are legal or not means a choice must be made between the least-harmful alternative—a safe legal abortion or one that is illegal and unsafe. In a certain sense, *Roe v. Wade* follows this line of reasoning. Women will continue to have abortions regardless of their legality—legal abortion, even though a far from desirable option—helps to ensure that the procedure is safe.

Finally, abortion politics has far more to do with the regulation or outlawing of abortion. Opposing abortion is often a conservative ideology strategy used to gain political mileage on other causes. Antiabortionists often oppose welfare entitlements, endorse the death penalty, and support an array of other conservative issues. Abortion politics has prevented the passage of laws helping children, women, and the elderly. For example, during the 2000 Missouri legislative session, legislation was introduced to prevent the abuse of the elderly in nursing homes in Missouri. Amendments concerning abortion were added to the bill, taking the proposed legislation away from its intended purpose, protecting the elderly, to the arena of abortion politics. The unfortunate outcome of this political ploy was that the legislation was not enacted. Thus, abortion politics continues; the elderly in turn continue to be abused in residential settings.

Abortion politics continues to occur in state legislatures throughout the United States. This kind of politics must end.

NO

Roland Meinert

It is widely believed, though undocumented, that the majority of professional social workers support the position that women of any age have an unequivocal right to abortion on demand. Despite the absence of definitive data, there are several reasons to support this belief. First, the social-work journal literature about abortion and reproductive rights is decidedly skewed toward pro-choice positions. One searches unsuccessfully through mainline social-work journals in an attempt to identify articles that espouse a pro-life position. In fact, there is every reason to believe that social-work editorial boards are heavily biased toward a pro-choice orientation. Second, the curricula in schools of social work have a blatant and one-sided pro-choice orientation, and in only a few programs is pro-life material fairly presented. Pro-life perspectives are not only routinely ignored in the instructional process, but they are frequently denigrated. The avoidance of pro-life content in the curriculum is one measure of the lack of intellectual, philosophical, and ideological diversity in social-work education. Third, the official policy of the National Association of Social Workers (NASW), representing about 155,000 social workers, supports abortion at any stage of pregnancy for any reason the woman selects (NASW, 2000). Although there is clear evidence that social work is firmly entrenched in the pro-choice camp and endorses abortion on demand, when the issue is examined in detail there are compelling, logical, persuasive, and science-based arguments that a central value should be pro-life. Thus, the answer to whether abortion should be an accepted social work value in my view is no.

IDEOLOGICAL FOUNDATIONS OF PRO-CHOICE RHETORIC

Social work has always occupied a marginal status within the helping professions and readily accommodated itself to influences and pressures from the environment. Lacking a firm theoretical framework to guide practice, it borrowed from other disciplines. These frameworks varied and the mission of social work changed depending on which theory was prominent at the time. For example, during the decades when social work was a prisoner of psychoanalysis, that theory defined both the purpose of the profession and the behavior of practitioners. During the time of the sexual revolution, it is not surprising that it adopted a pro-choice orientation bolstered by support from academic, mass media, entertainment, political and professional elites, most of whom were pro-life unfriendly. When the debate about abortion began in social work, the voices of those in the pro-life corner were drowned out by a cacophony of postmodern, radical feminist, existential, and moral relativistic voices. In most instances the proponents of the pro-life position were treated judgmentally as extremist Christians, far-right conservatives, and ignorant zealots whose intelligence was questionable. Given this stereotype the arguments of pro-life advocates were delegitimated as not befitting reasonable consideration.

By the 1960s and 1970s most abortion advocates were inextricably entwined in the emerging philosophy about reproductive freedom and the separation of sex for pleasure from parenthood and family life. The proposition was accepted that if men could be sexually promiscuous and irresponsible the same right should be available for women. This sexual revolution became prominent as the larger culture, including social work, came under the dominance of postmodernism, radical feminism, social constructivism, and moral relativism. The postmodern influence in social work resulted in the diminution of value systems such as the Judeo-Christian ethic, which had been the main philosophical orientation on which social work had been founded. It was replaced by the belief that individual subjective choice should be the supreme guide for human decision making. In postmodernism, individuals were free to behave in whatever way they selected, since overarching religious, cultural, and institutional standards were deemed irrelevant. These earlier standards for behavior were called meta-narratives by postmodernists, who argued that their elimination would enable persons to maximize their human potential.

The social and cultural implications of postmodern and moral relativistic positions should not be ignored. For centuries, humans have made decisions based on references to values that were transpersonal and lodged in culture, religious traditions, and institutional norms. These values existed outside the individual and served as guideposts and standards that informed the decision-making process and the behavior that emanated from it. Now, for the first time, it was argued that these systems of values should not only be ignored but should be demolished in favor of rampant individualism and subjectivism. This logic provided support for the pro-choice advocates, who maintained that women had an absolute right to freedom and need not be influenced by context, cultural values, established systems of morality, or institutional guidelines.

The profession of social work wholly accepted the absolute-freedom principle that was being espoused and promoted. The official policy on family planning and reproductive choice of NASW had a profound influence on social-work education. The principle of right-to-choose became a pro-choice mantra and was thought to be consistent with the concept of client self-determination, which has always been a central value in the profession. However, the major founders of social work, who developed its intellectual foundation, did not view the right of self-determination as an unqualified absolute. Self-determination was to be employed in a responsible fashion that did not violate the rights of others and the traditionally accepted beliefs of right and wrong. The NASW policy on abortion does not address this qualification. It maintains client self-determination is an absolute in terms of the decision to abort or not, and opposes any limits or restrictions on that decision, even with adolescents. Parenthetically, it describes those who support limits on absolute freedom of choice as members of a radical right wing who are assaulting the rights of women for religious reasons.

The social-work education establishment and its curriculum policy reflect a postmodern and relativistic influence. This is best understood when the curriculum policy at the graduate (M.S.W.) level is examined. Graduate programs are expected to offer concentrations (specializations) around a specific range of practitioner roles or functions. Each program has the total and complete right and freedom to design concentrations and their constituent courses. The only requirement is that concentrations must be relevant to the mission of social work. But there is wide disparity within the profession about the nature of this mission. The result of this policy concerning curriculum is an interprogram range of course offerings without conceptual boundaries. Programs create concentrations based on roles, target populations, problem categories, regional social needs, fields of practice, and even individualized student preferences. This limitless and expansive curricular scope is characteristic of the entire profession of social work, which has historically struggled to find a definitive conceptual and practice niche. The relevance of this to the abortion question is that social-work students are taught that absolute freedom, absolute client self-determination, and absolute pro-choice are unqualified values. Thus, abortion is to be endorsed at any time, under any conditions, and without consideration of any factors that exist outside the subjective decision-making sphere of the individual. This social construction of reality denies the existence of objective truth, and knowledge becomes relative to person, time, and place. It also removes social work from the family of professions based on truth seeking according to accepted canons of science. The entire structure of this line of thinking has been supported by radical feminist ideology, which has had an inordinate influence over both social-work practice and education.

THE NEGATIVE CONSEQUENCES OF ABORTION

In addition to the absolute right to choose, pro-choice proponents believe that abortions are justified because they result in very positive outcomes for the women who have them. Frequently cited are a better quality of life, economic advancement, educational advancement, development of work skills, broadening of life experiences, a better life for future children, enhancement of emotional well-being, more satisfaction in interpersonal relationships, and others. It is further argued that these outcomes are particularly important and beneficial for minority women and those of lower socioeconomic status. Feminists and pro-choice advocates found it necessary to publicize these alleged positive outcomes in order to destigmatize abortion and make it readily available. Most of these outcomes are related to the feminist conviction that women will only experience true happiness and fulfillment in careers and work outside the home. Along with the promotion of this belief it also became necessary to derogate women who sought their fulfillment as wives and mothers within the context of the family. It is my contention that the wide array of positive outcomes listed by abortion rights advocates has not been convincingly documented and confirmed. In fact, there are sound reasons to conclude that the negative consequences of abortion far outweigh the alleged positive ones.

Mounting evidence from sound research studies reveals that women who have abortions, particularly adolescents, experience major problems that until recently have been unknown or purposefully denied. A list of some, but not all, of these problems include: an increased risk of breast, cervical, and uterine cancers; significantly higher suicide rates during the postabortion year; emotional problems including severe depression, grief, shame, anxiety, remorse, uncontrollable crying and resentment; eating disorders; unrealistic expectations for replacement children; substance abuse; and damaged interpersonal relationships. The professional social-work literature rarely reports on these postabortion negative consequences. This constitutes a conspiracy of silence because to openly examine them weakens the entire proabortion movement and the possibility that freedom of choice should not be an absolute right. Space limitations preclude discussion of all these highly negative sequella from induced abortion, but there are two that are major public health problems—an increased risk for breast cancer and suicide.

Several reports especially a meta-analysis by Brind (1996) of 33 studies worldwide have shown a markedly increased risk of breast cancer for women who have had induced abortions. The risk varies from 30 percent to 50 percent based on age at time of the abortion and other factors. The finding calls attention to the pernicious effect of the intrusion and assault on the normal biological functioning of pregnant women. Following pregnancy there is an enormous increase in the level of estrogen and other hormones during the first trimester. This natural development stimulates the growth of the breasts in preparation for the production of milk. Toward the end of the pregnancy other hormones are activated which kill off the cells not needed to produce milk. These transitional cells increase carcinogenic susceptibility. In induced abortion, the maturing effects of the later hormones is absent and the changing and transitional cells have a much greater chance of becoming cancerous.

A study of over 9,000 women in Finland over a period of 7 years (Gissler, 1997) disclosed that the risk of dying within a year after an abortion was several times higher than the risk of dying after miscarriage or childbirth. Conclusions from the same data set reported the astonishing finding that the risk of death from suicide within the year of an abortion was seven times higher than the risk of suicide within a year of childbirth (Gissler, 1996). Also, the risk of suicide following induced abortion was about twice that in the general population of women.

One of the persistent myths is that a professional dialogue takes place between a pregnant woman and her physician, which leads to an informed decision about whether to abort or not. Evidence is hard to find that this actually occurs. To the contrary, most women who receive an abortion have had no prior contact with the physician who performs it, and the negative consequences of the procedure are never discussed. It is also likely that the pregnant woman has ended up in an abortion clinic that is more of a for-profit business than a medical facility. As abortions decline the number of clinics also decreases and the competition for patients becomes quite intense. In many cities, abortion clinics advertise for business, and price undercutting between them is becoming common. Legitimate questions can be raised about the ethics and the competence of physicians who work in such non-professional and blatantly commercial settings. The principle of informed consent should lead to the medical abortionists' sharing the information about breast cancer, suicide, and other risks, but it is unlikely, since it would mean a loss of income.

It is not known how many abortions in the United States are performed merely because one of the parents did not like the sex of the unborn child. Nor is it known if any abortionist has ever refused to perform the procedure because the unborn child was of the wrong sex. In India, figures from the last census make it very clear that females are being regularly aborted at a far greater rate than males (Dugger, 2001). This practice became a trend beginning in the 1980s, when ultrasound technology became widely available. For example, in the prosperous farming state of Punjab, the birth ratio of girls to boys has plummeted to 793 girls per 1,000 boys. The pronounced gender imbalance has long been a feature of life in India, and its acceleration will cause long-term social consequences and injustices. Feminists show no concern about this trend and ignore the possibility of similar consequences in the United States. Furthermore, feminists who express a desire for equity and justice for women strangely do not abhor the fact that at least half of those aborted are female and will never experience an equal opportunity for life.

As repeat abortions become more frequent, and it is estimated that about 45 percent are second ones, it is difficult to rationalize the supposed benefits of the procedure. It is not likely that women who have had more than one abortion are lifting themselves out of poverty and the myriad other difficulties facing them. In fact, the higher likelihood is that there are many more negative social, health, and psychological consequences resulting from induced abortion than there are positive benefits.

CONCLUSION

Communication between the majority pro-choice and minority pro-life social work advocates has been contentious, and occurs within contexts wherein the former group has the most organizational and programmatic power and controls the reward structure. Discussions have been narrow in scope, because pro-choicers begin and end the encounters with the presupposition that absolute freedom of choice closes off any other considerations. The imbalance in favor of pro-choice proponents increases due to enhanced support from political, medical, and media elites, thus placing pro-life proponents at a disadvantage. Social-work educators who endorse pro-life positions are very vulnerable because career advancement is in jeopardy within programs where strident pro-choice positions dominate. Pro-lifers seek engagement in a broader scope of questions such as: when life begins; the nature of human life; abortion surgical procedures; the proliferation of new knowledge about the development of the child during pregnancy; and the negative social and health consequences for women who abort. If it is true that knowledge becomes obsolete at an increasingly rapid pace then the social-work profession has an ethical obligation to reopen and reframe the abortion debate.

This should begin by examining the development of the child in the womb from the time of conception. Revolutionary advances in medical technology have confirmed that the heart begins to beat at day 18 in the womb and by day 42 brainwaves are recorded, the skeletal structure is complete and reflexes are present. Ultrasound and other technologies provide clear images of a child present in the womb. Pro-choice advocates need to confront the reality that these images confirm the existence of a living, growing human being rather than calling them "biological material," "disposable tissue," "property," "gangrenous growths," "noxious waste products" and "parasites" in the woman's body. These words are powerful in dehumanizing the unborn child and rationalizing the absolute right to choose (Brennan, 1999). After all, it is more semantically logical and emotionally reassuring to abort a parasite than a child.

As abortion facilities become more commercialized, medical staff will be under pressure not to share findings about the negative consequences of the procedure. To do so might result in a loss of income for abortion providers driven by market conditions and profit motives. This may account for the fierce resistance against informed-consent procedures. In this regard, profit seems to win out over medical ethics. If the predictions about the higher incidence of breast cancer, suicide, and other social and health effects of abortion in later life for women bear out, legal actions can be expected in the future. Women will feel justified in filing lawsuits against abortion providers for reckless endangerment to their health and rightly seek monetary damages. Just as tobacco companies failed to warn about the injurious effects of smoking on health, women who have abortions and later develop breast cancer will sue because they were not warned about the increased risks.

Perhaps the most difficult issue that needs to surface in reframing the abortion question is philosophical and cultural in nature. The excessive premium placed on individual subjective choice within a climate of moral relativism completely ignores the necessity for society to seek the common good. A central tenet and value in social work is the functioning and interaction of the individual with society and the larger environment. In formulating policies and implementing practices, both the individual and the common good must be considered. In the pro-choice movement, the subjective interests of the individual are elevated and the common good is diminished. It is no longer a profession of "social" work but of "individual" work. To ask the question whether abortion should be an accepted social work "value" is a perversion of the very concept. By definition, values are conceptions of the desirable that transcend the person and are lodged in larger cultural institutions. Values then serve to inform individual behavior and decision making. Support by the social-work profession for abortion is an occupational preference, but it is not a value. If social work is to retain any degree of legitimacy in regard to the abortion issue it should support an open dialogue about the topic; reexamine the pro-choice bias of the curriculum in educational programs; become open to new scientific knowledge about the beginning of life; admit the moral and ethical issues pertaining to abortion; and encourage research about the negative social and health consequences for women who abort. Also, pro-life practitioners and educators must be allowed to present their views without fear of sullied reputations, retaliation, or threats to their professional careers.

REFERENCES

Brennan, W. (1999). Anti-fetal rhetoric: America's best-loved hate speech. *New Oxford Review, 65*(5), 18–21.

Brind, J. (1996). Induced abortion as an independent risk factor for breast cancer: A comprehensive review and meta-analysis. *Journal of Epidemiology & Community Health, 50,* 481–496.

Childbirth by Choice Trust. (1995). *Abortion in law, history & religion.* Toronto, Canada: Author.

Dugger, C. (2001, April 22). Abortion in India is tipping scales sharply against girls. *The New York Times,* International Section, pp. 10–11.

Gissler, M. (1997). Pregnancy associated deaths in Finland—definition problems and benefits of record linkage. *Acta Obsetricia et Gynecologica Scandinavica, 76,* 651–657.

Gissler, M., Hemminki, E., & Lonnqvist, J. (1996). Suicides after pregnancy in Finland: 1987–94 register linkage study. *British Medical Journal, 313,* 1431–1440.

Harrison, B. W. (1983). *Our right to choose: Toward a new ethic of abortion.* Boston: Beacon Press.

National Association of Social Workers. (2000). Family planning and reproductive choice. In *Social work Speaks: National Association of Social Workers policy statements, 2000–2003* (5th ed.). (pp. 109–116) Washington, DC: Author.

Palley, M. L. (1991). Women's rights as human rights: An international perspective. *Annals of the American Academy of Political & Social Sciences, 515,* 163–179.

PART III

SOCIAL WORK AND SOCIAL-SERVICE DELIVERY ISSUES

■ ■ ■ ■ ■

IS FEDERAL GOVERNMENT SUPPORT OF FAITH-BASED SOCIAL-SERVICE AGENCIES CONSISTENT WITH SOCIAL-WORK VALUES?

Editor's Note:
Catholic Charities, the Salvation Army, Jewish Social Services, and a great variety of religiously affiliated food pantries, colleges, and hospitals have received federal funding for decades. There is little, if anything, new about the inclusion of faith-based organizations in the delivery of social services to the poor. What is new are the Charitable Choice provisions of the Personal Responsibility and Work Opportunity Reconciliation Act (PRWORA) of 1996. Charitable Choice removed many of the restrictions on the religious content associated with faith-based delivery of social services and treated faith-based organizations as equivalent to secular social-service agencies. With the devolution of federal responsibility for social services to the states coupled with severe budgetary constraints on social-service funding, conflict was likely inevitable.

Those opposed to the Faith-Based and Community Initiative of the current Bush administration perceive faith-based funding as a violation of the separation of church and state. Those advocating faith-based funding, especially those associated with the more conservative Christian denominations, often find much church opposition to the acceptance of federal funding for the same reason.

Gaynor Yancey, D.S.W., is the Associate Dean of Baccalaureate Social Work at Baylor University and Associate Research Director for the Faith and Service Technical Education Network (FASTEN). Her research interests include church social work, congregational-based social services, community organizing, and the development of faith-based services and organizations.

John R. Belcher, Ph.D., is a professor at the University of Maryland School of Social Work. He has authored over 76 publications that have focused on vulnerable populations. Dr. Belcher also teaches pastoral counseling part-time at

St. Mary's Seminary and University Ecumenical Institute of Theology. He also works as a pastoral counselor. His current scholarship focuses on vulnerable populations in the capitalist system.

YES
Gaynor Yancey

When the question is raised about government support of faith-based social-service agencies being consistent with social-work values, the relationship of social work and religion must be considered as well. The following discussion highlights the history of charity and social-welfare services, both informally and formally, and the dual relationship of the profession with religion and government.

CHARITY AND SOCIAL-WELFARE PROVISION

Caring for a member of one's society who is in need (social welfare or charity) has deep historical roots. The early-Egyptian concept of charity meant avoiding doing harm to others. Jewish tradition taught that one was obligated to do positive acts of goodness for those who were in need. The early Christian church added love and compassion to these traditions. Islam, one of the fastest-growing religions in the United States, emphasizes charitable acts to those in need as important to achieve individual perfection on the part of the giver.

The historical record shows that the early church cared for the needs of the poor through the giving of alms. Shelter was provided for those who were homeless. Monasteries served as hospitals for the sick and, at the same time, as a home for orphans and the elderly. It was difficult to discern the difference between the work of the church and government in the informal helping services for those in need because they were one and the same. In the European context, the church often became an arm of the government in providing social-welfare services. In America, religious charity tended to be more constrained and informal.

This is the way things were until industrialization brought masses of people to work and live in urban areas, straining these informal helping services of the church, which were not able to handle the volume of needs that arose. The church needed to formalize its care of the poor and needy. As a result of that need, social-work history reveals, three movements—the Charity Organization Society (COS), Settlement Houses, and institutions—helped spur the establishment of formalized social work.

The Charity Organization Society was begun in the early 1800s in Scotland by Thomas Chalmers, a minister who, appalled by the poverty he saw, divided his parish into 25 units and assigned a deacon from the church to each one. The units were composed of approximately 50 families each, and were overseen by the deacon, who was responsible for investigating what led a family to a point of need and then to help set forth a plan to correct it. By some accounts, the COS was known as the parent of social work. Chalmers was known for conceiving the person-centered philosophy that is at the heart of social-work practice. The COS movement spread to England in 1869 and to the United States in 1877, where a COS was established in Buffalo, New York, by another minister, Reverend S. Humphries Gurteen. By the early 1900s, nearly every major city in the United States had a COS, sometimes referred to as Associated Charities.

The first settlement house, Toynbee Hall, was founded in London in 1884 by Canon Samuel A. Barnett. Barnett's idea of helping improve the lives of the poor was to move university graduates into some of the poorest areas of London. His thought was that by living among the poor, the university graduates would see the world of the poor, and the poor would see their world. Perhaps, as they saw the world through each other's eyes, a spiritual reawakening would occur in their lives. The settlement house movement in the United States was started by laypeople who had little interest in its religious roots. It is true, though, that many of the women who led the settlement house movement in the United States were themselves religious. Some gave up missionary service overseas to work among the poor in the United States. Stanton Coit founded the Neighborhood Guild in New York. Jane Addams founded Hull House in Chicago. The focus of the settlement house movement was social change, even though the majority of these houses were denominationally based and led by women of strong religious faith.

The establishment of the Charity Organization Societies and the settlement houses coincided with the creation of institutions created to house persons who were in the midst of poverty and dependency. Asylums, orphanages, and poor houses were established as relief for the poor. Every religious denomination had homes for the aged or orphanages for children. Some even established community centers that focused on the needs of the poor, just as the settlement houses did. Rescue missions and homes were founded to meet the needs of alcoholics and derelicts. Homes for unwed mothers were opened.

Despite the religious roots of the social-work profession, the historical record shows that social work has always had leanings toward secularism. The works of Gurteen or Charles Loring Brace, a minister who started the Children's Aid Society, were based in secularism and not religion, even though they were ministers. By the 1960s, several social-work writers, including Spencer (1956), indicated that "social work literature is almost totally lacking in any treatment of the subject of man's spiritual needs and practices and their inter-relatedness with his other needs and adjustment" (p. 161).

Since then, there has been a resurgence of the importance of religion and religious institutions in providing social-welfare provision.

CONTEMPORARY SOCIETY SINCE THE 1980s

Ronald Reagan's election brought to prominence the questions, What is the obligation the more affluent have to the less fortunate? What is the proper role of government in realizing any collective objective? (Morris, 1986). Partially in answer to these questions, volunteering and the increased responsibility of private organizations to meet society's social-welfare needs became two major societal themes.

Thanks to the increased emphasis on volunteering, decreasing government spending on social-welfare initiatives became a cornerstone of the 1980s. Reagan's messages reiterated his expectation that the private sector would become more active in meeting the social-welfare needs of the country's citizens. In essence, Reagan threw down the gauntlet and challenged the private sector to meet the needs of society with little help from the government. In particular, Reagan called on churches to become more active in addressing the needs of the poorest citizens within the churches' neighborhoods. Reagan's view was of a society when mutual aid and self-sufficiency were promoted as concepts that were accepted by the generalized populace (Ellis & Noyes, 1990). In retrospect, this view may have helped reinforce a sense of pride in the citizens, but little attention seemed to be paid to the thousands who were falling through the proverbial safety net (Midgley, 1990).

As a result of the changing attitudes toward helping, social-welfare provisions were provided through a variety of organizational sectors and individuals (Harris, 1995). Much of this attention, however, focused on community organizations, self-help groups, and service-providing agencies. The involvement of the voluntary sector, in particular, received a great amount of attention by both policymakers and academics (Cnaan, 1997; Cnaan, Kasternakis, & Wineburg, 1993; Hodgkinson & Weitzman, 1994; Hodgkinson, Weitzman, Kirsch, Noga, & Gorski, 1993; Wuthnow, 1991). In the combined administrations of Presidents Ronald Reagan, George H. W. Bush, and Bill Clinton, little attention was paid and little credit given to the social-welfare contributions of religious congregations up until the mid-1990s, even though they expected to meet the social-welfare needs of the country's poorest citizens and were pressed to do more and more.

Baggett (1997) says that:

> while it is rightly acknowledged that a nation with an incredible 350,000 congregations would be unthinkable apart from the leadership and other resources gleaned from local communities, less is made of the importance of these

churches, synagogues and mosques for helping to sustain those same communities in the first place. The fact that nine out of ten congregations in the United States currently sponsor at least one social service program, for example, ought to disabuse anyone of the notion that the relationship between them and their surrounding communities is a one way street. . . . these numbers still do not capture one of the most significant, yet scantily recognized, contributions of congregations. This is their capacity for encouraging and empowering their members to become more community minded, actively engaged citizens. (pp. 1, 6–7)

Roozen, McKinney, and Carroll (1984) indicate that this phenomenon is a congregation's mission stance. Wind (1990) refers to this mission stance as "a mission orientation, or stance towards the world" (p. 34). Others may use words such as outreach, church and community ministry, ministry, social ministry, justice, or social action to describe the understanding of what religious congregations do. Feeding the hungry, clothing persons, helping the homeless, and visiting the sick or those in prison are all examples of social ministry. Social action, conversely, involves attempts to change social structures or systems in order to help those toward whom social ministry may be directed. Social action also includes advocacy and helping change policies that may adversely affect those who are needy. Macarov (1978) states that "social welfare actually overlaps with the activities of many other institutions" (pp. 22–23). Presidents Reagan, Bush, and Clinton, called on congregations to do in a public way what they had always done quietly (Harris, 1995)—become the primary safety net from which many needy people received help.

GEORGE W. BUSH AND FAITH-BASED AND COMMUNITY INITIATIVES

In 1996, the federal government moved away from "welfare as we have known it," as President Bill Clinton used to say. The passage of the Personal Responsibility and Work Opportunity Reconciliation Act (PRWORA) of 1996 put the major responsibility for social-welfare provision on the states and, at the same time, imposed time limits for government assistance on the recipients. By doing this, the federal government ended the entitlement of aid to families with dependent children. At the same time, churches, synagogues, and mosques continued to provide and expand their welfare services to the poor and indigent—as they had been encouraged to do in the midst of the federal government's retrenchment from social-welfare services. Questions emerged as to what, if anything, the federal government's role was in helping subsidize programs in faith-based organizations and congregations. Positive examples were shown consistently of faith-based organizations and congregations involved in substance-abuse-treatment programs, offering after-school children's care, feeding the hungry, and caring for the homeless. The reality, however, is that faith-based organizations and congregations need financial and volunteer help in meeting the on-going needs of so many people in our society who are poor and needy and who no longer qualify for government assistance.

Charitable Choice was a part of the first provisions of the PRWORA. Charitable Choice was the initial legislation that opened the doors for faith-based organizations to receive federal funding in helping them provide social services. Simply put, Charitable Choice has four basic tenets: (1) a level playing field that allows faith-based organizations to compete with secular social-service agencies for government funding; (2) a respect for the integrity of faith-based organizations by protecting their religious character in the provision of social services; (3) the protection of clients by not permitting discrimination because of religious beliefs or practice; and (4) maintaining church–state separation by limiting the use of government funds to public-service goals and not religious instruction (U.S. Dept. of Health and Human Services, 2002).

Within two weeks of his inauguration, President George W. Bush introduced his new public-policy initiative, the Faith-Based and Community Initiative, which permitted the federal government to provide funds for churches that offer social-service programs to the needy. This Initiative was the foundation of his "compassionate conservatism." According to Bush, "when we see social needs in America, my administration will look first at faith-based programs and community groups, which have proven their power to save and change lives. We will not fund the religious activities of any group, but when people of faith provide social services, we will not discriminate against them" (Bush Pushes, 2001). At another point, he elaborated on his understanding of the role of government in faith-based organizations by saying, "government should never fund the teaching of faith, but it should support the good works of the faithful" (Bush Pushes, 2001).

CONCLUSION

This historical account has centered on the history of the relationship between government, the church, and social work, from an informal network to a formalized structure of caring for the social-welfare services of the citizenry. The historical record shows that even though people of faith have always been a part of providing the services involved in social-welfare provision, there has always been a tension in this relationship. From the professionalization of social-service provision in the 1920s to the expanded federal role in the Social Security Act of 1935 to Reagan's renewal of voluntarism to the enactment of the Personal Responsibility and Work Opportunity Reconciliation Act of 1996 that established Charitable Choice to Bush's Faith-Based and Community Initiatives, history has shown us that the values of government and social work have been consistent; and have centered on the common good, on helping those who are poor and needy.

Social-work values find their best expression in addressing the needs of people within an environmental context. This type of social-work practice culminates in networking with other social-service agencies, churches, government agencies, and foundations in meeting the needs of the poor. Social welfare, at its core, is about the well-being of society's members. To accomplish this effectively and efficiently, it will take all these entities in the public and private sectors working together in more intentional ways in the future. It will take the public sector's accepting the nature of faith-based organizations. It will take faith-based organizations' understanding that government funding is just like any other funding; there will be expectations attached to the receiving of money.

Perhaps, in the end, the essence of the struggle over values between government, faith-based social-service agencies, and social-work is not about whether they are consistent. The real question is whether we are willing to collaborate with each other in bringing about the well-being of the poor and the needy in our society. The well-being of the citizenry is, after all, the common denominator. I am suggesting that instead of being in a culture that accentuates the separation of church and state, we are now in a culture that is emphasizing collaboration. Collaboration is a social-work value that is implemented on a daily basis in the lives of our clients in our helping process.

The needs of our society are so great that it will take, in my opinion, all of us learning to work together to ameliorate suffering. At the same time, we need to publicly acknowledge that the tensions between social work and religion may still be there. It is ironic that, in the end, it may be the tensions between social work and religion that cause more problems than the relationship between government and religion. Cnaan, Wineburg, and Boddie (1999) state it well:

> The separation of social work from its religious roots not only jeopardizes its moral foundation and public support but also makes it difficult for the profession to chart its future course—one that will undoubtedly find strong connections between secular and religious-based secular services at many levels. Post-1980 social policy is focusing on service development at the local level, welfare agencies, public and private, sectarian and secular, are using the resources of religious organizations. This, in turn, is forcing social work to reconnect with its religious roots. (p. 3)

NO

John R. Belcher

Piven and Ehrenreich (2005) make the point that "The New Deal/Great Society order was established during the middle decades of the twentieth century, from the 1930s until the 1970s, when the United States developed something approaching a modern European style welfare state" (p. 79).

Social work has historically attempted to help create structures in society that promote social justice and equality and eliminate poverty. Unfortunately, much of society chooses to see things differently. This discussion addresses the question: Is the federal government's support of faith-based social-service agencies consistent with social-work values? My answer is a resounding *no*. My familiarity: I am a former pastor in a mainline Christian denomination, a social-work professor, an adjunct professor at a local Christian seminary, and a Christian pastoral counselor. Thus, this discussion will focus on the Christian community.

Since the advent of the New Deal/Great Society, conservative forces have sought to dismantle and replace it with a "purer" capitalist structure (Belcher & Singer, 1988; Piven & Cloward, 1997). The organized right, a combination of political, business, and conservative religious forces, launched their campaign in earnest with the election of Ronald Reagan and, eventually, George W. Bush. Bush is a converted hedonist; before accepting Christ as his personal savior (a phrase used among conservative Christians to describe the time when they gave up their old self and became a new person), he allegedly womanized, abused alcohol, and was generally irresponsible. However, upon his conversion, he allegedly stopped all the aforementioned sins and became a responsible person. Thus, Bush believes (along with other members of the conservative Christian [CC] community), that their brand of faith provides the best avenue to escape poverty.

Bush immediately launched efforts to devolve the welfare system from government responsibility to the faith-based community. The social-work community needs to be particularly cautious about this effort because it masks what seems to be wholesome—the involvement of the faith-based community with the welfare system (Belcher, Fandetti, & Cole, 2004).

BACKGROUND

At one time, Christian theologians such as Walter Rauschenbusch (1917) and Max Stackhouse (1968) "argued that the church (the Christian community) had a responsibility for the poor and the disenfranchised" (Belcher, in press, p. 132). The traditional relationship of the mainline Protestant and Catholic Christian communities had been one of support for federal and state poverty programs. The church's role was to provide temporary assistance in the form of soup kitchens, food pantries, and emergency assistance.

A significant change took place with the growing presence of evangelicals and CCs. As Belcher notes:

> Conservative Christianity is hard to define because it is made up of many faith movements as well as denominations. Unlike their mainline Protestant counterparts, conservative Christian churches are not members of a body, such as the World Council of Churches; they do not seek unity. (in press, p. 129)

One of the most important distinctions between the CC community and the mainline Protestant and Catholic communities is how they address poverty. Mathew 12:28 states that the "kingdom of God has come upon you." Generally, mainline Protestants and Catholics have interpreted this scripture to suggest that a major thrust of the kingdom of God involves caring for the poor and maintaining a stance of Christian humility.

However, the CC community generally interprets Christ's message quite differently. Instead of being concerned with others in relation to issues such as sustenance, most CCs are primarily concerned with personal salvation. Thus, it is most important to CCs to save the souls of the poor. Some CC communities have historically sought to distance their members from concern for social problems such as poverty (Thomas & Dobson, 1999). Others do not seek to withdraw from society; instead, they seek to dominate it by imposing their values on it (Brown, 2002). James Skillen (1981, 1990) argues for CCs to enter political life with the goal of pursuing the fulfillment of God's ordinances. Even when not using the language of dominance, the CC community continues to seek to control public policy by putting their platform in place.

The most confusing point surrounding the discussion about the Faith-Based and Community Initiative is that the CC community claims to speak for Christendom because other Christians, such as mainline Protestants and Catholics, are apostate. When Bush and his colleagues discuss the Initiative, it is difficult to say whether they view faith as legitimate beyond the confines of CC communities. As Piven and Ehrenreich (2005) note, "what makes the typical evangelical (conservative Christian) church efforts sinister is their implicit—and sometimes not so implicit—linkage to the destruction of public and secular services" (p. 89).

CCs like to highlight a remark by President Bush that "Governments can spend money, but they can't put hope in the hearts or a sense of purpose in our lives" (Bush, 1999). Bush and the CC community assume that the government-led welfare state is bankrupt; it does not do enough to reduce welfare. The operative assumption is that welfare represents a hidden evil. Lakoff (2002) describes how conservatives regard certain people: "Those whose lack of self-discipline has led to a lack of self-reliance. Unwed mothers on welfare are high on the list, since their lack of sexual self-control has led to their dependence on the state" (p. 171). What Bush and the CC community overlook is that some people will never be able to escape welfare. No matter how much motivation, self-reliance, or faith a person has, disability, unaffordable housing, and low wages may prevent a person from escaping welfare.

Much of the CC community supports or at least overlooks reductions in federal poverty programs. Jim Wallis, the editor of the liberal evangelical Christian magazine *Sojourners,* commented on conservative religious leaders: "They have agreed to support cutting food stamps for poor people if Republicans support them on judicial nominees" (Weisman & Cooperman, 2005). Many CCs are consumed with issues such as abortion and school prayer and do not care if Republicans cut programs for the poor as long as judges are appointed who support these issues. In 2000, Bush received 40 percent of his votes from Christian conservatives (Brotherson & Teichert, 2001).

Bill Clinton and the Democrats bear much of the responsibility for the faith-based language in the 1996 welfare-reform package. Progressives in the Democrat party, such as pollster Stanley B. Greenberg (1991, 2005), argued that the party "needed to transcend welfare politics." That is, Democrats needed to dismiss the poor from their agendas because reducing poverty programs often enjoys widespread support (Abramovitz, 2001). The facts of poverty, such as the increasing inability of families to successfully "launch" their offspring, were overlooked (Schoeni & Ross, 2005).

The process of welfare reform has attempted to eliminate notions of collective responsibility and replace them with the idea that Americans should fend for themselves. Lakoff (2002, p. 33) describes the Bush Administration's policy toward the poor as acting out of the *strict father* model, in which men should be the sole provider for the family, and the welfare state interferes with this role. In essence, Christian conservatives have inverted the Judeo-Christian ethic: Instead of Christians reaching out to the poor (Belcher, 2003), the poor are abandoned. The thrust of the Faith-Based and Community Initiative is to uproot the poor and distance them further from the state. The president "is asserting that the individual person or family doesn't need mediating institutions and programs" (Gecan, 2005).

It is important to highlight the people that Bush has relied on to implement the Faith-Based and Community Initiative. These people include Stanley Carlson-Thies, a leading evangelical and CC who served as the White House Office's Associate Director for Law and Public Policy; Don Eberly, a leading evangelical who has written on civil society and served as Deputy Assistant for Faith-based and Community Initiatives and helped to launch the Initiative; Carl Esbeck, a CC lawyer who led the Department of Justice's Taskforce on Faith-Based and Community Initiatives; and John DubIulio, a Catholic social scientist (Lazarus, 2003). With the exception of DubIulio, all of these individuals are evangelicals and CCs. One would assume that, if Bush wanted to put forth a faith-based initiative with the participation of various religious groups, he would want the participation of people with a variety of faith backgrounds.

Instead, Bush ensured that the Faith-Based and Community Initiative would be narrowly conceptualized and focused. Despite rhetoric to the contrary (Lugo, 1998), the Initiative was designed to reengineer welfare to reflect the views of the CC community.

Conservative Christians do offer a response to poverty. CCs are convinced that most poverty will correct itself and it should not be addressed by what they label as "coercive redistributions of wealth of a nation by a burgeoning state that is oblivious to the realm of moral valuation" (Collins, 2005, p. 125). CCs believe that poverty has become a problem because liberals have "championed hedonistic freedom" (Collins, 2005, p. 125). The poor have become victims of a misguided social-welfare state. The CC solution for this malady is spiritual renewal. Olasky (2000) notes, "most poor people don't have the faith that they and their situations can change" (p. 3). The poor, according to CCs, are primarily poor because they do not believe.

The CC community seeks to change the fundamental relationship between the state and society. Lazarus (2003) notes, "Similarly a just state that recognizes institutional and religious diversity in society will not require faith-based groups to change their hiring policies when they accept the government's invitation to help address society's most pressing crises" (p. 310). Does this mean that CCs have the right to demand of their staff that they attempt to convert the client? Suppose the client is Jewish and won't convert? Will clients be denied services?

Ron Sider (2000) calls for CCs to "hammer out a manifesto of how biblical principles of justice should inform their work as public servants and servants of the kingdom of God" (Lazarus, 2003, p. 312). The Faith-Based and Community Initiative will help ensure that the CC community expands its values and ideas. Among the most conservative, the state, as defined by CCs, will become a theocracy in which CC principles determine citizenship.

Kenneth Collins (2005), an evangelical scholar, describes how CCs want to offer an alternative to "A radical, aggressive egalitarianism that grew out of—in a very idealized form—the earlier counterculture's Marxist and post-Marxist vision of a 'classless' society in which Trotsky was a prophet and Marcuse a saint" (p. 117). CCs generally believe that liberals and Marxists have formed a cabal, which is intent on creating a godless society. This sense of paranoia helps explain the CC tendency to lump liberals, Marxists, environmentalists, atheists, and supporters of the social-welfare state together with liberal Christians despite any evidence of collusion or cooperation between these groups. To assume that a liberal or a person who uses Marxist thought is a not a Christian represents a form of bigotry and discrimination.

Interestingly, CCs claim that they resent the very thing that they practice—the labeling of people with differing values in a derogatory manner. Ron Sider (2000) notes, "Please don't call me names. Just explain to me how the normative biblical framework I spell out is not adequately scriptural."

SOCIAL-WORK RESPONSE

Martin Rein (1976) noted, "I believe that skepticism is valuable, essentially because it seeks to confront people with the results of their actions" (p. 19). I would urge the profession of social work to approach the faith-based language with great skepticism. Various politicians have attacked the welfare state in the past and continue to do so. However, the alliance between the conservative Christian church and the state is one of the first that actively attempts to dismantle the welfare state. Everything that social work stands for is being discredited by this alliance.

Behind the scenes, the alliance is attempting to reestablish what Marx called "primitive accumulation—the earth-shaking use of force to restore social conditions of profitability" (Balakrishan, 2005, p. 6). The welfare state is perceived by the alliance as a threat to individual profitability because the welfare state attempts to set boundaries and enforce codes of behavior on business. In an interesting obfuscation, the alliance has blamed the poor for the economic conditions that contribute to their poverty; fewer government controls and regulations would result in more jobs, albeit these jobs might be unsafe, provide low wages and few, if any, benefits, and take advantage of workers by providing few, if any, worker rights. If the poor would "pray more" and not worry about the fact that they do not make enough to afford housing, food, and health care, they would not be poor.

Social work must stand against this injustice. CCs and Bush believe that liberals and social work were too successful in protecting the poor during the 1960s (MacDonald, 2000). As a result, social work has been assailed as the real culprit for poverty.

The National Association of Social Workers (NASW) does raise concerns about faith-based legislation; however, mere concern is not enough. Members of the profession need to examine their own beliefs about faith and determine whether their place of worship supports programs such as the Faith-Based and Community Initiative. Over the years, the profession has grown more conservative and no longer stridently resists encroachment on the welfare state.

Support for Initiative is not solely contained in the Office of Faith-Based and Community Initiatives. Bush has also worked to ensure that national research agencies, such as the Substance Abuse and Mental Health Services Administration (SAMHSA), control research so that paradigms that allow for client participation are limited. The social-work academy needs to be particularly cautious about this integration. Under the guise of a quest for good science, agencies such as SAMHSA have convinced academia that it should abandon certain research paradigms. Greenwood and Levin (2005) note, "Most social science disciplines have excused themselves from social engagement by defining social science as separate from the application of their insights" (p. 44). Many social-work researchers have unfortunately bought in to this idea, and much research is becoming devoid of advocacy in order to escape criticism. Lincoln and Cannella (2004) have spoken out against this trend.

Piven and Cloward (1997) make the point that "business is using its formidable propaganda resources to persuade workers and democratic publics about the inevitable primacy of markets over politics, and of capital over labor, in a global world" (p. 9). The profession has been warned before about the destructiveness of these forces (Piven & Cloward, 1971, 1982). Alas, we have become complacent. It is easy to be fooled. Straub (2006), commenting on George W. Bush's slim presidential victory in Ohio, noted, "Bush's Ohio victory did come about in part from a massive out-pouring of socially conservative evangelical Christians to the polls. A large majority of these Republican evangelicals were blue-collar Ohioans voting *against their self-interest, many mobilized by Burress's (a former union organizer) anti-gay marriage movement.*"

The secret to the success of the CC movement is their ability to get people to vote against their self-interest. One CC pastor claims that the person's self-interest is less important than supporting God. Even though George W. Bush is against unions, he is for godly principles, such as the continuing disenfranchisement of gays and lesbians. CCs are told they do not support God if they vote against Bush.

While so far I have been very critical of faith-based initiatives, I strongly urge the profession to support the traditional involvement of the church in the welfare state. Many mainline Protestant and Catholic churches have long and successful track records of providing temporary assistance to the poor (Unruh, 2004). These programs are not designed to replace the social-welfare state. More important, these programs do not make any attempt to convert the clients that approach these ministries for assistance. For example, I volunteer at a multiservice, church-supported food pantry and service center once a month. There are many such centers that rely on volunteers to provide emergency assistance to the poor. Ministers of the churches that support these centers do not call for the downfall of the social-welfare state. On the contrary, they support the efforts of the social welfare state. These centers are not what Bush or the CC movement had in mind in relation to the Faith-Based and Community Initiatives. Centers like these existed long before faith-based language was inserted into the welfare reform act of 1996. Such efforts are part and parcel of the mainline Protestant and Catholic outreach to the poor.

CONCLUSION

Where do we go from here? Clearly, the Faith-Based and Community Initiative juggernaut is designed to dismantle the social-welfare state and replace it with programs designed to convert the poor and blame them for their plight. However, it is beyond the scope of this essay to enter into a discussion of how welfare-state reforms could more responsive to the needs of the poor (Esping-Andersen, 2002). The Bush–CC era has seen the further dismantling of the welfare state, and as Gilbert (2002) notes, resulted in the "silent surrender of public responsibility."

Blackburn (2005) describes how the forces of capital will mobilize against attempts to limit it. Bush and the CC movement have joined forces to more carefully control the fate of the poor. Piven and Cloward (1997) have long argued that the forces of capital seek to "break the social compact." I urge social workers to heed Piven and Cloward's warning and not support faith-based initiatives.

REFERENCES

Abramovitz, M. (2001). Everyone is still on welfare: The role of redistribution in social policy. *Social Work, 46*, 297–308.
Baggett, J. P. (1997). Giving something back to the community: Congregations and civic participation. *Ethics and Policy, 1*, 6–7.
Balakrishan, G. (2005). States of war. *New Left Review, 36*, 5–151.
Belcher, J. R. (2003). Helping the homeless: Where is the Holy Spirit? *Pastoral Psychology, 50*, 63–76.
Belcher, J. R. (in press). Conservative Christianity: A new emerging culture. In E. T. Dowd & S. L. Nielsen (Eds.), *Exploration of psychologies in religion.* New York: Springer.
Belcher, J. R., Fandetti, D., & Cole, D. (2004). Is religion compatible with the Liberal social welfare state? *Social Work, 49*, 29–276.
Belcher, J. R., & Singer, J. (1988). Homelessness: A cost of capitalism. *Social Policy, 18*, 44–48.
Blackburn, R. (2005). Imperial Margarine. *New Left Review, 35*, 124–136.
Brotherson, S. E., & Teichert, J. B. (2001). Value of the law in shaping social perspectives on marriage. *Journal of Law and Family Values, 3*, 23–56.
Brown, R. M. (2002). *For a Christian America: A history of the Religious Right.* New York: Prometheus Books.
Bush, G. W. (1999, July 22). "The duty of hope" campaign speech. Indianapolis, IN.
Bush, G. W. (2001, May 20). Commencement address at the University of Notre Dame, South Bend, Indiana. *Origins, 31*(3), 46–48.
Bush pushes faith-based plans. (2001, January 29). *The Washington Post.* Retrieved from www.washingtonpost.com/we-srv/Onpolitics/elections/bushtext012901.htm.

Cnaan, R. A. (1997). *Social and community involvement of religious congregations housed in historic properties: Findings from a six-city study.* Philadelphia: Partners for Sacred Places.

Cnaan, R. A., Kasternakis, A., & Wineburg, R. J. (1993). Religious people, religious congregations, and volunteerism in human services: Is there a link? *Nonprofit and Voluntary Sector Quarterly, 22*(1), 35–51.

Cnaan, R. A., with Wineburg, R. J., & Boddie, S. (1999). *The newer deal—Social work and religion in partnership.* New York: Columbia University Press,

Collins, K. J. (2005). *The evangelical movement: The promise of an American religion.* Grand Rapids, MI: Baker Academic.

Ellis, S. J., & Noyes, K. H. (1990). *By the people: A history of Americans as volunteers* (rev. ed.). San Francisco: Jossey-Bass.

Esping-Andersen, G. (2002). *Why we need a new welfare state.* New York: Oxford University Press.

Gecan, M. (2005, April/May). Taking faith seriously. *Boston Review.* Available at http://bostonreview.net.

Gilbert, N. (2002). *Transforming of the welfare state: The silent surrender of public responsibility.* New York: Oxford University Press.

Greenberg, S. B. (1991, September). From crisis to working majority. *The American Prospect, 2.*

Greenberg, S. B. (2005, June). How we found—and lost—a majority. *The American Prospect, 16.*

Greenwood, D. J., & Levin, M. (2005). Reform of the social sciences and of universities through action research. In N. K. Denzin & Y. S. Lincoln (Eds.), *The Sage handbook of qualitative research* (3rd ed., pp. 43–64). Beverly Hills, CA: Sage.

Harris, M. (1995). Quiet care: Welfare work and religious congregations. *Journal of Social Policy, 24*, 53–71.

Hodgkinson, V. A., & Weitzman, M. A. (1994). *Giving and volunteering in the United States.* Washington, DC: Independent Sector.

Hodgkinson, V. A., Weitzman, M. S., Kirsch, A. D., Noga, S. M., & Gorski, H. A. (1993). *From belief to commitment.* Washington, DC: Independent Sector.

Lakoff, G. (2002). *Moral politics* (2nd ed.) Chicago and London: University of Chicago Press.

Lazarus, S. (2003). Evangelicalism and politics. In C. Bartholomew, R. Parry, & West, A. (Eds.), *The futures of evangelicalism.* (pp. 285–317). Grand Rapids, MI: Kregel.

Lincoln, Y. S., & Cannella, G. S. (2004). Qualitative research, power, and the radical right. *Qualitative Inquiry, 10,* 175–201.

Lugo, L. E. (1998). *Equal partners: The welfare responsibility of governments and churches.* Washington, DC: The Center for Public Justice.

MacDonald, H. (2000). *The burden of bad ideas: How modern intellectuals misshape our society.* Chicago: Ivan R. Dee.

Macarov, D. (1978). *The design of social welfare.* New York: Holt, Rinehart & Winston.

Midgley, J. (1990). The new Christian right, social policy and the welfare state. *Journal of Sociology and Social Welfare, 17*(2), 89–105.

Morris, R. (1986). *Rethinking social welfare: Why care for the stranger?* New York: Longman.

Olasky, M. (2000). *Compassionate conservatism: What it is, what it does, and how it can transform America.* New York: Free Press.

Piven, F. F., & Cloward, R. A. (1971). *Regulating the poor: The functions of public welfare.* New York: Vintage Books.

Piven, F. F., & Cloward, R. (1982). *The new class war: Regan's attack on the welfare state and its consequences.* New York: Pantheon Books.

Piven, F. F., & Cloward, R. (1997). *The breaking of the American social compact.* New York: New Press.

Piven, F. F., & Ehrenreich, B. (2005). The truth about welfare reform. In L. Panitich & C. Leys (Eds.), *The Socialist Register 2006: Telling the truth* (pp. 78–92). New York: Monthly Review Press.

Rauschenbusch, W. (1917). *A theology of the social gospel.* New York: Macmillan.

Rein, M. (1976). *Social science/public policy.* Kingsport, TN: Kingsport Press.

Roozen, D. A., McKinney, W., & Carroll, J. (1984). *Varieties of religious presence: Mission in public life.* New York: Pilgrim Press.

Schoeni, R. F., & Ross, K. E. (2005). Material assistance from families during the transition to adulthood. In R. A. Sattersten, Jr., F.F. Furstenberg, Jr., & R. G. Rumbaut (Eds.), *On the frontier of adulthood: Theory, research, and public policy* (pp. 396–416). Chicago: University of Chicago Press.

Sider, R. J. (1999). *Just generosity: A new vision for overcoming poverty in America.* Grand Rapids, MI: Baker.

Sider, R. J. (2000). Toward an evangelical political philosophy. In D. P. Gushee (Ed.), *Christians and Politics beyond the culture wars: An agenda for engagement.* Grand Rapids, MI: Baker.

Skillen, J. W. (1981). Politics, pluralism, and the ordinances of God. In H. V. Goot (Ed.), *Life is religion: Essays in honor of H. Evan Runner.* St. Catherines, Ontario: Paideig Press.

Skillen, J. W. (1990). *The scattered voice: Christians at odds in the public square.* Grand Rapids, MI: Zondervan.

Spencer, S. (1956). Religion and social work. *Social Work, 1*(3), 19–26.

Stackhouse, M. L. (1968). *The righteousness of the kingdom.* New York: Abingdon Press.

Straub, J. (2006). What was the matter with Ohio? *Monthly Review, 57,* 35–55.

Thomas, C., & Dobson, E. (1999). *Blinded by the light: Can the Religious Right see America?* Grand Rapids, MI: Zondervan.

Unruh, H. R. (2004). Religious elements of church-based social service programs: Types, variables and integrative strategies. *Review of Religious Research, 45,* 317–335.

U.S. Department of Health and Human Services. (2002). *What is Charitable Choice?* Retrieved December 12, 2002, from The Center for Faith-Based and Community Initiatives website: www.hhs.gov/faith/choice/html.

Weisman, J., & Cooperman, A. (2005, December 14). A religious protest largely from the Left. *The Washington Post,* p. A8.

Wind, J. P. (1990). *Places of worship: Exploring their history.* Nashville, TN: American Association for State and Local History.

Wuthnow, R. (1991). *Acts of compassion: Caring for others and helping ourselves.* Princeton, NJ: Princeton University Press.

SHOULD SOCIAL SERVICES BE PRIVATIZED?

Editor's Note:
Conservatives have vigorously attacked the belief that government should finance and deliver social services to the population. Critics claim that public social services are bureaucratic and wasteful in a time of scarce resources. Unlike commercial enterprises, which must be competitive to survive, governmental agencies involved in social welfare have no incentive for efficiency. Hence, some citizens bitterly complain about the quality of public services. Privatization is widely touted as an effective alternative to the governmental delivery of social services. Although proponents of privatization claim that commercial social services are more efficient and offer better value for money than government, supporters of governmental social services contend that the profit motive does not provide a suitable basis for meeting human needs. Social programs should be regarded as collective goods to be provided for all citizens in need, irrespective of their ability to pay.

David Stoesz, Ph.D., is a professor at Virginia Commonwealth University, Northern Virginia Branch. He is the coauthor (with Howard Karger) of *American Social Welfare Policy* (Allyn & Bacon, 2000). He is also the author of *Quixote's Ghost: The Right, the Liberati, and the Future of Social Policy* (Oxford University Press, 2005) and coauthor (with Howard Karger) of *The Politics of Child Abuse and Neglect in America* (Oxford University Press, 1995). Dr. Stoesz has published widely in the areas of international social development, social-welfare policy, and social-work education.

Ira C. Colby, D.S.W., is the dean and a professor of social work at the University of Houston. He serves on several national committees and has published widely in the areas of community-based practice, homeless teenagers, social-work education and social-welfare history. In addition, Dr. Colby has presented more than 50 invitational and refereed presentations around the world.

YES

David Stoesz

Privatization has become a volatile issue in social welfare, a paradoxical development because the private sector has been integral to service provision, actually preceding the welfare state. While it has been fashionable for leftists to view the private sector as symptomatic of a malevolent capitalism, this is duplicitous. Social workers who celebrate the public sector wouldn't deign to call the local welfare department in search of financial services from the income-maintenance division, let alone social services for a personal problem. While many vilify the private sector, it is worth pointing out that most of what Americans receive in the form of goods and services are provided via the market and, while it is not a panacea, it has almost always been preferable to government provision. How many human-service professionals would elect housing from the public-housing authority, opt to drive the government-issue auto, or look forward to the most recent flick from the government-information agency? Maybe a few romantic Bolsheviks, but not many more. Indeed, government provision is often reserved for the poor, an arrangement that is disingenuous at best, since it not only consigns them to inferior service, but segregates them from the mainstream in the process.

Given the private sector's dominant role in the culture, it is only prudent to incorporate it in discussions of social policy. After all, a substantial amount of social welfare in the United States is provided under nongovernmental auspices; to that extent American social welfare has *already* been privatized. For decades, the United Way has generated substantial revenues through hundreds of affiliates in virtually every American city for thousands of member agencies. Private philanthropy has provided billions of dollars in assistance for a range of social-welfare activities. Indeed, the training of radicals who strive to advance social justice is conducted by private organizations such as the Industrial Areas Foundation and the Highlander Center. Finally, many health and human service professionals work in the private sector, having found this preferable to government service. As these suggest, denying the historical role of the private sector in social welfare is simply myopic.

In fact, the private sector has become the preferred basis for addressing social problems for several reasons:

- *Virtually all social change originates in the private sector.* Social movements that have benefited workers, women, and minorities are oriented around such organizations as the AFL-CIO, NOW, the NAACP, and La Raza—all private organizations. *The private sector provides the freedom essential for innovation.* Virtually all management strategies to enhance organizational performance are derived from business.

- *The cultivation of civic culture is a function of the private sector.* Often taken for granted by Americans, the best evidence of this is to ask any resident of the former Soviet bloc about the value of government; invariably they prefer private initiatives.
- *The dynamism of the information age is a product of the private sector.* By now it is a cliché that the best thing government can do to facilitate the postindustrial economy is to get out of the way.

So what is all the brouhaha about privatization? Much of the fuss is the result of a rearguard polemic parroted by liberals who have been chagrined at the success of conservatism as public philosophy, signaled by the election of Ronald Reagan in 1980. Since then, the left has been frustrated about the limits imposed on expansion of the government welfare state, not only in the United States, but in Europe as well. Initially, this was aggravated by the far right's attempt to decimate public social programs while invoking the virtues of the private sector. More recently, a consensus has emerged that validates the private sector for its contributions to social welfare, portraying it as a complement of government. Republicans in particular have reinforced the value of nonprofits, evident in the Points of Light Foundation established by the elder President Bush, then reinforced by the faith-based social-services Initiative introduced by the younger President Bush, the funding for which was proposed at $24 billion over 10 years. Thus, leftist fears that privatization would be used to *replace* government would appear exaggerated.

Concomitantly, scholars began to explore the conditions under which the private sector might be desirable for service provision. John Donahue (1989) noted, "Governments in the United States spend roughly half a trillion dollars per year paying public workers to deliver goods and services directly. If only one-quarter of this total turned out to be suitable for privatization, at an average savings of, say 25 percent—and neither figure is recklessly optimistic—the public would save over $30 billion" (p. 216). Not long thereafter, David Osborne and Ted Gaebler (1992) proposed in *Reinventing Government* that the public and private sectors had different functions: optimally, government should establish the objectives of public policy, but assign the execution to the private sector. Subsequently, Osborne served as an advisor to the federal performance-review initiative.

The rhetorical virtues proclaimed by its proponents notwithstanding, privatization introduces difficult issues into the social-policy debate. Any discussion of the problems presented by privatization necessitates an appreciation of the primary sectors of American social welfare. As they have evolved historically, the *voluntary sector* consists of private, nonprofit organizations that populate localities by the thousands; the *government sector* is comprised of federal, state, and local departments, which either provide services directly or subcontract service provision through the private sector; the *for-*

profit sector is made up of private, commercial firms that have expanded rapidly during the past 3 decades. Details of each of these can be found in *American Social Welfare Policy* by Howard Karger and David Stoesz (2006).

Because each sector has different objectives, their interaction is not always synchronous, generating problems that are often associated with privatization. For example, government programs may be mandated by legislation, but the executive branch may have the option of subcontracting service provision. If government provides the service directly it will meet its mandated responsibility, though there is no necessary assurance as to the program's quality, accessibility, or efficiency; for those reasons, government can seek to emphasize those values by contracting with private vendors. To the extent that government funnels billions of dollars to purchase services, major industries evolve—as has been the case in health care—and these become powerful lobbies for the social programs on which they are dependent. Back in 1980, Arnold Relman (1980), the editor of the prestigious *New England Journal of Medicine,* warned of the power of "the medical-industrial complex" in health policy. This concern was amplified during the 2000 presidential election by Ralph Nader, who claimed that "corporate welfare" endowed American business with resources that it used to manipulate the political process.

For their part, voluntary agencies emerge as a result of a group of citizens agreeing that a community problem should be addressed, and convince the Internal Revenue Service to grant them tax-exempt status. As a result, there are now thousands of voluntary-sector programs; however, despite their ubiquitous nature, they appear irregularly throughout the society—AIDS prevention services tend not to appear in smaller, rural communities; child day care may be in short supply in the inner city. Two features have come to typify nonprofit agencies: (1) their mission is to address local problems, so they are strongly community based; and (2) because funding is often problematic, they resort to a variety of strategy to attract resources—recruiting volunteers, holding bake sales, applying to private foundations, negotiating government contracts, and charging fees for services.

For-profit firms must perform efficiently in order to generate profits on which investors insist. Beyond that, they enjoy a wide degree of latitude, providing they are managed responsibly, and they enjoy several advantages over their competitors in the governmental and nonprofit sectors. Commercial firms cannot be impeded from exploiting new markets they wish to enter, and they have immediate access to capital in order to expand their operations. These, coupled with business-expansion strategies—advertising, buying competitors, and acquiring sophisticated technology—often ensure growth. The conversion of *public utilities* into *social markets* is perhaps the most controversial aspect of privatization, because it appears to be at the expense of the governmental and voluntary sectors. While the contention that "profiteering from human misfortune" is often made by opponents of privatization, a fundamental question remains: how humane is it to maintain an archaic prison that violates inmates' rights or a foster-care system that routinely ignores the abuses inflicted on children, when a private provider can meet cost and quality standards for comparable care?

In practice, the varying motives and prerogatives of the voluntary, governmental, and for-profit sectors have been the source of seminal issues in social policy, many of which converge around privatization. As tax-exempt entities, voluntary-sector organizations should be more competitive than commercial firms because they do not have to pay taxes on income, nor do they have to generate profits to satisfy investors. Yet, nonprofit organizations have been poor competitors, often losing out to for-profit firms. The focus on community service, the absence of accountability, and chronic resource problems have all made nonprofits less competitive than commercial firms. As a result, when for-profit firms enter a market that has been traditionally served by the voluntary sector, they often takes a substantial portion of that market until nonprofits adopt many of the same management practices and become more efficient.

At a time when government must be judicious in its funding of mandated activities, contracting out services becomes a desirable option. Yet which strategy of privatization might be optimal? A good illustration of this has been evident in discussions of health reform: should government reserve the role of single-payer, as it has with Medicare, or reimburse a network of competing managed-care firms, as proposed under the Clinton Health Security Act? Should government favor nonprofit applicants because they claim to serve a broad spectrum of citizens, or for-profit firms because they boast the latest in technology? In making such decisions, should government officials be swayed by the influence of powerful lobbying agents who represent commercial providers or elected officials who respond to the appeals of community-based nonprofits?

Conscious of their public image, commercial firms often redouble their efforts to enhance the community's welfare. They encourage employees to contribute to the United Way, and they mount community-service programs. When Blue Cross–Blue Shield went from nonprofit to for-profit status, it established health foundations to support research and demonstration projects. When they suspect that they can generate a profit by providing superior service to a clientele, for-profit providers will seek subcontracts from government, as has been the case with managed-care firms seeking to enroll recipients of Medicaid and Medicare.

Unfortunately, human-service professionals have largely negated the opportunities associated with privatization. In some respects this has been an artifact of social work, the discipline traditionally associated with social welfare. As a result, social work has been dismissive of nonprofit agencies and outwardly hostile to for-profit firms. The professional education of social workers is virtually devoid of the knowledge and skills that are essential to business strategies in service provision, avoiding substantial content in finance, marketing, information systems, and contracting. For decades, social workers have managed programs to serve the public; yet rhetoric about client care notwithstanding, they have failed to generate any longitudinal data on the perceptions and experiences of clients about the services they receive.

As a result of a substandard education, it is not surprising that social workers are not competitive in the new human-services market. Having failed to generate data on cost-per-unit-of-service, it is no wonder that social workers are unsuccessful vis-a-vis commercial firms that make superior presentations to lawmakers and government officials seeking to optimize increasingly scarce tax revenues. Rather than redouble its efforts to generate such information, the response of social-work field has been to denigrate the motives of commercial firms. In this respect, social-work education is so retrograde that the altruist aspiring for a career in public service may be better prepared by a good ethics course and a program of study in the business school than studying social work.

Perhaps the most salient development relating to privatization has been the expansion of information technology. Combined with economic deregulation, this expansion has spawned a new generation of hybrid organizations that are flat, dispersed, and nimble. Not only have such organizations demonstrated their superiority in managing a range of services domestically, they have begun to exploit markets internationally. For social workers who were so wedded to government programs that they failed to take advantage of even industrial-era innovations, such as Employee Stock Ownership Plans, these hybrid entities are simply incomprehensible. Yet they are the future of human-service provision. As such, the best way to access the opportunities implicit in their development is to appreciate the virtues of the private sector—in a word, take privatization seriously.

NO

Ira C. Colby

To state that privatization is a controversial, polarizing, and emotional topic is at best an understatement of the obvious. Proponents of privatization offer well-thought-out and sometimes seemingly convincing arguments. Certainly the proposition that there is a better and more efficient way to provide social services is true; the belief that the provision of social-welfare services is not the sole domain of the public sector is correct. But the idea that privatization of basic public social services is the answer to creating an effective mechanism for the poor to move out of the throes of poverty is an insidious and grossly erroneous assumption.

Before moving any further into the discussion let me first define *privatization*. Doing so at the outset of a debate provides the required reference point for the ensuing discussion; not defining essential concepts is an interesting debate strategy when one's position is weak. Mixing or interchanging words and concepts, without establishing a baseline definition, subtly lures the listener, or in this case the reader, into a murky, often emotion-filled, controversy. But let us ignore the debater's trickery and be reasonable and logical in our discussion.

Privatization takes many forms, and is most recognized as the subcontracting of services with public dollars provided to nongovernmental groups to provide direct services. For our purposes, we'll refer to the straightforward definition set forth in Nightingale and Pindus (1977), "privatization refers to the provision of publicly funded services and activities by non-governmental entities" (p. 6).

Privatizing some social services is not a new phenomenon, but a well-established practice in the United States that dates back to the middle of the 20th century, when many private, nonprofit agencies contracted with the government to provide programs and services. Typical private nonprofit agencies that are contracted include United Way–funded agencies (e.g., the YMCA) and member agencies of the Family Association of America (e.g., Jewish Family Services and Catholic Social Services).

Social-welfare history reveals a rich past of social services firmly rooted in the church community, with later growth in private, nonsectarian-related organizations (Trattner, 1995; Axinn and Stern, 2000). Voluntary societies, such as the 17th-century Scots Charitable Society, and programs similar in design to the mid-19th-century Children Aids Society typify the array of social services in the private arena (Axinn and Stern, 2000). Additionally, the birth of the social-work profession can be clearly traced to mid-to-late 19th-century private sectarian and nonsectarian social-aid organizations.

So what is the fuss about concerning the privatization of social services? The recent proposals and movement to greater privatization seem to be nothing more than expanding and enhancing a model that is centuries old. Or, are they?

On the surface, privatization seems likes a workable strategy, particularly if one subscribes to a politically conservative or libertarian philosophy of government. Privatization implies that the government is no longer in the welfare business. Government's new role is twofold: funding and oversight. Based on a business model, the contracting agency or organization must meet the funder's requirements or the contract is cancelled. Provision of services becomes the province of the private sector and removes the government from a guardian and caregiver role. Competition, a source of pride in the private sector, presumably eliminates waste and incompetence, leaving only strong, efficient service providers in place.

Privatization sounds like a win-win situation for the body politic and the public, with numerous purported benefits. Private social services promises to reduce the size of the large federal and state government bureaucracies, such as the Federal Department of Health and Human Services. Private social services will introduce a local flavor that reflects local needs and issues rather than a national standard set by some obscure Washington, D.C., bureaucrats. The business model also implies that social agencies will be smaller, with less red tape, which in turn yields effective and purposeful services. And, of course, by adopting a business model, proponents suggest that contracts will be severed if outcomes are not realized or the organization is not efficient, saving the American public tax dollars in the long run.

With the new privatization efforts, a new, nontraditional welfare partner has emerged, *the for-profit corporation*. The Marriott Corporation and Lockheed Martin are among the many new welfare providers joining the ranks of traditional, private nonprofit social agencies.

Why would private for-profit corporations, ostensibly created to generate enormous profits for owners, board members, and stockholders, now take on social services? Are corporations expressing a new humanitarian philosophy, with the poor and at-risk populations their new concern? Or, are these mega-corporations looking for new avenues to increase and maximize their profit margins? Certainly an interesting twist by the mega-corporations, whose bottom line has always been the profit margin. The adage, "If you paint a zebra colors to conceal its stripes, you still have a zebra," raises a cautionary flag. Are we to believe that the mega-corporation social-service zebra no longer has it stripes? Or, is the new, corporate, for-profit, social-service zebra still a zebra?

We need only look back a few years to reacquaint ourselves with the purported efficient, cost-saving, minimal red tape and oversight programs of the for-profit corporations. This is the same sector whose track record with federal contracts reflects, at best, mismanagement of funds and projects for which the public and conservative commentators condemn the government. Social pundit Jim Hightower (2001) begins one of his many commentaries that warn of private, for-profit waste with the haunting phrase, "It's back." According to Hightower, the Pentagon's extravagant expenditures of the 1980s are commonplace once again (remember the $640 toilet seat?): $1,887 for a machine bolt that normally costs $40; a self-locking nut that listed for $2.69 but the government paid $2,185. Or, AlliedSignal overcharging the government 618 percent for spare parts or Boeing charging $403 for a regularly priced $25 metal cylinder; a $47 normally priced bell that the government paid $714 or the $.57 screw that sold for $76 (St. Clair, 2000).

So now we want to turn public social services over to the same sector that claims efficiency as its guardian philosophy? A system that will "save" the American public millions of dollars by eliminating waste and fraud and reducing the size of government? Well, if that's true, there *is* a bridge for sale in Brooklyn, some great swampland in Florida, and large estates in the desert of Arizona.

Our debate could rest on this plane, but we would be failing to address the central issue—why are we entertaining a "new" strategy of mega-corporations, with their newfound spirit, becoming the guardians and providers of social services to the most vulnerable and at-risk in our communities?

The ongoing privatization arguments are nothing more than an extension of the centuries-old debate concerning the role of government in welfare. As early as the 1601 Elizabethan Poor Laws, welfare was considered the sole province of the private community. The debate gained legal precedence with President Franklin Pierce's 1854 veto message of legislation that would have provided federal land to the states "for the benefit of indigent persons" (Axinn & Stern, 2000). As Pierce wrote,

> I can not find any authority in the Constitution for making the Federal Government the great almoner of public charity throughout the United States. To do so (would) . . . be contrary to the letter and spirit of the Constitution and subversive of the whole theory upon which the Union of these States is founded.

Following the Pierce veto, there were some publicly funded welfare programs, but these were more the exception than the rule. The historic public "hands-off" approach radically changed during the 1930s Depression with the advent of President Franklin D. Roosevelt's activist government. Public programs were quickly put in place and became the framework for the modern-day "welfare state." Yet even Roosevelt seemed ill at ease with the government's emerging welfare role when, in his 1935 State of the Union Address to Congress, he declared that "The Federal Government must and shall quit the business of relief" (Axinn & Stern, 2000).

Today's common catchphrases of "compassionate conservatism" and "faith-based social services" are nothing more than retreaded ideas from another era—fewer public services with a greater reliance on the private sector. It's as if President Pierce is again living in the White House.

Have some governmental programs been less than stellar? Yes, but just as often the private sector has failed in its delivery of services. How many automobile callbacks have there been for defective construction? Why are product defects, such as those in the recent Firestone and Ford Auto controversy, kept hidden from the public? How many airlines have 100 percent, or even 90 percent, on-time arrivals? How many utility "blackouts" or "brownouts" must the public suffer due to inadequate safeguards?

Mario Cuomo (1995) put it best: "With unemployment insurance, worker's compensation, Social Security, fair labor standards, Aid to Families with Dependent Children (AFDC), Medicare, and Medicaid, we improved our standards and working conditions, provided services that benefit and strengthen us, and protected and nurtured our most vulnerable members. In doing so, we amplified our potential for greatness" (p. 17). Government does play a central a role in providing services and is entrusted with a basic responsibility to ensure that all people, no matter their station in life, are provided needed services and supports that maximize individual, group, and community capacity to change, contribute, and participate in society.

Basic social services are the business of the government; contracting services to nonprofit social agencies is appropriate when *service*, not profit, is the ultimate end. The significant redirection of social-service programs by mega-, for-profit corporations marks a dangerous return to a compassionless period. Are we foolish enough to believe that for-profit, mega-corporations are the 21st century's new social altruists? Do we really believe that the government has failed us over time in its social agenda? If so, then government should remove itself from health care for seniors, preschool for poor children, civil rights laws, safety and security provided by the police and fire departments, funding of public education, and housing regulations.

If privatization is the answer to our collective good, then let's extend the privatization principle to other traditional governmental services. Let's privatize the United States military, including the Army, Navy, Air Force, Marines, and Coast Guard. Government costs would be greatly reduced through privatization by realizing significant savings from otherwise long-term expenditures that the government now pays. Under privatization, the private military contractors, not the government, would provide health care and other military benefits, now provided by the Federal Government through the Veteran's Administration. Closing down the Veteran's Administration alone could save U.S. taxpayers billions of dollars annually; in 1998, for example, the VA spent $43,150,218,825 on services (Veterans Administration, 2001).

Nor do we need locally funded public fire departments—let the individual citizen contract with a private, for-profit fire department. Why should the average person be forced to pay for a service, through taxes he probably will never use? Get the government out of fire protection and let the individual elect to contract (or not) with a private fire department. There is no need for public parks; let the private-sector recreation experts, such as Disney or MGM, manage our parks and compete for the contracts. Can you see a great roller-coaster ride at the Grand Canyon going up and down the canyon walls? And, while we're at it, let's privatize all libraries. If a library in one neighborhood doesn't meet its expected outcome, close it down and ship the books to a better-performing library. Give people vouchers to check books out and the strongest libraries will survive. Let's just go ahead and privatize all governmental service sectors and return to Pierce's minimalist view of government.

Privatization of public services certainly sounds ridiculous when extending the idea to other governmental domains. Most would agree that it is inappropriate to privatize the local fire department or military; if so, then why do some of these same individuals seriously entertain privatizing basic social services? The poor are often the focus and flash point for public-policy discussions and, for any number of reasons, are directly blamed for program failures; though they are rarely praised for program successes. In those instances, the elected officials or policymakers claim the positive recognition. Blaming the poor is very American. U.S. House of Representative and Republican party leader Dick Armey stated, "Poverty is a moral problem" while former Republican Speaker of the House Newt Gingrich noted that the poor "have to learn new habits" (Hudson, 1996). It is so easy to categorically blame the poor and devise reactionary policies and strategies, including contracting social services to private, for-profit corporations.

After decades of federal efforts we know it is difficult to marshal and sustain a national collective resolve to end poverty. Throwing money into a program is not the sole answer; shaming people for their life situations, a centuries-old intervention model, does little. Privatization is nothing more than washing our public hands of the poor under the guise of compassionate conservatism. We move human suffering and inequity into spreadsheets and bottom-line operations with the profit motive the driving factor for the new 21st-century for-profit corporate social agency.

Can we do better? Yes. Should we do better? Yes. Should we pass off our public responsibility to mega for-profit corporations? A resounding *No*.

REFERENCES

Axinn, J., & Stern, M. (2000). *Social welfare: A history of the American response to need* (5th ed.) Boston: Allyn & Bacon.
Cuomo, M. (1995). *Reason to believe.* New York: Simon & Schuster.
Donahue, J. (1989). *The privatization decision.* New York: Basic Books.
Hightower, J. (2001, February 14). *Jim Hightower, Hightower's common sense commentary.* National Public Radio.
Hudson, W. (1996). *Economic security for all: How to end poverty in the United States.* Vancouver, BC: Economic Security Project.
Karger, H. J., & Stoesz, D. (2006). *American social welfare policy* (5th ed.). Boston: Allyn & Bacon.
Nightingale, D. S., & Pindus, N. (1997, October 15). *Privatization of public social services: A background paper.* Washington, DC: Urban Institute.
Osborne, D., & Gaebler, T. (1992). *Reinventing government.* New York: Addison-Wesley.
Relman, A. (1980). The new medical-industrial complex. *New England Journal of Medicine 303*(17), 80.
St. Clair, J. (2000, July 11). *Rego and defense costs.* Retrieved July 9, 2001, from www.unrisd.org/engindex/publ/list/op/op7/op-07-01.htm.
Trattner, W. (1999). *From poor law to welfare state: A history of social welfare in America* (5th ed.). New York: Free Press.
Veterans Administration. (2001). Retrieved July 8, 2001, from www.bva.gov/about_va/history/expend.htm.

HAS WELFARE REFORM WORKED?

Editor's Note:
Welfare reform has been around—in one form or another—since the 1970s. Almost inevitably, each attempt at reforming public welfare has failed. That was true for former president Jimmy Carter's workfare program in the late 1970s, and for the Family Support Act of 1988, which, until the Personal Responsibility and Work Opportunity Reconciliation Act (PRWORA), was the most ambitious piece of welfare legislation since the New Deal. In part, these reforms failed because of inadequate federal funding and lackluster support from the states.

The PRWORA differed from previous reform legislation in several ways: (1) it was signed by Bill Clinton, a Democratic president; (2) it included specific sanctions against states that failed to comply with the bill; (3) it was the most ambitious and comprehensive welfare legislation to date; and (4) it set specific and irrefutable target goals for employing recipients. The PRWORA also rescinded 60 years of entitlement for public assistance and instituted a lifetime 5-year cap on welfare.

The question of whether the PRWORA has helped or hurt beneficiaries has been hotly contested. Conservatives argue that welfare reform has been an unqualified success, moving millions of people off welfare rolls and into jobs. Opponents claim that former recipients have moved from low-benefit public assistance into low-paying jobs that allow them to be "poor workers" instead of "poor recipients." Critics of welfare reform claim that little has changed in the socioeconomic lives of recipients.

Kirk A. Johnson, Ph.D., is a senior policy analyst at the Heritage Foundation. His work focuses on estimating the outcome of policies that affect low-income Americans. Dr. Johnson's commentary has been featured in the *Los*

Angeles Times, Forbes, the *Chicago Tribune,* the *Washington Post,* the *Miami Herald,* the *Detroit Free Press,* and on the Fox News Channel.

Robert Rector, M.A., is a senior research fellow at the Heritage Foundation and is considered a leading authority on poverty and the U.S. welfare system. His work focuses on a range of issues relating to welfare reform, family breakdown, and United States' various social ills. He played a major role in crafting the federal welfare-reform legislation passed in 1996.

Mimi Abramovitz, Ph.D., is a professor of social policy at Hunter College and the author of *Regulating the Lives of Women: Social Welfare Policy from Colonial Times to the Present* (2nd ed.) (South End Press, 1996); *Under Attack, Fighting Back: Women and Welfare in the United States* (2nd ed.) (2000); *The Dynamics of Social Welfare Policy* (2004) (with Joel Blau); and *Taxes Are A Women's Issue: Reframing the Debate* (with Sandra Morgen) (Feminist Press, 2006).

YES

Kirk A. Johnson and Robert Rector

When the welfare reform legislation was being debated in Congress about a decade ago, a heated debate transpired on the likely outcomes of the policy. An oft-cited Urban Institute report, for example (Center on Budget and Policy Priority, 1996), predicted that an additional 2.6 million individuals, and 1.1 million children would be thrown into poverty.

The consternation did not merely end when the bill passed, however. The late Senator Daniel Patrick Moynihan (D-NY) lamented that the law was the most "regressive and brutal act of social policy since Reconstruction" (DeWitt, 2005). Additionally, the late senator argued that the law would create substantial social unrest among affected individuals and families.

After Bill Clinton signed the Personal Responsibility and Work Opportunity Reconciliation Act of 1996 (P.L. 104-193), several Clinton administration staffers, most notably Peter Edelman, Assistant Secretary for Planning and Evaluation at the Department of Health and Human Services, and Wendell Primus, Deputy Assistant Secretary for Human Services Policy, resigned in protest. Edelman went on to write an article titled "The Worst Thing Bill Clinton Has Done," arguing that the new law was "awful" and would do "serious injury to American children" (1997). Wendell Primus wrote similarly of the catastrophe that would befall children in particular in the wake of the new law.

In order to evaluate whether welfare reform has worked, three questions must be answered. First, what were the changes to welfare enacted in 1996? Second, what happened after welfare reform in terms of the social indicators of poverty, dependency, and employment? Third, what can we conclude? Has welfare reform worked?

HOW DID THE LAW CHANGE WELFARE?

The old Aid to Families with Dependent Children (AFDC) program was transformed into a new program called Temporary Assistance to Needy Families (TANF). TANF changed welfare in a variety of noteworthy ways. In particular, welfare became a "reciprocal agreement" between society and the recipient. Society would only provide welfare benefits if able-bodied recipients work, or prepare for work, in exchange for aid. To that end, federal work requirements required the state welfare agencies that administer TANF funds to move welfare clients into work activities.

Besides reducing dependency and increasing employment, the law had a number of other goals, including reducing child poverty, reducing illegitimacy, and strengthening marriage. The program also established a 5-year lifetime time limit for welfare benefits.

WHAT HAPPENED AFTER WELFARE REFORM?

In the 10 years since the bill became law, welfare reform has been intensely studied and scrutinized for its effects on a broad range of social indicators, such as poverty (and in particular, child poverty), hunger, employment, and dependency. From the broad range of social indicators, most have been positive in the post–welfare reform era.

First and foremost, welfare dependency dropped in a substantial way. In the first few years post-reform, welfare caseloads dropped by nearly 60 percent nationwide (Rector & Fagan, 2003). Some would immediately argue, however, that the decrease in welfare dependency centered predominantly on the easy to employ, and that the group with the greatest tendency toward long-term dependence would be the most disadvantaged, and least-employable single mothers. But dependence has fallen most sharply among young, never-married mothers who have low levels of education and young children (O'Neill & Hill, 2001), indicating that welfare reform is not just affecting the easy-to-employ population. O'Neill and Hill also note that a number of important employment metrics for this disadvantaged group improved in post–welfare reform. In particular:

- Employment of never-married mothers has increased nearly 50 percent.
- Employment of single mothers who are high school dropouts has risen by two-thirds.
- Employment of young single mothers (ages 18 to 24) has nearly doubled.

Again, these employment statistics demonstrate that welfare reform was particularly good for this hard-to-employ population. Decreases in dependence and increases in employment among single mothers are evidence of the success of welfare reform.

Some critics argue that increased work rates among hard-to-employ populations do not mean that the jobs are sufficient to raise people out of poverty. This contention, however, is not supported by the data. A casual review of the poverty statistics clearly shows that between 1994 and 2004:

- The overall poverty rate dropped from 14.5 percent to 12.7 percent.
- Child poverty dropped 4 percentage points, from 21.8 percent to 17.8 percent, and black child poverty dropped more than 10 percentage points, from 43.8 percent to 33.6 percent, respectively.
- The poverty rate for children in female-headed families dropped by more than 10 percentage points between 1994 and 2004, from 52.9 percent to 41.9 percent. (U.S. Census Bureau, 2005)

1994 is used as a starting point in this analysis because a number of welfare-reform waivers were granted to certain states beginning in 1995. Many of these waivers implemented on a local level policies that were later adopted in the 1996 law.

But why was welfare reform so important in improving these outcomes, particularly on child poverty? Rebecca Blank, a former member of the Council of Economic Advisers in the Clinton White House, examines the link between welfare reform and child poverty (Blank & Schoeni, 2003). Blank analyzes the income of families with children from 1992 to 2000 and finds that incomes rose for all but the bottom 2 percent of families with children. Moreover, poor families showed large income gains, "suggesting that most poor families experienced larger income gains than did most middle- and upper-middle income families."

Blank's study demonstrates how important incentives are in welfare policy. States with "strong work incentive" policies showed greater increases in the incomes of single parents with children than did states with weak work incentives. Indeed, "at the bottom of the distribution, states with strong work incentives have the smallest share of children in families with negative changes in income, while states with the weakest work incentives show the highest share of children with [decreases in income]" (Blank & Schoeni, 2003). So, strong incentives correlate to fewer families losing income. States with weak incentives had more families losing income. Blank attributes these differences to incentives in the state welfare policies themselves, not to states' economic differences.

Blank also investigates the effects of tough welfare-reform "penalties" on the incomes of poor, single-parent families. She notes that the effect of welfare time limits and other pro-work-sanction policies "provide a strong enforcement mechanism for women to participate in welfare-to-work programs" (Blank & Schoeni, 2003). To reiterate, states with stricter time limits and stronger sanction policies were more successful in raising the incomes of poor children than were states with lenient policies. Specifically:

> States with strict or moderate penalties for not working consistently show higher income gains among poor children throughout the income distribution than do states with lenient penalties. . . . [I]t is the more lenient states with softer penalties where children's income seems to have grown least. (Blank & Schoeni, 2003)

Other researchers have analyzed the role of incentives in the differential outcomes of welfare reform on a state-by-state basis. Rector and Youssef (1999), for example, noted that the early welfare-reform experience varied based on the kinds of incentives states enacted. Those with strict sanction policies saw their caseloads decline faster than those states that did not.

Another study (O'Neill & Hill, 2001) examined changes in welfare case-loads and employment from 1983 to 1999. This analysis shows that after welfare reform, policy changes explained about three-quarters of the increase in employment and decrease in dependence.

The final important metric to be discussed is child hunger. The U.S. Department of Agriculture (USDA) notes in its annual food security report that child hunger has fallen dramatically since welfare reform (Nord, Andrews, & Carlson, 2005). In 1995, the first year of comparable USDA data, some 887,000 children were hungry at some point in the year. In 2004, that number had been cut nearly in half (545,000).

CONCLUSION

It is instructive that in the past few years, Wendell Primus, one of the Clinton administration officials who resigned in protest, changed his opinion on the law. After reviewing the evidence, he admits to the success of welfare reform and has tempered his earlier pessimism (Harden, 2001). "In many ways," he stated, "welfare reform is working better than I thought it would. The sky isn't falling anymore. Whatever we have been doing over the last five years, we ought to keep going" (p. 1).

Recently, Congress did just that. As part of the Budget Reconciliation Act passed in early 2006, the work requirements begun in the original 1996 reform legislation have now been strengthened. In the original reform, states were required to engage some 45 percent of their TANF caseloads in work activities, to reduce caseloads by a similar percentage, or to achieve some combination of the two.

Most states were not required to have strong work incentives because caseloads dropped so dramatically and so quickly. By the late 1990s, then, federal requirements were met on the basis of caseload reductions. Therefore, states did not have to enact work requirements for the caseloads that remained. Not surprisingly, over the past 4 years the caseload population has remained largely unchanged.

With the reauthorization of the 1996 law, states must now place 45 percent of their TANF recipients into work activities or reduce future caseloads by an equivalent amount, although the base against which future caseload reduction will be measured is now the low caseload levels of 2005 as opposed to the high 1995 levels under the original law. Therefore, the work requirements have been substantially strengthened.

In looking at the bulk of the evidence, work-based welfare reform has been effective in reducing caseloads, increasing employment, and reducing poverty. Looking to the future, more could be done to reduce poverty, because merely increasing work is not enough.

In the United States, about one-third of all children are born out of wedlock, which has a disastrous effect on children and is the prime cause of child poverty and welfare dependence. In addition, children who grow up in single-parent families are more likely to become involved in crime, to have emotional and behavioral problems, to be physically abused, to fail in school, to abuse drugs, and to end up on welfare as adults.

Although as noted, the original welfare-reform law set some goals for increasing marriage and reducing out-of-wedlock childbearing, most states focused squarely on caseload reduction and ignored the law's other goals. The recent reauthorization changed that. The law now sets aside $100 million a year for local groups dedicated to fostering healthy marriages, especially for populations at risk of single parenthood. Even though the funding amounts to only 1 cent to strengthen marriage for every 15 dollars the government spends subsidizing single parenthood, this is a step in the right direction. Through this initiative, the federal government is acknowledging what social science has known for years: children are better off if they are raised by two parents in a stable marriage.

Naturally, this is an initiative whose fruits will not be evident for years, or even decades, to come. The out-of-wedlock birth crisis did not happen overnight, and it will take time to solve the problem. Certainly, though, this is an innovative step in welfare reform, with great promise to alleviate the problems of dependency and poverty in the decades to come.

NO

Mimi Abramovitz

In 1996, the U.S. government transformed the 60-year-old federal welfare program for single mothers into a state-administered block grant. The new PRWORA replaced the long-standing Aid to Families with Dependent Children (AFDC) program with Temporary Aid to Needy Families (TANF).

Billed as a way (1) to increase "self-sufficiency," (2) promote marriage, and (3) limit the domestic role of "big government," the controversial welfare overhaul moved families from welfare to work, discouraged single mother-hood, and shifted federal responsibility for welfare to the states.

Now that 10 years have passed, we can ask, Has welfare reform worked? The law's stated goals suggest that welfare reform should have (1) lowered welfare rolls without eliminating the safety net, (2) increased employment at wages that permitted "self-sufficiency," (3) raised marriage and reduced nonmarital birth rates, and (4) reduced federal and increased state control of welfare programs.

If merely lowering the welfare rolls and limiting the role of the federal government were the main goals of welfare reform, we could celebrate, because fewer women rely on welfare today, and states have more control over the program. However, evidence of the program's other outcomes suggest that we may want to hold our applause. The data reveal that welfare reform did not work. Instead, we now know that (1) the reformers used misleading numbers to build support for transforming welfare, (2) the resulting caseload decline reflected changes in the economy more than the changes in welfare, (3) the falling caseload numbers left many former recipients out in the cold, (4) the emphasis on "work-first" did not yield "self-sufficiency," (5) the new policy failed to reverse marriage and childbearing trends, (6) welfare reform increased family hardship, and (7) welfare reform perpetuated "welfare racism." In the final analysis, welfare reform did not work for the poor because it was part of a wider effort to redistribute income upward.

MISLEADING NUMBERS

The reformers spoke of a "welfare explosion" and a "welfare mess" to build support for stripping AFDC of its entitlement status and otherwise restricting eligibility. However, they based their claims on misleading numbers. Yes, the absolute number of AFDC recipients jumped from 4.5 million in 1965 to a pre-TANF peak of 14.2 million in 1994 (U.S. Department of Health and Human Services, n.d.). But rather than reflecting the "irresponsible" behav-ior of women on welfare, as claimed by the advocates of welfare reform, the enlarged welfare rolls reflected legitimate need in poor communities, pres-sure from the welfare rights and other social movements, the post–World War II liberalization of welfare's eligibility rules, and population growth. A more accurate picture of welfare's growth emerges when caseloads are adjusted for population size. This calculation, based on readily available numbers, reveals that caseloads actually peaked in the mid-1970s—long before welfare reform. More specifically, the AFDC caseload reached a high of 5.2 percent of the *total* population in 1975 and 46.7 percent of the *poverty* population in 1973 (U.S. Department of Health and Human Services, 2005a). By 1996, despite higher total numbers, the welfare caseload fell to 4.5 percent of the *total* and 33.3 percent of the *poverty* population. In brief, prior to welfare reform poor women did not need the strong arm of the state to leave welfare. Given lower poverty rates, the availability of jobs, and the desire of many women to leave, the always meager and punitive program, most women left welfare when they could.

WELFARE REFORM CANNOT CLAIM FULL CREDIT FOR THE SMALLER CASELOAD

The welfare caseload continued to fall after the enactment of the 1996 federal welfare law. It dropped to 5.4 million recipients in 2003, or 1.9 percent of the total population, and 15.1 percent of the poverty population (U.S. Department of Health and Human Services, 2005a). The post-1996 decline has been attributed to both welfare reform and the economic boom in the late 1990s. However, a recent study that echoes many others found that welfare reform accounted for the smallest share of the decrease. The study ascribed one-fifth of the falling caseload to welfare reform's time limits and sanctions, a quarter to the economy, a third to a residual policy bundle, and the rest to unexplained time effects (Danielson & Klerman, 2004). In sum, welfare reform cannot claim all the credit for the smaller caseload.

WELFARE REFORM LEFT POOR WOMEN OUT IN THE COLD

In contrast, welfare reform can claim significant credit for leaving many poor women and children out in the cold. As poverty and unemployment rates began to mount in 2000, the welfare system responded poorly to the resulting need for assistance. As noted earlier, the welfare caseload fell to a low of 1.9 percent of the *total* population and only 15.1 percent of the *poverty* population (U.S. Department of Health and Human Services, 2005a). Even more troubling, the number of eligible families who actually received benefits plummeted sharply from a pre-TANF high of 84.3 percent in 1995 to a low of 48 percent in 2002 (U.S. Department of Health and Human Services, 2005b). The welfare reformers continued to tout the low numbers, even though this historic change in public policy shredded an already tattered safety net.

The anti-poor, antigovernment spirit of welfare reform also spread to other social programs. This included tax cuts for the rich; the resulting loss of revenues needed to support social programs (Abramovitz & Morgen, 2006); the effort to privatize major social programs serving the middle class (e.g., Social Security and Medicare) (Shapiro & Greenstein, 2005); the conversion of housing, health, education, nutrition, and other social programs into block grants; and deep spending cuts in programs serving the poor. When it comes to rates of poverty and inequality, the United States compares unfavorably to most other Western industrialized nations (Shapiro & Greenstein, 2005).

"WORK-FIRST" DID NOT YIELD "SELF-SUFFICIENCY"

The welfare reformers promised that the "work-first" emphasis of TANF would make women "self-sufficient" (I prefer the term *economically secure*). That is, employment would yield enough income to cover basic costs for former recipients without resorting to state aid. Instead, welfare reform failed as the jobs women found either did not pay enough or did not last.

Jobs

It is generally agreed that immediately following the 1996 welfare overhaul, about 66 percent of women who left the program became employed—just 6 percent more than the 60 percent of women who left AFDC for work prior to welfare reform (Moffitt, 2002). In the booming 1990s, the demand for low-paid women workers was especially high in a small number of industries that had gained more jobs and wage growth than the overall economy, especially retail business and eating and drinking establishments (Boushey & Rosnick, 2004; Bilby, 2005). By the end of the 1990s, the overall unemployment rate for low-income single mothers had dropped faster than the national rate (Chapman & Bernstein, 2003; Fremstad, 2004).

Unfortunately, this successful job picture was fleeting. By 2000, as the economy sagged, the women exiting welfare had a harder time finding work than those who had left in the prosperous 1990s. Sadly, three of the nine private-sector industries that had hired welfare recipients recorded greater job losses than elsewhere in the private sector (Boushey & Rosnick, 2004). The promise of economic security vanished as the previously low unemployment rate for low-income single mothers rose from 9.8 percent in 2000 to 12.3 percent in 2002 (faster than the national rate); as the proportion of women who left welfare but never found work rose from 50 percent in 1999 to 58 percent in 2002; and as the number of women who left welfare with no job, no working partner, and no TANF or SSI benefits rose from 9.8 percent in 1999 to 13.8 percent in 2002 (Bilby, 2005; Fremstad, 2004; Loprest, 2003). Referred to as "disconnected" by researchers, the last group of families report significantly more health problems, fewer high school degrees, more long-term joblessness, many employment barriers, and a greater likelihood of being homeless and receiving help from charities (Bilby, 2005; Fremstad, 2004; Loprest, 2003).

Wages

The promise that work-after-welfare would pay also failed to materialize. A small number—about 25 percent—of the women who left welfare for work landed "good jobs," defined as full-time jobs that paid at least $7 an hour and that provided health insurance or that paid at least $8.50 an hour with no health benefits (Fremstad, 2004; Pavetti & Acs, 2001). At this hourly rate, their annual pay amounted to about $12,000, somewhat above the minimum wage but $2,000 to $2,500 below the official poverty line for a family of three. However, since only one-third of the women worked full-time or full-year, about two-thirds of the former recipients earned much less. Between 50 and 75 percent of the women who left welfare in the 1990s remained poor 2 to 3 years after leaving the program (Blank, 2002; Fremstad, 2004). And between 2000 and 2004 the poverty rate increased from 33.0 percent to 35.4 percent for all single mothers with children under age18; from 41 percent to 43.3 percent for black single mothers and from 42.9 percent to 45.9 percent for Hispanic (any race) single mothers (U.S. Census Bureau, n.d.).

When former recipients found that they could not make ends meet, they rightly sought help. Some turned to their equally poor families. Others supplemented their meager earnings with the Earned Income Tax Credit (EITC) or other government programs such as Food Stamps. Still others reapplied for TANF—if they had not exhausted the lifetime limit for receipt of benefits. In 28 states, the TANF caseloads grew by an average of 16.2 percent from 2001 to 2003—but rising as high as 49.7 percent in Arizona and 40.3 percent in Nevada. In the 22 other states the caseloads continued to fall—on average by 12.5 percent, but dropping as much as 43 percent in Illinois and 35.4 percent in New York (Rahmanou, Richer, & Greenberg, 2003). Either way, welfare reform did not work. The rising caseloads helped to meet the real needs faced by women who fell on hard times, but belied the promise that work would pay for those who try hard and play by the rules. The declining caseloads in the midst of rising poverty suggests that the government turned its back on thousands of families faced with unemployment, low wages, and mounting hardship.

Who Benefits?

If keeping people off welfare did little to help poor women, children, and communities, flooding the labor market with thousands of desperate workers certainly helped to lower labor costs for business. *The New York Times* recently reported that the influx of women into low-wage jobs since the welfare overhaul had depressed the median wage of all women workers (Uchitelle, 2004). Increased competition for jobs made it easier for employers to pay less, and harder for unions to negotiate good contracts. And corporate profits soared, comprising 12.4 percent of the national income in March 2004—not a record high, but significantly above its average level of 9.5 percent from 1970 to 2003. Meanwhile, only 51.7 percent of the national income went to wages and salaries, the lowest share since 1929 (Kamin & Shapiro, 2004; U.S. Bureau of Economic Analysis, 2006).

FAMILY VALUES: SINGLE MOTHERS AND NONMARITAL BIRTHS

The second major goal of welfare reform sought to promote heterosexual marriage as the foundation of society by encouraging the formation of two-parent families and reducing the incidence of single motherhood and non-marital births. Although the population experts had refuted the claim that access to welfare benefits undercut marriage and encouraged women to have "kids for money," the 1996 law included several provisions that promoted marriage by stigmatizing single motherhood. This included the family cap (no aid for children born to women on welfare); abstinence-only grants to high schools (that taught no sex before marriage but nothing about contraception and safe sex); and the "illegitimacy" bonus (extra funds for the five states achieving the highest reduction in nonmarital births without any increase in their abortion rate). The data show that welfare reform failed to enforce this narrow version of "family values." Neither TANF nor President Bush's subsequent marriage promotion campaign have changed long-term marriage and childbearing trends. Beginning before and continuing after welfare reform, these developments had a life of their own (Fein, Burstein, Fein, & Lindberg, 2003).

Marriage Rates

Welfare reformers argued that access to welfare benefits discouraged marriage and that limiting access to cash aid would reverse the downward trend. The data suggest otherwise. For one, millions of married couples use a wide variety of government programs, suggesting that access to assistance does not break up marriage. In 2003, among all recipients, the married share ranged from 13 percent for rent subsidies to 66 percent for workers' compensation benefits. Married women accounted for about one-fifth of all women who received TANF and food stamps and nearly half (46 percent) of all women with a family member registered for Medicaid (Fein, 2004).

Second, the loss of welfare benefits has not increased marriage rates of poor women. Despite the effort to promote marriage by stigmatizing single mothers and denying them aid, the marriage rate for women living at or below 100 percent of the poverty line continued to drop, falling from 37 percent in 1991 to 33 percent in 2001. This mirrors the declining marriage rate of all U.S women (Fields, 2003). The proportion of never-married women in the United States rose from 17.3 percent in 1960 to 21.2 percent in 2003, while the divorce rate mounted steadily from 2.9 percent in 1960 to 11.5 percent in 2003 (Statistical Abstract of The United States, 2006)

Still other data suggest that it is the lack of income rather than access to welfare benefits that may break the marital bond. Economically disadvantaged adults up to age 30 actually are more likely to marry than advantaged adults, but they are also more likely to split up (Fein, 2004). According to Fein (2004), "poverty brings a substantial array of stresses that spill over into marriages and create abundant marital distress" (p. 9). Reflecting this, the percent of married women with income at or above 300 percent of the poverty line fell from 69 percent in 1991 to 68 percent in 2001. That is, it barely changed. During the same period, as noted above, the marriage rate for poorer women (those with incomes below 100 of the poverty line) dropped from 37 percent to 33 percent. The rate for even poorer women (those with incomes at or below 50 percent of the poverty line) fell even more from 37 percent to 31 percent (Halle, 2002).

Childbearing

Nor has welfare reform led to changes in childbearing by unmarried women, which skyrocketed before, during, and after welfare reform. The percentage of children born outside of marriage rose from 4.0 percent in 1940 to 5.3 percent in 1960 to 32.3 percent in 1995 to 35.7 percent in 2004 (U.S. Department of Health and Human Services, 2005c; Hamilton, Ventura, Martin & Sutton, 2005; Child Trends, 2005b). Similarly, the birth rate per 1000 unmarried women age 15 to 44 increased from 22 births in 1960 to 44 in 1995 to 46 in 2004 (Child Trends, 2005a). The rise of births outside marriage during the past 60 years has little to do with welfare reform. Rather, it reflects shifts in the rate at which women marry and the rate at which both married and unmarried women have children. And more women are choosing to cohabit, to postpone marriage, to raise children on their own, or to otherwise respond to changed sexual and gender norms (Child Trends 2005b).

While the overwhelming majority of births to teens take place outside marriage, the birth rate per 1,000 unmarried teens age 15 to 19—the icon of welfare reform—began its steady decline prior to welfare reform. This rate dropped from a peak of 89 births per 1,000 unmarried teens age 15 to 19 in 1960 to 56.8 per 1,000 in 1995 to 41.7 per 1,000 in 2003 (Child Trends, 2005a). The pre-1996 declines of teen births appeared in all racial and ethnic groups, but was especially marked among black teens. It reflected the greater use of contraception, exposure to sex education, fear of AIDS, and changes in the economy. Despite recent abstinence campaigns, the long decline in the teen birth rate seems to have slowed in 2004 (Child Trends, 2005b).

Whether or not one believes that nonmarital births are problematic, it appears that welfare reform has had little or no impact on the trend. Like the opposition to abortion and same-sex marriage, however, the pro-marriage rhetoric fueled the effort to impose a monolithic set of family values on everyone else and successfully mobilized conservative voters.

INCREASED FAMILY HARDSHIP

Welfare was ostensibly created to help poor women in need. Aid to Dependent Children (ADC)—the forerunner of TANF—was included in the 1935 Social Security Act to support children deprived of male-breadwinner support and to allow single mothers to stay home with their children. For more than half a century the program provided a limited but crucial safety net that enabled low-income women to escape unsafe or unhappy marriages and ensured that their children had supervision and did not starve.

Although the goals of TANF do not include poverty reduction, increased hardship could not have been one of them. Yet in 1997, the first year following welfare reform, an Urban Institute (UI) survey found that many families scored high on a stress index that measured deprivation of food, housing, and health care. Family stress was linked to less engagement in school, more behavioral and emotional problems for children, and parental distress (Moore & Vandivere, 2000). In 2002, 6 years after welfare reform, more than half of all *poor* Americans—those most likely to use welfare—continued to report hardships, including lack of food, utility shutoffs, lack of a stove or refrigerator, or crowded or substandard housing (Chase-Lansdale, Coley, Lohman, & Pittman, 2002; Sherman, 1997). A 2003 survey of unemployed workers found mothers with children at home faced more hardships than all unemployed workers (National Employment Law Project, 2003). Parents preoccupied with such stressful circumstances often cannot provide an optimal home environment for their children. When overwhelmed, some may become harsh or coercive (Moore & Vandivere, 2000). Reflecting these pressures, the rate per 1,000 children under 18 in foster care jumped from 4.2 percent in 1982 to 7.8 percent in 1998, falling only slightly to 7.3 percent in 2002. (Paxton & Waldfogel, 2002). So much for the benefits of welfare reform for children.

PERPETUATED WELFARE RACISM

Welfare reform also failed because it did not protect women of color against the discrimination that made it harder for them to leave welfare for work than for white women. Existing evidence points to the perpetuation of what some call "welfare racism" (Neubeck & Casenave, 2001). Researchers have documented that welfare-department case workers are more helpful to white than to black recipients regarding access to information about jobs and child care and that local employers preferentially hire white over black job applicants with the same welfare and employment histories (Gooden, 1999, 1998; Jones-DeWeever, Peterson, & Xue 2003).

In the past, women of color were overrepresented on the welfare rolls relative to their number in the overall population (but not in relation to the number of women of color who are poor due to racial discrimination). Between 1992 and 2002, the proportion of white recipients fell from 38.9 percent to 31.6 percent, but that of African American rose from 37.2 percent to 38.3 percent and that of Latinos jumped from 17.8 percent to 24.9 percent. Today, women of color outnumber white women on the welfare rolls both absolutely and proportionately. This shift in the composition of caseloads risks a revival of the invidious racial and gender stereotypes that prior to 1996 were evoked by more than a few reformers to build support for ending welfare. The negative discourse was fueled by the media, which regularly linked poverty and welfare to race. Many white people turned against welfare, thinking (wrongly) that they had nothing to lose.

CONCLUSION

Welfare reform did not achieve its own stated goals or lead to the well-being of poor women, children, or low-income communities. Both of these failures can be explained by understanding that the real goals of the welfare overhaul lay elsewhere. Welfare reform is best understood as part of a broader strategy adopted by conservatives to promote economic growth by (1) limiting the role of the federal government, (2) shrinking the welfare state, (3) lowering labor costs, and (4) reducing the influence of popular movements best positioned to resist the overall austerity plan. It was also an effort to win votes by enforcing the family-values agenda of the far right that had gained a strong grip on U.S. public policy by the 1980s (Abramovitz, 2006a, 2006b, 2004). Neither accidental nor simply mean-spirited, welfare reform has not worked for poor women because the real goal of the reform was to help redistribute income upward and downsize government on the backs of the poor.

REFERENCES

Abramovitz, M. (2004, Fall/Winter). Saving capitalism from itself: Whither the welfare state? *New England Journal of Public Policy*, 21–32.

Abramovitz, M. (2006a). Neither accidental, not simply meanspirited: The context for welfare reform. In K. Kilty & E. Segal (Eds), *The promise of welfare reform: Rhetoric or reality*. New York: The Haworth Press.

Abramovitz, M. (2006b). Welfare reform in the United States: Race, class and gender matters. *Critical Social Policy, 26,* 336–364.

Abramovitz , M., & Morgen, S. (2006). *Taxes are a women's issue: Reframing the debate.* New York: Feminist Press.

Bilby, S. B. (2005, August). Path to job can be rocky for many women. Mott Memo. Charles Stewart Mott Foundation. Retrieved February 28, 2006, from www .mott.org/publications/pdf/memov4n1.pdf.

Blank, R. M. (2002, December). Evaluating welfare reform in the United States. *Journal of Economic Literature, 40*(4), 1105–1166.

Blank, R. M., & Schoeni, R. (2003). Changes in the distribution of children's family income over the 1990s. *American Economic Review, 93*(2), 304–308.

Boushey, H., & Rosnick, D. (2004, April 1). For welfare reform to work, jobs must be available. Center for Economic and Policy Research. Retrieved February 22, 2006, from www.cepr.net/publications/welfare_reform_2004_04.htm.

Center on Budget and Policy Priorities. (1996, July 26). Urban Institute study confirms that welfare bills would increase child poverty. Available from www.cbpp.org/URBAN726.HTM.

Chapman J., & Bernstein, J. (2003, April). Falling through the safety net: Low-income single mothers in the jobless recovery (Economic Policy Institute Brief #191). Retrieved February 22, 2006, from www.epinet.org/content.cfm/issuebriefs_ib191.

Chase-Lansdale, P. L., Coley, R. K., Lohman, B. J., & Pittman, L. D. (2002). Welfare reform: What about the children? *Welfare children and families study.* (Policy Brief 02-01). Baltimore: Johns Hopkins University.

Child Trends. (2005a, March). Facts at a glance (Publication #20004-02). Retrieved March 2, 2006, from www.childtrends.org/Files/Facts_2005.pdf.

Child Trends. (2005b, October 17). New trends in U.S. birth and fertility rates. Retrieved March 2, 2006, from www.childtrends.org/_pressrelease_page .cfm?LID=739191BF-CE3A-4BB4-B3C621BED7125A95.

Danielson, C., & Klerman, J. A. (2004). Why did the welfare caseload decline? (National Poverty Center Working Paper #04-12). Retrieved March 10, 2006, from www.npc.umich.edu/publications/workingpaper04/paper12/04-12.pdf.

DeWitt, L. (2005, October). Moynihan, welfare reform, and the myth of "benign neglect." Retrieved November 10, 2005, from www.larrydewitt.net/Essays/Moynihan.htm.

Edelman, P. (1997, March). The worst thing Bill Clinton has done. *The Atlantic Monthly, 279*(3), 43–58.

Fein, D. (2004). Married and poor: Basic characteristics of economically disadvantaged married couples in the U.S. Retrieved March 7, 2006, from www.mdrc.org/publications/393/workpaper.pdf.

Fein, D. J., Burstein, N. R., Fein, G. G., & Lindberg, L. D. (2003). *The determinants of marriage and cohabitation among disadvantaged Americans: Research findings and needs.* Rethesda, MD: Abt Associates, Inc.

Fields, J. (2003). America's families and living arrangements: 2003. *Current Population Reports,* (P20-553). U.S. Census Bureau, Washington, D.C. Retrieved March 10, 2006, from www.census.gov/prod/2004pubs/p20-553.pdf.

Fremstad, S. (2004). Recent welfare reform research findings: Implications for TANF reauthorization and state TANF policies. Center on Budget and Policy Priorities. Retrieved February 10, 2005, from www.cbpp.org/1-30-04wel.htm.

Gooden, S. (1998). All things not being equal: Difference in caseworker support toward black and white welfare clients. *Harvard Journal of African American Public Policy, 4,* 23–31.

Gooden, S. (1999). The hidden third party: Welfare recipients' experiences with employers. *Journal of Public Management and Social Policy, 5*(1), 69–83.

Halle, T. (2002). Charting parenthood: A statistical portrait of fathers and mothers in America. (Child Trends research brief). Retrieved February 23, 2006, from www .childtrends.org/Files/ParenthoodRpt2002.pdf.

Hamilton, B. E., Ventura, S. J., Martin, J. A., & Sutton, P. D. (2005). Preliminary births for 2004, Tables 1 and 2. National Center for Health Statistics. Retrieved March 2, 2006, from www.cdc.gov/nchs/products/pubs/pubd/hestats/prelim_births/ prelim_births04.htm.

Harden, B. (2001, August 12). Two-parent families rise after change in welfare laws. *The New York Times,* p. 1.

Jones-DeWeever, A., Peterson, J., & Xue, S. (2003). Before and after welfare reform: The work and well-being of low-income single parent families. Institute for Women's Policy Research. Retrieved February 20, 2006, from www.iwpr.org/ pdf/D454.pdf.

Kamin, D., & Shapiro, I. (2004). An uneven recovery: New government data show corporate profits enjoying unusually large gains, while workers' incomes lag behind. Center on Budget and Policy Priorities. Retrieved March 5, 2006, from www.cbpp.org/9-3-04ui.pdf.

Loprest, P. (2003, August). Disconnected welfare leavers face serious risks. Urban Institute. Retrieved December 30, 2005, from www.urban.org/publications/ 310839.html.

Moffitt, R. (2002, January). From welfare to work: What the evidence shows. The Brookings Institute (Policy Brief #13). Retrieved February 15, 2006, from www .brookings.edu/es/wrb/publications/pb/pb13.pdf.

Moore, K., & Vandivere, S. (2000). *Stressful family lives, child and family well-being.* (New Federalism Brief, B17). Washington, DC: The Urban Institute.

National Employment Law Project. (2003). Women workers and their children especially hard hit by unemployment. Retrieved December 30, 2005, from www .nelp.org/news/pressreleases/pr073003b.cfm.

Neubeck, K., & Casenave, N. (2001). *Welfare racism: Play the race card against America's poor.* New York: Routledge.

Nord, M., Andrews, M., & Carlson, S. (2005, October). *Household food security in the United States, 2004.* USDA Economic Research Service (Report No. 11). Washington, DC: USDA.

O'Neill, J. E. & Hill, M. A. (2001, July). *Gaining ground? Measuring the impact of welfare reform on welfare and work.* (Civic Report No. 17). New York: Manhattan Institute.

Pavetti, L., & Acs, G. (2001, Fall). Moving up, moving out, or going nowhere? A study of the employment patterns of young women and the implications for welfare mothers. *Journal of Policy Analysis and Management, 20*(4), 721–736.

Paxton, C., & Waldfogel, J. (2002). Work, welfare, and child maltreatment. *Journal of Labor Economics, 20*(3), 435–474.

216 PART III SOCIAL WORK AND SOCIAL-SERVICE DELIVERY ISSUES

Rahmanou, H., Richer, H., & Greenberg, M. (2003, October 16). Welfare caseload remains relatively flat in second quarter of 2003. Center for Law and Social Policy. Retrieved February 28, 2006, from www.clasp.org/publications/caseload_2003_Q2.pdf.

Rector, R., & Youssef, S. (1999, May 11). The determinants of welfare caseload decline. Heritage Foundation Center for Data Analysis (Report #99-04). Retrieved from www.heritage.org/Research/Welfare/CDA99-04.cfm.

Rector, R., & Fagan, P. (2003, February 6). The continuing good news about welfare reform. Heritage Foundation, (Backgrounder No. 1620). Retrieved from www.heritage.org/Research/Welfare/bg1620.cfm.

Shapiro, I., & Greenstein, R. (2005, February 9). Cuts to low-income programs may far exceed the contribution of these programs to deficit's return. Center on Budget and Policy Priorities. Retrieved February 28, 2005, from www.cbpp.org/2-4-05bud.pdf.

Sherman, A. (1997). *Poverty matters: The cost of child poverty in America.* Washington DC: Children's Defense Fund.

Statistical Abstract of the United States. Infoplease. (2006). Marital status of the population by sex, 1900–2003. Retrieved from www.infoplease.com/ipa/A0110389.html.

Uchitelle, L. (2004, June 5). Healthy Growth of 248.000 jobs reported in May. *The New York Times,* p. A1.

U.S. Bureau of Economic Analysis. (2006, March). Current and historical data, national charts, D55. *Survey of current business, 86*(3). Retrieved March 31, 2006, from www.bea.gov/bea/ARTICLES/2006/03March/D-Pages/0306DpgD.pdf.

U.S. Census Bureau. (2005). Historical poverty tables, 1959–2004. Retrieved March 5, 2006, from www.census.gov/hhes/www/poverty/histpov/perindex.html.

U.S. Census Bureau. (n. d.). Historical poverty tables, Table 4: Poverty status of families, by type of family, presence of related children, race, and Hispanic origin: 1959 to 2004. Retrieved February 1, 2006, from www.census.gov/hhes/www/poverty/histpov/hstpov4.html.

U.S. Department of Health and Human Services. (2005a). Indicators of welfare dependence (Annual Report to Congress, TANF Table 2). Retrieved February 16, 2005, from http://aspe.hhs.gov/hsp/indicators05/apa.htm#tbt1.

U.S. Department of Health and Human Services. (2005b). Indicators of welfare dependence (Annual report to Congress. Table IND4a). Retrieved February 16, 2006, from http://aspe.hhs.gov/hsp/indicators05/ch2.htm#ch2_1.

U.S. Department of Health and Human Services. (2005c). Statistics, U.S. Welfare Caseloads Information. Administration for Children and Families News. Retrieved February 16, 2006, from www.acf.hhs.gov/news/stats/6097rf.htm.

CAN CHILD PROTECTIVE SERVICES BE REFORMED?

Editor's Note:

The issue of child abuse has been periodically driven into the headlines by sensational stories of a child's death or physical and sexual abuse. This creates a maelstrom of concern resulting in some minor reforms, at least until the next big news story hits. The problem of child abuse then quietly recedes into the background until the next egregious case emerges. This roller coaster of public concern typically results in little real change in the quantity or quality of services, or in funding levels.

Some critics of Child Protective Services (CPS), the public agency charged with protecting vulnerable children, maintain that the system is so rife with incompetence, inadequate training, hierarchal and unimaginative administration, chronic overload of caseworkers, high turnover rates, and poor pay as to make it not salvageable. Others believe that CPS can and must be reformed.

Kristine E. Nelson, D.S.W., is the dean and a professor in the Graduate School of Social Work at Portland State University in Oregon. For nearly a decade, she was the director of research at the National Resource Center on Family-Based Services at the University of Iowa, 1 of 10 national child-welfare resource centers. She has been the principal investigator on six federally funded studies of family preservation services and of child neglect and has participated in several national symposia and expert panels on research and research methodology in these areas. Dr. Nelson is coauthor of *Reinventing Human Services: Community- and Family-Centered Practice* (Aldine, 1995), *Evaluating Family-Based Services* (Aldine, 1995), and *Alternative Models of Family Preservation: Family-Based Services in Context* (Charles C. Thomas, 1992).

Diane K. Yatchmenoff, Ph.D., is a research assistant professor at Portland State University and assistant director of the Regional Research Institute for

Human Services (RRI), the research arm of the Graduate School of Social Work (GSSW). Her research interests include the prevention and treatment of child abuse and neglect and the intersection of public child-welfare and children's mental-health service systems. Dr. Yatchmenoff is a principal investigator for the evaluation of Oregon's statewide child-welfare system of care and for a federally funded initiative to transform the children's mental-health system for young children and their families in Multnomah County, Oregon. Dr. Yatchmenoff teaches graduate-level courses in research methods and child-welfare policy at the GSSW.

Katharine Cahn, Ph.D., M.S.W., is the executive director of the Child Welfare Partnership and an assistant professor at the Graduate School of Social Work (GSSW) at Portland State University. Her professional social work encompasses training, consultation, education, and research to promote systems improvement in child welfare. Recent research projects include her dissertation research on the adoption of innovation in child welfare, and a community-based action-research project to address disproportionality in child welfare. Recent consultation and training projects include work to promote wraparound services, family group conferencing, and culturally responsive engagement practices in public child welfare in the Pacific Northwest. In addition, Dr. Cahn has been the principle investigator or consultant for several grant-funded projects to develop management and supervisory curricula for public child-welfare agencies. She teaches in the social services and administration concentration at the GSSW and is a guest lecturer in child-welfare policy and practice courses at the graduate and undergraduate level.

David Stoesz, Ph.D., is a professor of social policy at Virginia Commonwealth University and the director of policyAmerica. He has been a caseworker and a welfare department director, and is the author of several books, including *Quixote's Ghost: The Right, the Liberati, and the Future of Social Policy* (Oxford University Press, 2005), and *American Social Welfare Policy* (with Howard Karger) (5th ed., Allyn & Bacon, 2006).

YES

Kristine E. Nelson, Diane K. Yatchmenoff, and Katharine Cahn

It has been said that how we care for our children and our elderly is the true test of the humanity of a society. Given this, the only possible answer to the question posed in this chapter is yes. Child protective services not only can, but must, be reformed. To be successful requires (1) an understanding of how we got to the current situation and what that situation is, (2) clarity on the shape of a more desirable system, and (3) a keen understanding of the dynamics of change in large complex systems (how to get there from here).

PURPOSE, HISTORY, AND CURRENT SITUATION

Purpose

The purpose of the Child Protective Service (CPS) system is to protect children from abuse and neglect. Though shaped by federal legislation, CPS is codified in state laws mandating that services be provided to families identified as abusing or neglecting. Services are usually delivered by state or county agencies funded with a combination of state and federal dollars.

History

A commitment to child rescue emerged from general concerns about child welfare in the late 19th century. During the 19th and early 20th centuries, a legal framework for child protection emerged along with the establishment of the major services provided to abused and neglected children: orphanages, institutions, foster-family care, adoption, and in-home services. Throughout this time period, the system maintained a culture of child rescue and mother blaming (Abramowitz, 1996; Gordon, 1994.)

It wasn't until Henry Kempe identified the battered child syndrome using X-ray technology to detect old injuries (Kempe Silverman, Steele, Droegemueller, & Silver, 1962) that the shape of the current system of child protection was established. Based on a medical model, parental pathology was defined as the source of the problem. In response to Dr. Kempe's well-publicized work, Congress passed the Child Abuse Prevention and Treatment Act of 1974 that called for mandatory reporting and suggested— although it did not pay for—services to ameliorate parental problems. Encouraged by this bill, a successful public education campaign led to a tenfold increase in reports of child abuse and neglect by the early 1980s (Daro & Donnelly, 2002). However, a dramatic decline in funding for child welfare under the Reagan administration assured that legislatively mandated services to support parental functioning and family preservation were never widely available (Nelson, 1997). This lack of funding has been exacerbated by a chronic shortage of trained workers to carry out this difficult work (Zlotnik, 2003).

CURRENT SITUATION

Child and family problems have also become more serious. Illegal drugs such as methamphetamine and crack cocaine now join the devastating impact of alcohol on family functioning. Research documents the trauma and brain impairments that stem from domestic violence, neglect, and parental mental-health problems (Harden, 2000). Nationally, the majority of cases that come to the attention of child-welfare agencies are due to child neglect, a problem that responds best to longer-term, multifaceted intervention that is precluded by the categorical funding of the current CPS service-delivery system. It is, therefore, not surprising that many conclude there is a crisis in child protection.

There are other indications that the system as currently configured is failing to meet the needs of all children. In over 26 jurisdictions, lawsuits have been successfully filed against state or county agencies for violations, from caseload size to lost children to lack of attention to mental-health needs (Sallee & Shaening, 1995; Schorr, 2000). There is particular concern about the disproportional occurrence of negative outcomes for children of color (Brown & Bailey-Etta, 1997; Roberts, 2003). For example, despite similar rates of abuse, children of color are more likely than white children to be placed in out-of-home care (Morton, 1999). Children of color also receive fewer services while in out-of-home care and leave the system less prepared for adulthood (Courtney et al., 1996; Courtney & Skyles, 2003).

THE DESIRED SHAPE OF REFORM

In the most promising approaches to reform in recent years, CPS acts as a gateway for children and families who are in need of assistance, support, or intervention to ensure their safety, health, and well-being. This implies that CPS is closely linked with a larger network of child and family-serving systems in the community and that it is effective in engaging families, identifying needs, and providing bridges to other services. It also implies that child protection is a community responsibility involving prevention, education, and supportive services to a greater extent than legal or criminal sanctions (U.S. Advisory Board on Child Abuse and Neglect, 1993).

One such approach is to *embed child protection in community-based, family-driven, and culturally competent Systems of Care*. The Systems of Care movement has grown exponentially over the past 20 years in the field of children's mental health (see, for example, Lourie, Stroul, & Friedman, 1998; New Freedom Commission on Mental Health, 2003; Pires, 2002), providing integrated services to maintain children in the least restrictive placements and to wrap individualized formal and informal services and supports around children and families.

Recently, a federally sponsored initiative has encouraged states to model their public child-protection systems on the core principles in the children's mental-health Systems of Care program (U.S. Department of Health and Human Services, 2003). This transformation is intended to result in a number of significant reforms, including:

- An integrated, comprehensive service-delivery system in which state and local child- and family-serving entities collaborate at every level to provide seamless, noncategorical, and effective services.
- A single plan of care for children and families entering the CPS system, one that destigmatizes their involvement and puts families in charge of service planning.
- Accountability at all levels (case level, practice level, system level) for the experience of children and families with families at the table and taking leadership roles.
- Responsiveness to cultural needs and cultural differences, driven by the voice of the consumer in determining what cultural responsiveness means and how it is to be accomplished.
- Willingness to address the unique and individual needs identified by families (including youth), using flexible funds as necessary.

The federal funds allocated to implement System of Care principles in 2003 both highlighted and contributed additional resources to reform efforts that have been ongoing in many states, thereby increasing the potential for a more significant and widespread impact on the CPS system nationally.

A second approach to CPS reform that rests on some of the same core principles is the *two-tiered* or *alternative response* system (National Clearinghouse on Child Abuse and Neglect Information, 2005). This approach recognizes that relatively few families who are reported for alleged maltreatment of their children require the coercive intervention that has become the hallmark of CPS and that many could be helped instead through a lower level of service provided on a voluntary basis. Alternative response systems rely on careful assessment of the safety and level of future risk to the child(ren) as well as the capacity to successfully engage families on a voluntary basis (English, Wingard, Marshall, Orme, & Orme, 2000; Loman & Siegel, 2005). Such a system, to be effective, requires highly skilled intensive outreach and engagement strategies with families who have multiple problems and may be reluctant to accept services. In turn, available, accessible, and *effective* community-based services are critical. In an alternative response system, court involvement would be rarely invoked, and only when absolutely necessary. Such an approach represents a genuine paradigm shift from our current system.

This paradigm shift appears to have been successfully accomplished in a number of states (Hernandez & Barrett, 1996; Siegel et al., 1998), while in others the necessary level of outreach and engagement has been hampered by resource constraints combined with the challenges of engaging high-risk families (English et al., 2000). As a result, the impact of these important reform efforts on CPS practice has been limited. This is true also of Systems of Care principles. In Oregon, for example, a 5-year evaluation of a statewide initiative to develop individualized, strengths/needs-based service delivery demonstrated substantial impact in some locations and much less in others (Cahn, 2003; Shireman et al., 2001). This suggests that reform is possible but not inevitable, even in the face of good ideas, strong advocacy, and the infusion of at least some resources.

So what is required to translate good ideas into significant lasting practice—or system-level reform—that would result in widespread improvements in the outcomes for children and families?

REFORMING LARGE COMPLEX SYSTEMS

In most states, child protection services are delivered by state and county bureaucracies. Bureaucracies by their very nature institutionalize practice, make work products consistent, and resist change. Therefore CPS reform will require major systems change. An extensive organizational change literature points to elements necessary to successfully take innovative practices up to scale. Drawing from this literature one can say thatsystems change *is* possible in the presence of: (1) a strong and sustained leadership message, (2) strategies to engage line staff, (3) changes in formal and informal organizational culture and structures, and (4) support and alignment (even pressure) by community groups, other professionals, and advocates.

A sustained leadership message is critical and has been present in most notable child-welfare systems changes. Only a clear leadership message can counteract the two most potent forces blocking systems change: (1) the designed-in inertia of bureaucracies noted in classic organizational literature (Weber, 1958) and addressed specifically in child welfare (Hagedorn, 1995; Littrell & Zurcher, 1983), and (2) change or initiative "fatigue"—observed in staff who have been subject to repeat short-term (and often conflicting) agency-change projects with no overarching vision (Kettner, Daley, & Nichols, 1985). This second dynamic is an artifact of the highly politicized context of agenda setting in the public sector. Public concern is often triggered by dramatic media coverage of a case with a poor outcome. In response, legislators propose quick fixes and demand results within the short, 2-year election cycle (Altshuler & Behn, 1997). Against this backdrop, change efforts are almost impossible to launch and to sustain over longer periods. Staff and middle managers can become inoculated against and cynical about change efforts (Smale, 1998), adopting an attitude of "this too shall pass." For this reason a strong sustained leadership message is critical. It needs to be clear that "this change will *not* pass." Staff must hear that they will have to come to terms with the change one way or the other (adopt it, pretend to adopt it, or leave).

But top-down messages are not enough. Although the formal structure is a top-down bureaucracy, a great deal of discretion rests with professionals on the line. Staff must be engaged in the change on their own terms. Staff will greet any change in child welfare with one or both of the following two statements: (1) "We do that already; it's just good social work" or (2) "We can't possibly do that because of workload" (Cahn, 2003). The change needs to offer immediate benefits not just to children and families, but to the staff themselves. Sustainable change will be consistent with good social work principles and will offer relief to workload pressures, saving time rather than taking more time.

The organizational structure must also be changed to align with the new practices. Where cultural responsiveness and family-driven planning are part of the reform, new contractors, new relationships with the community, and new relationships with kin and extended family networks must be established. If the reform includes an emphasis on individualized case plans, more flexible contracting and payment mechanisms must be established. New office locations must be provided to put staff close to the community. It is not possible to implement changes in practice and attitude without changing the hard-wiring of the organizational structure.

Changes in informal culture must be made as well. Language and reward structures and symbolic values can be shifted to align with the reform. For example, in the late 1980s, Oregon workers began to refer to contract agencies, kinship networks, and courts alike as "community partners," heralding the beginning of a breakdown in the traditional walls that separate public child welfare from the private and community sectors. While language changes do not in and of themselves cause change, they can help embed a change if accompanied by structural change and financial rewards. Without accompanying structural change, changes in slogans only add to staff resistance and cynicism. Organizations with positive climates have better outcomes (Glisson & Hemmelgarn, 1998).

Organizational culture is set in part by the characteristics, values, and skills of the workforce who make up the culture. Offices with a majority of workers who have had professional education or training prior to hiring will be more innovative. Education that teaches strengths-based, collaborative, culturally responsive work will be supportive to reform. Recent national initiatives to "re-professionalize" the child-welfare workforce (increase the number of staff with social-work undergraduate and graduate degrees) and to retain educated staff are examples of such efforts (Briar-Lawson & Zlotnik, 2003; Fox, Miller, & Barbee 2003).

Finally, the external environment must align with, and even demand, the change. Sustained pressure from outside groups will help dislodge the inherent stability of bureaucracy. A lawsuit or the threat of a lawsuit has been key to change in several states (Sallee & Shaening, 1995; Shireman et al., 2001). However, the threat must be combined with new resources. Legislative investment (such as adding new positions to reduce caseloads or providing flexible funds that workers can spend to customize planning or offer concrete services) and new coalitions have been key parts of change efforts (Glisson & Hemmelgarn, 1998).

CONCLUSION

It is clear that change in CPS is not only necessary, but possible. The current system fails to meet the needs of children and families, particularly children and families of color, who turn to the system for protection, support, and safety. The nature and shape of the change has emerged in pilot projects and systemwide change efforts across the country. We have guidance from other fields, as well, to aid the change effort. A strong leadership message, a change that engages staff, congruence in organizational structure and culture, and meaningful advocacy and support from the community will all be elements of a successful reform effort.

The care of children is the most important task of society. There is no alternative to reform of the current system and it can be done.

NO
David Stoesz

Child protective services is irreparably broken and should be replaced by a new infrastructure that assures vulnerable children and troubled families the services they need. Evidence of systemic collapse is extensive. Critical examinations of child protection by social workers (Costin, Karger, & Stoesz, 1996; Gelles, 1996, Epstein, 1999) and journalists (Horwitz, Higham, & Cohen, 2000; Bernstein, 2001) reveal a nonsystem that employs too few capable professionals; rations services, often with disastrous results; uses confidentiality to cover bureaucratic bungling; and even defies court orders to assure care for maltreated children. The child-welfare scandals of the 1990s, so poignant in New York City and Washington, D.C., have been supplanted by tragedies in Florida, Washington, and New Jersey.

Yet newspaper headlines miss the more quotidian indicators of program failure. The rates of reported as well as confirmed cases of abuse and neglect in the United States are more than double those of the United Kingdom or Canada (Waldfogel, 1998). Yet child protection, the most urgent of child welfare services, often fails its mandate to intervene effectively on behalf of maltreated children. The "system has faced confusion about its purposes and methods, declining professionalism, and progressive disorganization," noted eminent child-welfare scholar Alvin Schorr (2000), "In many places the debasement of services, the decline of staff, and the absence of sustained citizen engagement are so advanced that it is difficult to see how these may be reversed" (pp. 124, 131).

In 2003 the Federal Administration on Children and Families reported the performance of 32 states with respect to seven basic outcomes central to child welfare: not one state was in full-compliance with all outcomes; not one state could assure that children had a permanent living arrangement or that their families were better able to care for them (Administration on Children and Families, 2003). States have proven unable to provide an accurate and timely picture of their performance. For 1998, North Dakota reported improbably that not one incident of maltreatment had occurred. For 2001, Kansas and Maryland failed to provide any data on allegations of maltreatment. Of those states reporting, allegations ranged from Kentucky's high of 159.5 per 1,000 children in 1998 to Pennsylvania's low of 7.9. In 2001, founded cases ranged from Alaska's high of 82.6 per 1,000 children to Pennsylvania's low of 1.6 (Ways and Means Committee, 2004). Such disparate data indicate that federalism, the complementary relationship between the federal government and the states, has failed in child protection.

An insufficient number of professionally prepared staff contributes to the crisis in children's services. "Right now," researchers from the Annie E. Casey Foundation (2003) concluded, "the conditions of frontline human services jobs create a serious shortfall between the kind of workers we have and ones who can effectively and compassionately address the enormous problems of vulnerable children and their families" (pp. iv–40).

> Frontline jobs are becoming more and more complex while the responsibility placed on workers remains severely out of line with their preparation and baseline abilities. Many are leaving the field while a new generation of college graduates shows little interest entering the human services sector. *Millions of taxpayer dollars are being poured into a compromised system that not only achieves little in the way of real results, but its interventions often do more harm than good.* It is clear that frontline human services jobs are not attracting the kinds of workers we need and that regulations, unreasonable expectations, and poor management mire workers and their clients in a dangerous status quo (emphasis added). (Annie E. Casey Foundation, 2003, p. 2)

Inadequate training, high caseloads, and poor supervision conspire to subvert child protection: Perhaps 50 percent of children who die from maltreatment are known to local child-welfare agencies at the time of their death (Lindsey, 1994). Inexplicably, the nation's schools of social work have failed to provide a sufficient number of child-welfare professionals to staff an adequate level of child protective care. Despite annual federal training, expenditures exceeding $280 million, there is no accounting of how many students, staff, and parents are trained; indeed, no one knows how many schools of social work receive federal training funds.

Inferior care leaves indelible marks on troubled children. Most children who enter foster care do so as a result of maltreatment that comes to the attention of child protective services. For abused and neglected children, foster care fails to provide an adequate, nurturing environment. The Northwest Foster Care Alumni Study revealed that post-traumatic stress disorder rates for former foster children were "up to twice as high as for U.S. war veterans" (Pecora et al., 2005, p. 32). The University of Chicago's Chapin Hall reported that children who had aged-out of foster care had significantly higher rates of pregnancy, unemployment, and homelessness (Davey, 2005). Violence among youth and young adults is associated with earlier experiences of maltreatment, and subsequent incarceration exacerbates problematic behavior (Garbarino, 1995, 1999).

These factors converge into a "perfect storm" in children's services: rather than receive constructive care, troubled children are confronted with defective programming and inadequate staff; tragically, their circumstances are often worsened. Too often, a child's induction into child welfare initiates a vicious cycle of dysfunction; rather than provide substantive assistance to abused and neglected children, child protective services inducts them into a programmatic purgatory. The utter failure of child welfare in general, and child protective services in particular, justifies replacing a nonsystem that has been associated with damaging children and their families with a network that promises to provide essential services in a prompt and accountable manner. The following principles provide benchmarks for the future care of maltreated children:

- Reorganize child welfare through a local children's authority, which would be held accountable for provision of a range of services for children and their families.
- Require the children's authority to institute a validated risk-assessment instrument integrated with a management-information system that allows aggregating data and following families longitudinally.
- Construct a national database that follows abusers and children who are under the supervision of a children's authority across jurisdictions.
- Open public access to records of cases where children have been seriously injured or died after being placed under agency care.
- Require the children's authority to report accurate data on the disposition of cases on a monthly basis in exchange for public funding.
- Publish annually a report on child welfare comparing children's authorities with respect to specific variables relating to child abuse and neglect.
- Consolidate funding for categorical programs into a block grant that is open-ended as long as children's authorities meet specific performance standards.
- Establish a national certification of child-protection supervisors that includes training in forensics, investigation techniques, family and juvenile law, management information systems, research, and ethics.

- Required educational institutions in receipt of child-welfare training funds to conduct state-of-the-art research in child protection, especially field experiments designed to demonstrate the effectiveness of various interventions.
- Reassign all data relating to child morbidity and mortality to the Centers for Disease Control and Prevention.

The Savannah/Chatham Youth Futures Authority illustrates the deployment of such a model, and the Harlem Children's Zone appears to be moving in this direction.

Two caveats are essential to the successful replacement of the present nonsystem of child welfare with a nationwide network of integrated children's authorities. First, children's authorities should be phased-in, designated by the Administration of Children and Families, only after they have met rigorous standards. Second, states must be included in the process, making provision for the legal designation of the children's authority as well as leveraging resources.

Historically, intervention on behalf of maltreated children became a societal issue during the Industrial Revolution over a century ago (Leiby, 1978; Trattner, 1999). The child-welfare project, conceived during the Progressive Era, foundered on the shoals of two institutions. First, Title IV of the 1935 Social Security Act allowed the states to define child welfare, funded through federal entitlements. Our legacy from this period has been the bureaucratic, uncoordinated, and unaccountable nonsystem of child welfare. Second, social work was to provide the professional staffing for child welfare, arguably the preeminent mission of the profession (Young, 1964). Instead of demonstrating increasing proficiency in helping maltreated children, social work has effectively abandoned child welfare, not only failing to inspire capable young people to enter the field, but neglecting to conduct state-of-the-art research on interventions or to maintain even the most basic management-information systems. Duncan Lindsey's (1994) observation of over a decade ago still holds today: "The amount of scientifically validated research on child abuse and neglect is vanishingly small" (p. 117).

Most inexcusable about the institutional miasma of child protection has been the unwillingness of child-welfare professionals to acknowledge the inadequacy of current programming. Rather than take a stand on professional ethics and defend standards of practice, child-welfare workers have preferred to take shortcuts in casework, ration care when necessary, and complain about inept supervision and impossible caseloads. In many public agencies, the institutionalized inadequacy of contemporary child protection should invite a strike, but child-welfare professionals have been loath to consider a strategy so empowering. Short of this, child-welfare workers might consider reinventing their work, taking advantage of organizational innovations and information technology, but there is little indication that these are occurring either. Evidently, child-welfare professionals prefer to take a "mental-health day" whenever possible, and when this no longer suffices, simply quit. The result, of course, is extraordinarily high staff turnover, with entire caseloads shifted from worker to worker in quick succession, leaving vulnerable children adrift. That this should occur at public expense is the shame of the nation; that it continues under the guise of professional care is the embarrassment of social work.

REFERENCES

Abramowitz, M. (1996). *Regulating the lives of women: Social welfare policy from colonial times to the present* (2nd ed.). Boston: South End.

Administration on Children and Families. (2003). *Summary results of the 2001 and 2002 Child and Family Service Reviews.* Washington, DC: Author.

Altshuler, A. A., & Behn, R. D. (Eds.). (1997). *Innovation in American government: Challenges, opportunities, and dilemmas.* Washington, DC: Brookings Institute.

Annie E. Casey Foundation. (2003). *The unsolved challenge of system reform.* Baltimore: Author.

Bernstein, N. (2001). *The lost children of Wilder.* New York: Vintage.

Briar-Lawson, K., & Zlotnik, J. (2003). *Charting the impacts of university-child welfare collaboration.* New York: Haworth Press.

Brown, A. W., & Bailey-Etta, B. (1997). An out-of-home care system in crisis: Implications for African American children in the child welfare system. *Child Welfare, 76,* 65–83.

Cahn, K. (2003). Getting there from here: Variables associated with the adoption of innovation in public child welfare. (Doctoral dissertation, Portland State University). *Dissertation Abstracts International, 65*(03), 1114. AAT 3127385.

Costin, L., Karger, H., & Stoesz, D. (1996). *The politics of child abuse in America.* New York: Oxford University Press.

Courtney, M. E., Barth, R. P., Berrick, J. D., Brooks, D., Needell, B., and Part, L. (1996). Race and child welfare services: Past research and future directions. *Child Welfare, 75,* 99–137.

Courtney, A., & Skyles, A. (2003). Racial disproportionality in the child welfare system. *Children and Youth Services Review, 35,* 355–358.

Daro, D., & Donnelly, A. C. (2002). Charting the waves of prevention: Two steps forward, one step back. *Child Abuse and Neglect, 26,* 731–742.

Davey, M. (2005, May 19). Those who outgrow foster care still struggle, study finds. *The New York Times,* p. A14.

English, D. J., Wingard, T., Marshall D., Orme, M., & Orme, A. (2000). Alternative responses to child protective services: Emerging issues and concerns. *Child Abuse and Neglect, 24,* 375–388.

Epstein, W. (1999). *Children who could have been.* Madison: University of Wisconsin.

Fox, S., Miller, V., & Barbee, A. (2003). Finding and keeping child welfare workers: Effective use of training and professional development. *Journal of Human Behavior in the Social Environment, 7,* 67–81.

Garbarino, J. (1995). *Raising children in a toxic environment.* San Francisco: Jossey-Bass.

Garbarino, J. (1999). *Lost boys.* New York: Free Press.

Gelles, R. (1996). *The book of David.* New York: Basic Books.

Glisson, C., & Hemmelgarn, A. (1998). The effects of organizational climate and interorganizational coordination on the quality and outcomes of children's services systems. *Child Abuse and Neglect, 22,* 401–421.

Gordon, L. (1994). *Pitied but not entitled: Single mothers and the history of welfare, 1890–1935.* New York: Free Press.

Hagedorn, J. M. (1995). *Forsaking our children: Bureaucracy and reform in the child welfare system.* Chicago: Lake View Press.

Harden, B. J. (2000). Safety and stability for foster children: A developmental perspective. *Future of Children, 14*(1), 36.

Hernandez, M., & Barrett, B. A. (1996). *Evaluation of Florida's family services response system.* Tampa: University of Southern Florida Mental Health Institute.

Horwitz, S., Higham, S., & Cohen, S. (2000, March 16). "Protected" children died as government did little. *The Washington Post,* p. A1.

Kempe, C. H., Silverman, F., Steele, B., Droegemueller, W., & Silver, H. (1962). The battered child syndrome. *Journal of the American Medical Association, 181,* 17–24.

Kettner, P. M., Daley, J. M., & Nichols, A. W. (1985). *Initiating change in organizations and communities.* Monterey, CA: Brooks/Cole.

Leiby, J. (1978) *A history of social welfare and social work in the United States.* New York: Columbia University Press.

Lindsey, D. (1994). *The welfare of children.* New York: Oxford University Press.

Littrell, B., & Zurcher, L. A. (1983). *Bureaucracy as a social problem.* Greenwich: JAI Press.

Loman, A. L., & Siegel, G. (2005). Alternative response in Minnesota: Findings of the program evaluation. *Protecting Children, 20*(2,3), 78–92.

Lourie, I. S., Stroul, B. A., & Friedman, R. M. (1998). Community-based systems of care: From advocacy to outcomes. In M. H. Epstein, K. Kutash, & A. Duchnowski (Eds.), *Outcomes for children and youth with emotional and behavioral disorders and their families* (pp. 3–20). Austin, TX: Pro-Ed.

Morton, D. T. (1999). The increasing colorization of America's child welfare system: The overrepresentation of African-American children. *Policy & Practice of Public Human Services, 57*(4), 23–30.

National Clearing House on Child Abuse and Neglect Information. (2005). How does the child welfare system work. Retrieved April 17, 2006, from http://nccanch.acf.hhs,gov/pubs/factsheets.cpswork.cfm.

Nelson, K. E. (1997). Family preservation—What is it? *Children and Youth Services Review, 19,* 101–118.

New Freedom Commission on Mental Health. (2003). *Achieving the promise: Transforming mental health care in America: Final report* (DHHS Pub. No. SMA-03-3832). Rockville, MD: Author.

Pecora, P., Kesslen, R. C., Williams, J., O'Brien, K., Downs, A. C., English, D., et al. (2005). *Improving family foster care.* Seattle, WA: Casey Family Programs.

Pires, S. A. (2002). *Building systems of care: A primer.* Washington, DC: Human Service Collaborative.

Roberts, D. (2002). *Shattered bonds: The color of child welfare.* New York: Basic Civitas.

Sallee, A., & Shaening, M. A. (1995). Child welfare system litigation: Achieving substantial compliance. *Journal of Law and Social Work, 5,* 14–23.

Schorr, A. (2000, March). The bleak prospect for public child welfare. *Social Service Review, 74*(1), 124–136.

Shireman, J., Rodgers, A., Alworth, J., Wilson, B., Gordon, L., & Poirier, C. (2001). *Strengths/needs based services evaluation final report 2001.* Portland, OR: Portland State University Regional Research Institute in Human Services.

Siegel, G. L., Loman, A. L., Sherburne, D. S., Aldrich, D., Bergsma, J. L., DeWeese-Boyd, M., Collins, M., Loman, M. J., & McGhee, B. (1998). *Child protection services family assessment and response demonstration impact evaluation: Digest of findings and conclusions.* St. Louis, MO: Institute of Applied Research.

Smale, G. (1998). *Managing change through innovation.* London: The Stationery Office.

Smale, G. (1999). Three dimensions of managing change in service reform. *Prevention Report, 1,* 20–25.

Trattner, W. (1999). *From poor law to welfare state.* New York: Free Press.

U.S. Advisory Board on Child Abuse and Neglect. (1993). *Neighbors helping neighbors: A new national strategy for the protection of children. Fourth report.* Washington, DC: Administration for Children and Families, Department of Health and Human Services.

U.S. Department of Health and Human Services. (2003). *Improving child welfare outcomes through systems of care 2003B.* Retrieved April 17, 2006, from www .acf.dhhs.gov/programs/cb/programs_fund/discretionary/2003.htm.

Waldfogel, J. (1998). *The future of child protection.* Cambridge, MA: Harvard University Press.

Ways and Means Committee. (2004). *Overview of entitlement programs.* Washington, DC: Government Printing Office.

Weber, M. (1958). *The protestant ethic and the spirit of capitalism.* New York: Scribners.

Young, L. (1964). *Wednesday's children.* New York: McGraw-Hill.

Zlotnik, J. L. (2003). The use of Title IVE training funds for social work education: An historical perspective. *Journal of Human Behavior in the Social Environment, 7* (1-2), 5–20.

■ ■ ■ ■ ■

ARE FAMILY DRUG COURTS WORKING IN CHILD WELFARE?

Editor's Note:

People sentenced for drug crimes accounted for 21 percent of state prisoners and 55 percent of all federal prisoners in 2004. More than 500,000 prisoners are now incarcerated in the United States for drug crimes. Drug arrests are climbing, with 1.7 million arrests in 2003. Especially notable is the continuing increase in women prisoners, their numbers rising 4 percent a year—double that of men. A large percentage of women prisoners (31 percent compared to 21 percent of men) are doing time for drug crimes. Women and minorities are more likely to be locked up for a drug offense. At an annual cost of over $23,000 an inmate, this takes a large chunk out of public coffers.

It is therefore not surprising that society is looking for a lower-cost alternative to incarceration. One alternative that has emerged is drug and family drug courts. More than $200 million has spent on these courts since 1995. A study by the National Institute of Justice estimates a recidivism rate of 16.4 percent for drug-court graduates in the first year after graduation, and a recidivism rate of 27.5 percent in the first two years after graduation. That is considered good given the population that drug courts serve. But are they really working? This debate will examine that question.

Patricia Sandau-Beckler, Ph.D., is a professor of social work in the College of Health and Social Service, New Mexico State University. Her research and publications are in the area of child welfare and family preservation. She is the coeditor (with Elaine Walton and Marc Mannes) of *Balancing Family-Centered Services and Child Well-Being* (Columbia University Press, 2001).

Scott W. M. Burrus, M.A., is a senior research coordinator for NPC Research in Portland, Oregon. He conducts program evaluation and development in academic, clinical, and urban community settings. Burrus specializes in program collaboration, evaluation design, database management, and qualitative data analysis.

Michael J. Beckler, L.I.S.W., L.C.D.C. (Texas), is a clinical social worker in Las Cruces, New Mexico. He coauthored "Infusing Family-Centered Values into Child Protection Practice" (with Patricia Sandau-Beckler, Richard Salcido, Marc Mannes, and Mary Beck) (*Children and Youth Services Review,* 2002).

YES

Patricia Sandau-Beckler and Scott W. M. Burrus

The Family Treatment Drug Court (FTDC) is a fast-growing approach to delivering treatment to parents and children in the child-welfare system. Prior to 1998, Family Treatment Drug Courts were unheard of. Presently, according to the OJP Drug Court Clearinghouse (2005), there are nearly 153 Family Treatment Drug Courts (also known as Family Drug Treatment Courts, or FDTCs) in the United States; this number grows monthly.

According to the U.S. Department of Health and Human Services (DHHS) (2004), during fiscal year 2003–2004 over 900,000 children were determined to be victims of parental neglect or abuse. Over 60 percent of the confirmed child-welfare cases resulted from neglect, and children ages 0 to 3 had the highest rate of victimization. Over 1,500 children died during this period, the majority neglect-only victims. It is estimated that between 40 and 90 percent of all child-welfare cases have substance abuse as a contributor to the parents' involvement with the child-welfare system. Moreover, parental substance use has been linked to severe child abuse and neglect as well as to neglect-related child fatalities.

Given the prevalence of substance abuse as a contributor to parents' involvement with child welfare, both the child-welfare system and the substance-abuse-treatment community are faced with the daunting task of serving these families. Family Treatment Drug Court is one example of how these systems have attempted to serve families involved with child welfare due to substance abuse.

This debate addresses the significant components and practices of FTDC programs shown to support the niche that they occupy in the court system, and demonstrates their potential value to the overall system of care for substance-abuse families. Following this will be a description of how this model benefits the child-welfare, treatment, and judicial systems; and finally, the key reasons why Family Drug Treatment Courts benefit families.

KEY COMPONENTS

A key component of the FTDC is the coordinated approach involving judicial personnel such as judges; drug court coordinators; and trackers who give random urine analysis, monitor high-risk behaviors, and closely supervise the behavior of the substance-affected parent. Substance-abuse treatment-agency professionals include therapists, supervisors, medications monitors, child-welfare workers, child therapists, and parent educators and medical personnel. These teams may also include extended-family members. Often, these teams are highly consensual, reflecting a team effort. The plan can call for either outpatient services or, at times, in-patient treatment services. Accountability for all parts of the system is assured, with this highly partici-patory group meeting in the court system to review progress. Judicial access and attention predominate through the entire process, thus leading the case disposition.

The parent(s) have the opportunity to develop a relationship with the team members. Isolation of the substance abuser from family members is a normal by-product of the dynamics of substance addiction. The ongoing contact of every team member makes this approach more effective than the frag-mented system that parents experience when being referred to many agencies to obtain care for an addiction.

The cost of drug treatment has been the subject of much evaluation. It is clear that drug courts are much less costly than formal prosecution and incarceration. The daily rate of sending these parents to jail when they have engaged in criminal behavior and the cost of foster care, group care, or resi-dential care for the children of these families is much higher than the outpa-tient treatment approaches of child-welfare drug court. The cost to the juvenile justice, education, and health-care systems for the children is also significant if the family is left untreated. Treating addiction can reduce recidi-vism rates for criminal activity and further decreases abuse and neglect. These human and social savings alone are enough to demonstrate the bene-fit of these programs. Children who have experienced child neglect or abuse grow up to be more frequently unemployed; have less schooling; experience more physical and mental health problems that interfere with employment; have lower educational levels; are twice as likely to fall below the federal poverty guidelines; have more substance-abuse problems, criminality, and incarcerations; and are often victimized again in adulthood (Zielinski, 2004).

The FTDC provides many benefits for child-protection service agencies as well. First, the treatment-participation rate is higher for those going through drug court than for those who are not. Individuals or families ordered to treatment experience many barriers, including long waiting lists, high treatment costs, long distances to treatment programs, and varying treatment effectiveness. Still other barriers include programs with inadequate resources for child care, thus not allowing the child to come along with the parents; and the lack of insurance coverage—or worse yet—coverage for any-thing longer than detoxification.

Also, the enhanced supervision of these cases decreases the likelihood that the parents will be lost in the system. This issue is pervasive given the high re-referral rates in child-welfare cases when parents are addicted. The chronic nature of addiction has a profound impact on the continuing deterioration of family life. The impact on children whose parents did not receive treatment is felt into adulthood.

The most frequent benefit stated by judges is that they have more information on which to base court decisions (Marlowe, Festinger, & Lee, 2004). Direct and ongoing knowledge of the progress of defendants is helpful. Traditionally, reports by workers or treatment agencies were used to determine permanency decisions, which frequently led to an adversarial process in child-welfare courts, often pitting the family against the child-welfare agency. The FTDC can be more flexible in handling issues such as relapse, due to their powers to apply or remove sanctions. This is critical to the support of family functioning and helping family members gain sobriety.

Judges are also in a better position to obtain resources and community support because of their knowledge of the family's needs. Judicial staff also become aware of the helpers and their roles at a more personal level, allowing for more direct communication and knowledge of what is available for the family members. Finally, the judge may serve as a motivator for family members to make significant changes. Research suggests that the most important element for change processes is the relationship with the helper. FTDCs provide an opportunity for the judges to develop that role.

The FTDC plan is based on a comprehensive assessment, with the treatment plan being a part of the court expectations. Consequently, the multidisciplinary treatment team is assured that all barriers to treatment—like transportation, waiting lists, insurance coverage, parent cooperation, and services availability that incorporate parenting needs—are addressed.

An equally important support offered to the multidisciplinary team members by FTDCs is the ability to work with treatment compliance. For high-risk participants, the intense court involvement assures more oversight of compliance. Most often, the FTDC serves the highest-risk families with chronic substance abuse, compared to other families who voluntarily enter treatment. High-risk defendants are best served by the intensive supervision and monitoring that is administered in the family drug court process.

Judges are the only ones who have the authority to administer significant sanctions and rewards to these parents. The court has at its discretion multiple positive and negative reinforcements to influence treatment outcomes. Examples of positive reinforcers are more freedom to travel or take jobs, more visitation privileges with less supervision, and graduation enhancements for completing steps in the treatment process. Examples of negative reinforcements may include such activities as more community service, house arrest, short jail times for violations, returning to higher levels of supervised visitation with family members, increased therapy sessions, and a return to former levels of low independence in daily routines.

ADVANTAGES TO FAMILIES

The major benefit for families is the goal of preserving or reuniting the family during the treatment process. The defendant is told that cooperation and work will help in achieving independence from legal procedures. Substance abuse is a family disease, and the services are targeted to all members of the family. FTDC can also help parents have access to their children for family treatment, which is not so when they are incarcerated.

The most striking feature of FTDCs is the large number of benefits that accrue to the children. FTDC reduces the risk of children entering and/or languishing in the foster-care system. Children of addicts have a high rate of behavior problems and are at greater risk for out-of-home placement, and these programs can help children get treatment for their depression and anxiety. Treatment teams are better able to understand the context for the child's hypervigilance, anger, or grief, and to meet their needs for consistent care.

Another advantage is better visitation plans for children placed out of their home; especially if they focus on treatment goals and provide an opportunity to encourage the parent–child bond.

In FTDC, treatment plans are developed for the whole family. They help parents better understand the negative effects of substance abuse on children. These plans also help prepare families for potential relapses, and for living with someone who has a chronic relapsing condition.

Extended-family members and foster parents are critical caregivers to the children and supports to the recovering parents. They have often been worn out and distressed by the behaviors of the addicted family member. In FTDC, extended-family and foster parents play critical roles in providing support in the recovery process for both the children and the parents. These key supporters will often be the persons assisting children in understanding the disease process of substance abuse and helping them with relapse and recovery issues. When parents start recovery and take on more ambitious parenting roles, there is a great need for a well-coordinated transfer of duties back to the recovering parent. Foster parents and extended-family members have firsthand involvement with the parents in the process. The perception of the extended family is greatly enhanced as they see the court actively involved instead of merely administering punishment.

CONCLUSION

Family Treatment Drug Court is a family-centered experiment in progress. The potential to treat families for substance abuse, which is characterized as a family disease, is a model that honors and supports families through combined resources coordinated by the court system. This new collaboration can bring to the table the resources and support that families need for recovery. It is an innovation that is working to meet the needs of children who have come to the attention of the child-welfare system. It represents the combined talents and resources of several systems that, when coordinated, can help these children and their parents in unprecedented ways. FTDCs have more potential than any other collaboration that currently exists to treat families in the child-welfare system. Nationally, yearly costs for child abuse total about $93 billion for treatment, hospitalization, health problems, child-welfare care, and judicial expenses. Another $69 billion is spent in indirect expenses related to children's physical and mental health, including depression, alcoholism, drug abuse, obesity, and the additional costs of meeting children's special needs in schools (Fromm, 2001). If the FTDC approach can contribute in any way to reducing parental substance abuse, treating children, and helping prevent substance abuse in the next generation, then it is working. The benefit to the public both is both financial and humane.

NO

Michael J. Beckler

The existence of the drug court model presupposes the status quo in terms of fighting drug abuse in the United States. Namely, that drug abuse is a crime. The War on Drugs creates numerous criminals who either must be punished and incarcerated—which we don't have the resources to do—or rehabilitated in such away as to affirm that our current policy on drugs is correct. The drug court is based on the belief that drug abuse is a legal problem whose solution is control and treatment. If drug abuse was regarded as a public-health problem, the need for drug court would be greatly reduced and would focus only on drug behavior that violated other laws. Illegal usage would not, by itself, constitute sufficient grounds for legal intervention. The extensive use of drug courts makes them a political solution for what is possibly a medical problem. Either way, negative behavior and drug usage can be destructive, but having a medical problem is less stigmatizing to one's future success than being labeled a criminal.

The War on Drugs costs between $40 to $50 billion annually. It costs about $26,000 a year to incarcerate a defendant, while it costs about $1,800 for traditional outpatient services, and $6,880 for long-term residential treatment services (Lapidus, Luthra, Verma, & Small, 2004). While drug courts don't address the root cause of the incarceration; namely, the law itself, they do provide an alternative that is more humane than incarceration. Unfortunately it is estimated that 10 million people need treatment but are not getting it (Substance abuse and Mental Health Services Administration [SAMHSA], 2000).

PROBLEM-SOLVING COURTS

The drug court is one example where the court has become involved in problem solving through collaboration. Other examples are domestic-abuse courts, mental-health courts, and DUI courts (Skove, 2002). These courts are a widely accepted part of the justice system, but questions exist about the degree and quality of representation for those placed under these helping systems. Is their protection equal to defendants with greater resources? Most enter into these systems through plea bargaining, and defendants with less money and resources need to plea bargain more. Nevertheless it would be difficult to ethically argue that they are not better off than being incarcerated.

The drug-court movement addresses one of the major deficits of the traditional model of incarceration for drug-abuse behaviors: it attempts to assure treatment and accountability rather than only punishment. In short, drug courts represent a major innovation in addressing the increased incarcerations rates and family problems resulting from drug abuse and correlated crimes. Since the first drug court appeared in 1991, the number of courts have proliferated to 1,621 by 2004 (Huddleston, Freeman-Wilson, Marlowe, & Roussell, 2005). Drug courts have a core set of central principles that assure the "fidelity" of the model. These principles define the drug-court model and delineate minimal components assumed necessary to assure success. According to the National Report Card on Drug Courts and other problem-solving court programs in the United States:

- Drug courts integrate alcohol and other drug treatment services with justice-system-care processing.
- Using a nonadversarial approach, prosecution and defense counsels promote public safety while protecting participants' due-process rights.
- Eligible participants are identified early and promptly placed in the drug court programs.
- Drug courts provide access to a continuum of alcohol, drug, and other related treatment and rehabilitation services.
- Abstinence is monitored by frequent alcohol and other drug testing.
- A coordinated strategy governs drug-court responses to participant compliance.
- Monitoring and evaluation measures the achievement of program goals and gauges effectiveness.
- Continuing interdisciplinary education permeates effective drug court planning, implementation, and operations.
- Forging partnerships among drug courts, public agencies, and community-based organizations generates local support and enhances drug-court effectiveness. (Huddleston et al., 2005)

As these principles illustrate, there are a number of actors in drug court besides the defense and prosecution, judge, and defendant. It is important to note that, by far, the major contribution of the drug-court model is the coordinated effort of the system to assure that accountability follows treatment. Alcohol and drug-treatment programs—beyond the self-help movement of AA—have existed for decades, but access was and is limited to the substance user's funding or by financially stretched public coffers. Additional factors are also important. First is the involvement of the judge, which is of primary importance to assure accountability (Hora, 2002). Second, objective measures are used to assure compliance (i.e., drug tests), and mandated attendance at treatment is verified by the program itself (Hora, 2002). In short, the drug court is an approach that incorporates accountability with treatment. To have treatment available at the early-intervention stage is a major step toward rehabilitation, not just punishment.

SUMMARY OF THE RELATIONSHIP OF THE DRUG COURT MODEL TO THE WAR ON DRUGS

The War on Drugs has resulted in massive arrests, incarcerations, and a need to find alternative ways of dealing with these offenses other than prison. Drug court is one method that offers more than just punishment. It has demonstrated considerable success when comparing participants with those of equal offenses that are not in the program. There is a decrease of drug use during enrollment in the program—as demonstrated by drug testing—and a decrease in recidivism (U.S. Government Accounting Office [GAO], 2005). However, the necessity for this model is due to the laws and priorities of the judicial system; namely, that drug use is a crime. In addition, it could be argued that the disproportionate number of minorities and women incarcerated due to drug-related crimes is more destructive to the fabric of society than the crimes they committed. Finally, with drug courts reaching such a small number of the defendants facing incarceration, they are more of a bandaid than a solution. Redistributing funds from the War on Drugs to prevention and treatment may, in the end, do more to decrease drug use than the failed attempts to control supply. This is not to advocate legalization, but rather to point out the disproportionate allocation of resources to control access than is allocated to prevention and treatment. In addition, a public policy that focuses on addiction and harm reduction may reduce the glamorization of drugs that the crime model does not successfully do, as evidenced by the profit inherent in distribution. It can also be argued that if harm reduction was the focus, movies and pop culture that tend to glamorize drug usage as rebellion and coming-of-age would have less meaning. Use alone is not the issue for a harm-reduction model, but rather, destructive use to self and others. It is clearly more difficult to glamorize self-destructive behavior than rebellious behavior. Again, a shift does not have to mean legalization, but rather a redirection of the focus to clinical rather than criminal intervention. Assuring access to treatment, and promoting prevention, might change the culture of use and abuse of substances more than the current efforts of criminalization and incarceration.

FAMILY DRUG COURT

FTDC is a hybrid of the drug-court model and is specifically used for cases where the children have been impacted by the substance abuse of the parent. Drug abuse alone is not usually the sole criterion for a family's being referred to drug court. Normally there has been child abuse or neglect and, during the assessment stage, a determination made that chemical use is a contributing factor to the abuse or neglect. In this sense, the FTDC differs from other drug courts where drug use and abuse may be the only offense bringing the defendant into the criminal justice system. At first glance, one of the major criticisms of drug courts does not apply; namely, that the law creates the problem necessitating the intervention, and by changing the law, the focus could change from a legal to a medical problem. However, this might not be the case. Available research does not indicate the patterns of neglect or abuse that warrant involvement in drug court, but rather that the drug abuse was a primary factor. This again raises the question of whether good prevention and treatment as public policy might not bring families to resources before the neglect or abuse occurs.

Also, family drug-court treatment becomes possible with cases that historically might not have always had access to such services. Specifically, the question is whether there was availability of treatment resources prior to the FTDC involvement. If treatment would be readily available, based on marketplace concepts, would there be a need for the intense controls inherent in the FTDC model? The current system seems somewhat conflicted in that it requires seeing defendants both as deviant and as suffering from a disease. As a deviants need to avoid detection, which makes treating the disease more difficult because their energy is going into not getting caught. In some cases, this avoidance may be the precipitating factor to the abuse or neglect because the user cannot use resources and use substances and still provide for the family because their activities are illegal. Research as to the types of abuse and neglect, and situations that bring the family to drug court might help clarify whether prevention and early intervention services might alleviate the problems before needing legal intervention. Again, it should be emphasized that a major strength of FTDC is its focus on the behavior that endangers the child, rather than just the illegal use. This creates an atmosphere where treatment becomes a solution for the problem, rather than punishment for the problem, assuming that there is acceptance that the behavior needs to be changed. Theoretically, this should increase the potential for success as the goal of successful treatment is correlated with stabilizing the family. However, the definition of success in the long term is not clear. If any use is seen as failure the success of the model may be less than if the focus is on reducing risk behavior for the children. Existing research for family court is relatively new so longitudinal studies are not available. With the high recidivism rate for drug and alcohol abuse, longitudinal studies would be helpful. Even with good research, however, a harm-reduction model would create a greater opportunity for success, because recidivism alone would not reflect failure, but child endangerment would. Clearly, not all substance-using parents abuse or neglect their children.

Another question is whether the family court judge, at least in all cases, would be necessary for success to occur if the system were geared more toward treatment as a whole. The court's ability to address treatment barriers such as child care, transportation, and cost may be the primary factor, more important than the drug-court model with the intense involvement of the judge. Stated another way, would a comprehensive health-care system that addressed barriers be sufficient to address these families' needs?

In summary, the existing research of FTDC tends to compare those in the program to those who are not. This is true about drug courts as a whole, not only FTDCs. What is lacking is an understanding of the components of the system that work, for whom (i.e., what type of situations or clients), and how much is needed to assure an acceptable outcome. For example, is abstinence the goal, or is it the elimination of endangering behaviors? Is the judge's intensive involvement necessary in all cases, or only those that are "high risk," as defined by having had prior treatment, or in displaying certain patterns of abuse or neglect? Does the degree of control exercised by the system relate to outcome or is it more availability of resources? What types of treatment are more effective? Treatment models are not noted in the research, so it is not known what "treatment" means in the programs described by existing research. Existing social-science research indicates that any treatment is more effective than no treatment, with little differentiation made as to the type of treatment. Is it possible that treatment and the removal of barriers to get treatment account for the success of the model more than the coercion and power of the court to punish or reward?

CONCLUSION

The position taken in this paper is not that FTDCs are wrong, ineffective, or bad public policy; instead, their need is a by-product of a War on Drugs that is inherently flawed and failing. The current policy is directing precious resources toward control of supply at the expense of adequate prevention and treatment. Although this argument is less germane to FTDC, the fact that this court is a by-product of the current culture of control makes it difficult to separate it from the questions raised about the War on Drugs. Stated another way, would a society where an accessible and good public-health model drove treatment decrease the need for these coercive and costly systems? Does the current incarceration rate from women and minorities for drug-related offenses cause more family destruction than the crimes they commit? Would a harm-reduction model better focus available resources and increase the overall health outcome for all involved?

REFERENCES

Fromm, S. (2001). *Total estimated cost of child abuse and neglect in the United States.* Chicago, IL: Prevent Child Abuse America.

Hora, P. H. (2002). A dozen years of drug treatment courts: Uncovering our theoretical foundation and the construction of a mainstream paradigm. *Substance Use & Misuse, 37*(12–13), 1469–1488.

Huddleston, C. W., Freeman-Wilson, K., Marlowe, D. B., & Roussell, A. (2005). *Painting the current picture: A national report card on drug courts and other problem-solving court programs in the United States.* Washington, DC: Bureau of Justice Assistance, National Drug Court Institute.

Lapidus, L., Luthra, N., Verma, A., & Small, D. (2004). Break the chains: Communities of color and the war on drugs. American Civil Liberties Union & The Brennan Center at NYU School of Law.

Marlowe, D. B., Festinger, D. S., & Lee, P. A. (2004). The judge is a key component of drug court. *Drug Court Review, 4* (2) 1–35.

OJP Drug Court Clearinghouse. (2005). *Drug court activity update: March 1, 2005.* Washington DC: American University.

Skove, A. E. (2002). Specialized and problem-solving courts: Trends in 2002: The ethics of problem solving. In *Report on trends in the state courts.* National Center for State Courts. Retrieved May 18, 2006, from www.ncsconline.org/D_KIS/Trends02MainPage.html.

Substance Abuse and Mental Health Services Administration. (2003). *Blueprint for change: Ending chronic homelessness for persons with serious mental illnesses and co-occurring substance use disorders.* (DHHS Pub. No. SMA-04-3870). Rockville, MD: Author.

U.S. Department of Health and Human Services. (2004). *Child maltreatment: 2003.* Washington, DC: Author.

U.S. Government Accounting Office. (2005, February). *Evidence indicates recidivism reductions and mixed results for other outcomes.* (Report to Congressional Committees. GAO-05-219): Washington, DC: Author.

Zielinski, D. S. (2004). *Child maltreatment and adult socioeconomic status: Support for a mediation model.* Unpublished doctoral dissertation, Cornell University, Ithaca, NY.